THE GREAT WALL OF MONEY

A volume in the series
Cornell Studies in Money
edited by Eric Helleiner and Jonathan Kirshner

A list of titles in this series is available at
www.cornellpress.cornell.edu.

The Great Wall of Money

Power and Politics in China's
International Monetary Relations

Edited by Eric Helleiner
and Jonathan Kirshner

Cornell University Press
Ithaca and London

First published 2014 by Cornell University Press
First printing, Cornell Paperbacks, 2014

Printed in the United States of America

Library of Congress Cataloging-in-Publication Data

  The Great Wall of money : power and politics in China's international
monetary relations / edited by Eric Helleiner and Jonathan Kirshner.
    pages cm. — (Cornell studies in money)
  Includes bibliographical references and index.
  ISBN 978-0-8014-5309-0 (cloth : alk. paper)
  ISBN 978-0-8014-7959-5 (pbk. : alk. paper)
  1. Monetary policy—China. 2. China—Foreign economic relations.
I. Helleiner, Eric, 1963– editor of compilation. II. Kirshner, Jonathan,
editor of compilation. III. Cohen, Benjamin J. China question. Contains
(work):
  HG1285.G74   2014
  332.4'50951—dc23   2014011483

Cornell University Press strives to use environmentally responsible
suppliers and materials to the fullest extent possible in the publishing of
its books. Such materials include vegetable-based, low-VOC inks and
acid-free papers that are recycled, totally chlorine-free, or partly composed
of nonwood fibers. For further information, visit our website at
www.cornellpress.cornell.edu.

Cloth printing   10 9 8 7 6 5 4 3 2 1
Paperback printing   10 9 8 7 6 5 4 3 2 1

Contents

PREFACE

In our earlier volume *The Future of the Dollar,* we took as our point of departure a basic question: What is the future of the US dollar as an international currency? We quickly realized that searching for the (elusive) answer to that question was less intellectually satisfying than considering why experts from distinct academic specializations and perspectives came to divergent conclusions. A similar philosophy informed our approach to this project. Looking beyond the dollar and toward the future of the international monetary system more generally, it was clear to us that China would play a larger role in that evolving order. In addition, it seemed equally clear that the nature and significance of that role would be determined by policy choices made by the People's Republic. But what will inform these choices and what kinds of international monetary power is China acquiring? These political questions have often been overlooked in the growing literature on Beijing's monetary management, most of which has been dominated by questions rooted in economics. This book is about the essential role that politics and power play in forging China's international monetary relations. By bringing together scholars with distinct points of departure—students of the international political economy of money and China specialists—our goal once again is to illuminate the way in which particular analytical pathways yield varying expectations. By analyzing the various political sources and motivations of China's policy choices, we hope that scholars will be better positioned to anticipate and understand them. Some names in this book are transliterated using the old Wade-Giles system, when the historical analysis concerns a time period in which this system was in use.

We have incurred many debts in putting this book together. We are, of course, particularly grateful to the contributors for their participation in this project over the course of its evolution and for their diligence in meeting deadlines. Several scholars also provided very insightful and helpful feedback on the chapters and the book, including Sarah Eaton, Wendy Leutert, Odette Lineau, Carla Norrlof, Tom Pepinsky, and two anonymous reviewers. For their invaluable logistical support as well as help in the preparation of the manuscript, we thank Elaine Scott, Sandra Kisner, Wendy Leutert, and Antulio Rosales. As always, Roger Haydon provided excellent evaluations and advice, and we are grateful for his support for this project. The editorial work of Gavin Lewis and Susan Specter was also extremely helpful. And finally, for their financial assistance, we thank the Reppy Institute for Peace and Conflict Studies, the Social Sciences and Humanities Research Council of Canada, and the Trudeau Foundation.

Contributors

Gregory Chin is Associate Professor in the Department of Political Science at York University (Canada).

Benjamin J. Cohen is Louis G. Lancaster Professor of International Political Economy in the Department of Political Science at the University of California, Santa Barbara.

Eric Helleiner is Faculty of Arts Chair in International Political Economy and Professor in the Department of Political Science at the University of Waterloo and the Balsillie School of International Affairs.

Yang Jiang is Senior Researcher at the Danish Institute for International Studies.

Jonathan Kirshner is the Stephen and Barbara Friedman Professor of International Political Economy in the Department of Government and Director of the Reppy Institute for Peace and Conflict Studies at Cornell University.

Bessma Momani is Associate Professor in the Department of Political Science at the University of Waterloo and the Balsillie School of International Affairs.

David A. Steinberg is Assistant Professor in the Department of Political Science at the University of Oregon.

Andrew Walter is Professor of International Relations in the School of Social and Political Sciences at the University of Melbourne.

Hongying Wang is Associate Professor in the Department of Political Science at the University of Waterloo and the Balsillie School of International Affairs

ABBREVIATIONS

ABC	Agricultural Bank of China
ACU	Asian Currency Unit
ASEAN	Association of Southeast Asian Nations
BIS	Bank for International Settlements
BOC	Bank of China
BRIC	Brazil, Russia, India, China
BRICS	Brazil, Russia, India, China, South Africa
BSAs	Bilateral swap arrangements
BWCC	Bretton Woods Conference Collection
CCB	China Construction Bank
CCP	Chinese Communist Party
CDB	China Development Bank
CIC	China Investment Corporation
CMI	Chiang Mai Initiative
CMIM	Chiang Mai Initiative Multilateralization
DM	Deutsche mark

EMDCs	Emerging market and developing countries
EMU	Economic and Monetary Union
EU	European Union
FBIS	Foreign Broadcast Information Service
FTA	Free trade agreement
G5	Group of Five
G7	Group of Seven
G20	Group of Twenty
GATT	General Agreement on Tariffs and Trade
GDP	Gross domestic product
GFC	Global financial crisis
GNP	Gross national product
HDWP	Harry Dexter White Papers
ICBC	Industrial and Commercial Bank of China
IMF	International Monetary Fund
IMFC	International Monetary and Financial Committee
KMT	Kuomintang
MD	Morgenthau Diary
MFN	Most favored nation
MOF	Ministry of Finance
MOFCOM	Ministry of Commerce
NATO	North Atlantic Treaty Organization
NDRC	National Development and Reform Commission
NPC	National People's Congress
OECD	Organisation for Economic Co-operation and Development
OPEC	Organization of the Petroleum Exporting Countries
PBOC	People's Bank of China
PLA	People's Liberation Army
PRC	People's Republic of China
RMB	Renminbi
ROC	Republic of China
SAFE	State Administration of Foreign Exchange
SASAC	State Asset Supervision and Administration Commission
SCO	Shanghai Cooperation Organization
SDR	Special Drawing Right
SOE	State-owned enterprise

SWIFT	Society for Worldwide Interbank Financial Telecommunication
WB	World Bank
WTO	World Trade Organization

THE POLITICS OF CHINA'S INTERNATIONAL MONETARY RELATIONS

Eric Helleiner and Jonathan Kirshner

The Chinese government has become an increasingly important player in international monetary relations in recent years. Once the IMF's latest quota review is implemented, China's voting share in this institution at the center of global monetary governance will be the third largest after those of the United States and Japan. Its foreign exchange reserves have become the largest in the world—ever—at a staggering $3.5 trillion by mid-2013. Its exchange rate policy has become a major subject of international economic diplomacy and is closely scrutinized, and often shadowed, by countries around the world. The internationalization of the renminbi is also attracting growing attention in international policy circles. And all of this, of course, takes place in the context of China's continuing emergence as a great power, which both conditions and complicates its own policies and the reactions of other states to those initiatives.[1]

---

1. On the political implications of China's rise, see Goldstein 2005, Johnston 2003, Ross and Zhu 2008, Christensen 2006, Friedberg 2011, Beckley 2011/12, Kirshner 2012.

To date, the study of China's increasingly important role in the international monetary system has focused primarily on economic questions and technical issues, with much less detailed attention given to the *politics* of China's international monetary relations. This volume aims to help redress this imbalance by considering the following questions: What kinds of power is China acquiring in international monetary relations? What are the priorities of the Chinese government in this sphere? What explains its preferences? Answers to these questions should help inform our understanding of the future of the global economy, the prospects for international relations, and the trajectory of China's continuing emergence in the coming decades.

In this introduction, we elaborate on these three questions, highlighting essential variables, considering the range of possible outcomes, and situating the perspectives and contributions of the chapters that follow. The authors in this volume occasionally disagree with regard to their expectations, and in their choices of different levels of analysis seen as crucial for explaining and anticipating outcomes. But collectively they reveal the extent to which China's choices, and global monetary affairs, will be shaped by political factors.

What Kinds of Power Is China Gaining in International Monetary Relations?

International monetary relations concern issues such as the relative values and exchange of countries' currencies, the choice and management of international currencies, and financing of and adjustment to international payments imbalances. Market dynamics certainly shape outcomes across these various issues. But state choices and political contestation at both the domestic and the international level also play a crucial role, with outcomes often determined by the exercise of power.

The study of state power in international monetary relations has in fact attracted considerable scholarly attention among political scientists in recent years.[2] Some analysts have focused on episodes in which one state

2. See for example Kirshner 1995, Andrews 2006.

directly forces another to change its behavior. Other scholars have emphasized more indirect "structural" forms of power involving manipulation of international monetary rules or the unilateral shaping of the international monetary environment—whether by active measures or even by passive inaction—in which foreigners must operate in ways that prompt changes in the latter's behavior and even their interests.[3] Important distinctions have also been drawn between "power-as-influence" and "power-as-autonomy." The former involves the ability to change others' behavior, while the latter is the capacity to act without restraint, independently from external influence.[4]

This volume explores how China's power is growing in an uneven manner across several key dimensions of international monetary relations, including the financing of payments imbalances, the politics of macroeconomic adjustment, its role in international institutions, and the international use of its currency. Perhaps the most visible aspect of this power has been China's growing role as a provider of balance of payments financing for deficit countries around the world. This role reflects not just the country's creditor status which emerged in the early 2000s but also the fact that the vast majority of China's foreign claims are state-controlled because they are held as official exchange reserves or owned by state-owned banks, sovereign wealth funds, and other investment vehicles.

There is no question that China has acquired new power because of its creditor status and its provision of balance of payments finance. When China has offered such finance directly to countries, its influence over those countries has been enhanced. But the extent of this power-as-influence is hotly debated, particularly in the case of the United States whose current account deficits China has helped finance. Some scholars argue that China has acquired influence over the United States because of the latter's dependence on Chinese financing. Others are less sure, arguing that the situation is better characterized as one of mutual vulnerability because of China's dependence on both the US export market and the depth of US financial markets. As China's holdings of US assets have grown to enormous levels, analysts have also noted that Chinese policymakers have felt increasingly compelled to support the United States economically.[5]

---

3. Strange 1987, Helleiner 2006a.
4. Cohen 2008.
5. Setser 2008, Drezner 2009, Chin and Helleiner 2008, Kirshner 2008.

As the Chinese government has helped boost the IMF's capacity to offer balance of payments finance, it has also successfully demanded greater influence in that multilateral institution. As noted above, under quota revisions agreed to in 2010 (but not approved by all members as of late 2013), China's voting share is set to grow from 3.81 percent to 6.07 percent, leaving it with the third largest voting share in the institution behind the United States (16.5 percent) and just behind Japan (6.14 percent). In mid-2011, a Chinese official, Zhu Min, was for the first time appointed as one of the Fund's deputy managing directors.

China is also one of the top two contributors (alongside Japan) to a new multilateral East Asian fund created in 2010—originally with $120 billion and then doubled in 2012—to provide balance of payments finance to countries in the region. Again, the size of its contribution—almost a third of the total size of the fund—has given it influence in designing this institution. This Chiang Mai Initiative Multilateralization (CMIM) arrangement built on a network of bilateral swaps that had been first established in 2000 as the Chiang Mai Initiative (CMI), in which China had also played a lead role.

China's creditor status, and the growing size and openness of its economy, have also transformed the country into a more powerful player in international debates on the politics of macroeconomic adjustment. Such adjustment is the stuffing of international monetary politics, as countries jockey to shift often painful burdens abroad. (The recent upheavals in the eurozone illustrate how bitter, and contested, those costs can be.) Powerful states are often able to shuck off some of these costs onto other countries, as when the United States unilaterally "closed the gold window" in 1971, forcing its economic partners to adjust to its new policies.[6] This type of power is visibly accruing to China; as Cohen has noted, its large creditor position has insulated the country from the kinds of external pressures for adjustment that are often experienced by debtor countries. Additionally, foreign dependence on Chinese investments has discouraged foreign governments from pressuring China too strongly in areas such as exchange rate policy.[7]

---

6. Odell 1982, Gowa 1983.
7. Cohen 2008, Blustein 2012.

The changing balance of monetary power is also evident in Sino-American relations. The United States has found that its ability to pressure China indirectly to assume more of the burden of adjustment to "global imbalances" through dollar depreciation has been less effective than it had been vis-à-vis other foreign surplus countries such as Japan or Germany. Over the course of the 1970s, for example, under American pressure and despite Japanese foot-dragging, the yen doubled in value, from 360 to 180 to the US dollar; a decade later it appreciated from 160 to 80.[8] But the Chinese government has more successfully resisted the US "dollar weapon" through large-scale currency interventions that have been sterilized via the state-controlled financial system to minimize the kinds of domestic inflationary pressures that Germany and Japan experienced when they defended their currencies.[9]

Alongside its growing power in the politics of payments finance and adjustment, China has acquired additional influence within key international institutions that address these and other international monetary issues. In addition to its role in the IMF and CMIM, China has become a key player in the new G20 leaders' forum created in November 2008. This body quickly replaced the G7 (of which China was not a member) as the premier venue for international economic cooperation among the leading powers. In a regional context, China has also emerged as a key player in the ASEAN + 3 grouping which has been fostering East Asian monetary cooperation through the CMI/CMIM and other regional initiatives.

China's growing power in international monetary relations is thus multidimensional. But it is also uneven, and its trajectory still uncertain. (In particular, its upward trend might be set back if the country's notable internal debt and financial problems take a turn for the worse, or if the country experienced an internal financial crisis.) A defining question centers on the prospects for the RMB's international role, which, although growing, is still relatively modest. As Chin notes, the Chinese government is very aware of the enduring "structural power" in international monetary relations that the United States derives from the dollar's international

---

8. Hamada and Patrick 1988, McKinnon and Ohno 1997, Grimes 2001. On why disagreements between the United States and China are likely to be chronic and even more difficult to manage, see for example Bowles and Wang 2008.

9. For the dollar weapon, see Henning 2006.

dominance. United States management of the dollar shapes the international monetary environment within which countries, including China, operate. The dollar's global role also enables the United States to more easily finance payments imbalances and deflect the costs of adjustment onto foreigners. American policy-as-autonomy is also boosted by the fact that its monetary authorities need not be so concerned about how exchange rate movements might affect domestic balance sheets because very little of the country's public and private debt is denominated in foreign currencies. Foreign dependence on dollar liquidity during international financial crises has also given US monetary authorities enormous international influence at those moments.

What is the international destiny of the RMB? There is an observable historical pattern in which great powers have sought to extend the reach and influence of their currencies. But in more recent history, states poised to emerge as players on the monetary scene have been more cautious about internationalizing their currencies. They have been less geopolitically ambitious, wary of the costs involved, and averse to the risk of sacrificing domestic macroeconomic policy autonomy. As Cohen notes, both West Germany and Japan were reluctant to encourage the internationalization of their currencies after the breakdown of the Bretton Woods monetary system in the early 1970s, lest they lose control of monetary policy. These states also had reasons to be cautious about their geopolitical aims, as they were dependent for their security on the incumbent issuer of the key currency. West Germany's unique position led some scholars to label it a "semisovereign state." Japan's security dependence on the United States was also very high, although its policymakers in the 1990s, first with rising political ambition and later in search of greater economic insulation, became much more receptive to the idea of a greater international role for the yen.[10]

The leaders of the Chinese Communist Party are especially sensitive to encroachments on their policy autonomy, and place a great premium on stability, which suggests that they will be cautious about the extent to which they loosen their control over their currency. This will shape the nature of RMB internationalization, but so will other factors, including

---

10. Katzenstein 1987, Grimes 2003, Katada 2002, Helleiner 1992.

China's distinct geopolitical position and aims. Internationalization is clearly coming; the question is largely a matter of how much, how fast, to what extent, and with what "ceiling."

The RMB's use is already increasing in the East Asian region, and a number of key Southeast Asian countries now are linking their exchange rate management more closely to the RMB than to the dollar. Some analysts, such as Arvind Subramanian, have predicted that the RMB's broader international role may soon expand very quickly. Drawing on over a century of data, he highlights a statistical correlation between a country's size in the world economy—measured by GNP, share of world trade, and net creditor status—and the international reserve role of its currency. Based on this past experience, Subramanian predicts that the RMB should overtake the dollar as the primary reserve currency by the early 2020s. Other analysts analyses are much more skeptical; Mallaby and Wethington, for example, argue that the "rise of China's currency will be slower than commonly predicted, and the yuan is more likely to assume a place among secondary reserve currencies." The World Bank splits the difference, anticipating a "multi-currency scenario" (dollar, euro, yuan) in place by 2025.[11]

Whatever the scenario, a common denominator is that the outcome will be determined more by politics than economics, as both the RMB "optimists" and "pessimists" explicitly recognize. Subramanian acknowledges, for example, that his prediction is "conditional" on the Chinese government launching "far-reaching" financial reforms to allow the currency to be held in more liquid markets, including full currency convertibility and the cultivation of domestic financial deepening.[12] Mallaby and Wethington, on the other hand, argue that Chinese policymakers might be wary of unleashing such reforms. Several chapters in this volume emphasize how the Chinese government has begun to undertake financial reforms to promote RMB internationalization. China has also sought to bolster the RMB's international role in more direct ways by establishing a number of swap arrangements with foreign authorities as well as bilateral agreements that encourage the signatories to use each other's currencies in bilateral trade. Other chapters stress the limited and qualified nature of those reforms, but all contributors see politics as determining the ultimate outcome.

---

11. Subramanian 2011; Mallaby and Wethington 2012, 136; World Bank 2011, 126.
12. Subramanian 2011, 9.

If these initiatives intensify and are successful in boosting the RMB's international role, China's power in international monetary relations will be considerably strengthened. But the contributors to this book have different perspectives on the strength of the Chinese government's commitment to RMB internationalization. Jonathan Kirshner argues that the RMB's growing international role is a "virtual certainty" and that it will provide China with new structural power, particularly in the East Asian region. Yang Jiang, however, is more cautious, noting the considerable concerns that exist within the Chinese government about the loss of financial and monetary control associated with financial liberalization. She emphasizes that the bilateral approach favored by China leaves its monetary diplomacy "shallow, symbolic, pragmatic, and short term–oriented," suggesting a cautious and gradualist approach to RMB internationalization. Gregory Chin shares with Jiang the view that China's leadership prioritizes stability and order, but he nevertheless detects signs of considerable monetary ambition.

China's International Monetary Priorities: Taker, Maker, or Breaker?

Regardless of the pace and disposition of the RMB's international role, it is clear that China's international monetary power is growing. Thus it is important to try and discern the priorities and intentions of Chinese policymakers in the international monetary system. In broad brush, a rising power can be a "taker," "maker," or "breaker" of an existing international order. Obviously, these are idealized, abstract possibilities— practice will be much less pristine than theory—but they nevertheless capture the basic options open to China in the future, and reflect the different choices made by states in the past. In the first role, China would remain a rule-taker, essentially supporting the international monetary status quo—playing a larger role in a game governed by the same rules. In the second role, it would emerge as more of a rule-maker, demanding significant reforms to that status quo. In the third role, as a rule-breaker, China would challenge the existing system either by demanding wholesale transformation or by exiting that system to create its own arrangements.

These choices have profound consequences for the nature and pattern not only of international monetary affairs but for world politics more generally. Japan in the half-century from 1881 to 1931 was a classic example of a taker—going to heroic (and at times misguided) lengths to embrace the classical gold standard system that then represented a Good Housekeeping Seal of Approval for economic management. Those who bought into this system understood that to join it was to take a seat at the grown-ups' table as defined by the established great powers. Japan achieved this only through the painful "Matsukata deflation" of the 1880s, and the even more draconian measures undertaken in order to restore (and then maintain) the gold standard in the 1920s. (Interestingly, although Finance Minister Matsukata aspired to join the existing system, he was a nationalist, suggesting, importantly, that assuming the role of taker need not imply a lack of international ambition.) And for better or worse (actually, entirely for worse) Japanese banking elites were such takers that they became, as late converts often are, "holier than the pope," and stuck with the gold standard even after Britain itself was forced to abandon it, with catastrophic consequences for Japan's domestic politics.[13]

Interwar France, on the other hand, illustrates the tumult that can be brought about by an influential participant in monetary politics that chooses to play the role of a breaker (even though breakers rarely self-identify as such). France dissented from the gold exchange standard system that emerged from the Genoa monetary conference of 1922. France did not play by the rules of the system, registered its opposition regularly and loudly, often made mischief, and accumulated vast stores of gold at a rate and in a manner that storm-tossed the rickety monetary regime. The French subversion of the Genoa system contributed to the catastrophic collapse of the international monetary order in 1931, in the wake of the uncontained global financial crisis that emerged after the failure of the Austrian Creditanstalt bank, and this in turn considerably deepened the Great Depression. The Genoa system was broken, and France was a key breaker. Of course it takes at least two to disagree, and both international political discord as well as a divergence of ideologies about proper international monetary governance caused this collapse. The interwar experience

---

13. Shinjo 1962, Goldsmith 1983, Smethurst 2007, Metzler 2006, Kirshner 2007. On Matsukata's nationalism, see Helleiner 2003, 86–87.

suggests potentially alarming parallels for the present day, should political relations between the United States and China deteriorate.[14]

Finally, the United States, of course, provides the archetypical example of a maker. Determined to avoid the mistakes of its interwar isolationism and short-sighted foreign economic policies, and driven by various economic and strategic motivations, the United States set up (and bankrolled) the Bretton Woods international monetary system. Learning, ideology, interest, and geopolitical imperatives went hand in hand (and were each essential) as the United States carried the heaviest stones, and coordinated the effort, that built the postwar monetary order.[15]

Handicapping the nature of China's integration and expanding role in the international monetary order will not be easy. As Benjamin Cohen notes, even if the Chinese government were to embrace the path of a relatively socialized taker of the rules of the game, accommodating the changes implied by such a trajectory would still tend to be naturally, even inherently, disruptive. A complicating factor, he adds, is that "Beijing appears to be working hard to tilt the global balance of monetary power as much as possible in its favor, quite unlike anything attempted at a comparable stage by Germany, Japan, or Saudi Arabia." This is certainly related to the fact that, unlike those other states as they emerged as more prominent players on the postwar world's monetary stage, China is neither an ally nor a client of the United States, but, even in the most benign sense of the concept, a geopolitical rival. Indeed, as Kirshner also emphasizes, it is the first newcomer on the monetary scene in seventy years that can be seen as a potential adversary to the system's most prominent participant, and this matters, given the political challenges that are inherent to managing international monetary relations.[16] This would present challenges even in a "best case scenario." In fact, the evidence to date on the Chinese government's intentions is mixed. Jiang observes, for example, that it has been very critical of

---

14. For France, see Kindleberger 1972. Both disagreements about economic ideology and the cooperation-inhibiting intensity of the security dilemma in Europe contributed to the collapse of the interwar monetary order. Vehemently opposed ideas about monetary management were regularly debated in the public sphere—see the various essays collected in Royal Institute of International Affairs 1932 and League of Nations 1932. See also Einzig 1931 and Aguado 2001.

15. Gardner 1980, Ikenberry 1992, Helleiner 2014a, Pollard 1985.

16. Kirshner 2009, 196. On geopolitical rivalry shaping monetary affairs in Asia more generally, see Grimes 2008.

the conditionality that the IMF has imposed on developing countries and registers its opposition to neoliberal ideology in global monetary governance. Yet at the same time, she emphasizes that the People's Republic has not offered a clearly articulated or ambitious alternative vision, proffering instead only "symbolic gestures," and motivated by defensive instincts.

Not surprisingly, then, scholars—including contributors to this volume—hold different perspectives on this question and each can cite evidence to support his or her position. These very different views of the priorities of the Chinese government in international monetary relations are not necessarily irreconcilable. Chinese priorities may have shifted over time. Indeed, some contributors to this volume (especially Chin and Kirshner) argue that the global financial crisis was an important watershed, encouraging Chinese officials to embrace more ambitious and experimental goals in international monetary relations. Chinese officials may also assign different priorities to distinct issue areas within international monetary relations. Equally important, it is necessary to avoid overstating the unity of Chinese officialdom itself; different Chinese policymakers have different perspectives, and the resulting constellation of policies might not reflect a singularly coherent driving vision.[17]

From one perspective, the Chinese government has to date been very much a supporter of the status quo. With its accumulation of massive dollar reserves, China has reinforced the dollar-based international monetary order. Its conservatism was also apparent during the 2008 global financial crisis when some had predicted that China might pull back its US investments, perhaps even as a kind of "payback for the American bungling of the 1997–98 East Asia crisis."[18] Instead of acting as a destabilizer, China bolstered the system by providing crucial ongoing support for the dollar and for US current account deficits. In the words of one critic, China served as America's "head servant" in this episode.[19] The contrast with the behavior of the United States during the Great Depression—when it refused to support European countries in distress—was striking.

Some scholars point to significant material incentives that nudge China in this direction. John Ikenberry, in particular, has emphasized the extent

---

17. On this issue see for example Shih 2009.
18. James 2009, 224.
19. Hung 2009. For China's stabilizing role, see also Helleiner 2014b.

to which the Western order—and this encompasses the entire Organisation for Economic Cooperation and Development, not simply the United States—is very large, very robust, and features a system that is "hard to overturn and easy to join." There are also limits to China's capabilities, something that outside observers tend to minimize.[20] And in this volume, Andrew Walter argues that although Chinese officials object to perceived biases in international macroeconomic surveillance, their fear of foreign criticism and "stigmatization" by the IMF encouraged them to commit after the 2008 global financial crisis to an enhanced surveillance process under the auspices of the G20. Some analysts also highlight how China has been a supporter, rather than a challenger, of the IMF. It is often forgotten that China was in fact one of the founding members of the IMF, playing an active role in the negotiations that created its Articles of Agreement which formed the international legal foundation for postwar international monetary affairs. After the 1949 revolution, mainland China was forced out as Taiwan assumed its IMF seat but Eric Helleiner and Bessma Momani stress how the People's Republic of China later sought to join the body rather than reject it. When it assumed membership in 1980, the Beijing government also maintained good relations with the Fund and did not rock the boat. Indeed, when Japan proposed an Asian Monetary Fund in 1998 that would have challenged the IMF's role in the region, Chinese officials opposed the scheme.[21] Although it subsequently supported the more modest CMI arrangement, the Chinese government was one of the leading advocates of making CMI lending conditional on the adoption of an IMF program.

Still, other scholars see Chinese policymakers as having more reformist ambitions, particularly since the 2008 global financial crisis. They often cite a prominent essay of March 2009 by China's central bank governor Zhou Xiaochuan that called for international monetary reform to reduce the dollar's central role and strengthen that of a supranational reserve currency. Zhou couched his ideas in the spirit of a long line of reformist liberal multilateralism from John Maynard Keynes to Robert Triffin, and he

---

20. Ikenberry 2008, 14; 2013. Chin and Helleiner 2008.
21. Sohn 2008, 311. China was also motivated by geopolitics, in this case the desire to undercut an effort by Japan to assert greater regional leadership (Green 2003, 230, 267; Grimes 2003, 173; Grimes 2008, 205).

stressed the need for gradual change that built on past efforts to strengthen the IMF's Special Drawing Rights (SDR). As Chin notes, Zhou's proposals situated him as a champion of rule-based multilateralism. The essay left little mystery in this regard: the crisis was "an inevitable outcome of the institutional flaws" of relying on a single national currency to serve as the world's money.[22] Chin also reminds us that Zhou's analysis built directly on ideas already expressed by Chinese policymakers over the previous decade. He argues that the 2008 global financial crisis generated new political impetus among them to support the cause of international monetary reform, and that "China's actions aim to induce institutional adaptation."

Indeed, Chinese officials have become strong advocates of IMF reform. They have devoted particular attention to governance issues such as the need for a more merit-based selection of the managing director and for a larger voice for emerging-market countries in the institution. As Chin and Walter both note, Chinese policymakers have also urged since the late 1990s that IMF surveillance focus more on the surveillance of the policies of major developed countries, particularly "reserve-issuing countries." (Interestingly, as Helleiner and Momani observe, the government representing China at the 1944 Bretton Woods conference also pushed for a symmetrical adjustment of obligations of creditor and deficit countries.) This push for greater symmetry intensified after the early 2000s when the IMF began to urge the Chinese government to allow currency appreciation, advice that many Chinese officials resented and saw as driven by the United States. Despite their frustrations, however, Chinese officials were consistently reformist rather than radical in their goals; they never objected to the right of the Fund to do surveillance of its members (although the Chinese government did withdraw temporarily from bilateral surveillance discussions in 2007–8). Indeed, as noted above, Walter points out that Chinese officials have been supportive of the G20's efforts since 2009 to resolve global imbalances through its Multilateral Assessment Program (in which the IMF plays an important advisory and analytical role). Helleiner and Momani also highlight how Chinese officials' skepticism of full capital account liberalization, and their calls for the IMF to "effectively monitor

---

22. Zhou 2009, 1; David Barboza, "China Urges New Money Reserve to Replace Dollar," *New York Times,* March 24, 2009; Chin and Wang 2010.

and regulate international capital flows," actually position Chinese policy-makers as "important defenders of the content of the original IMF Articles of Agreement." The monetary initiatives of the Chinese government to date, they emphasize, have all been consistent with support for the Fund, the very hallmark of a reformist agenda.

Nevertheless, other analysts do suggest that Chinese policymakers are increasingly interested not just in reforming but in challenging core fea-tures of the existing international monetary order. For example, despite its reformist content, Zhou's 2009 essay is perceived by Kirshner and others as a thinly veiled challenge to the dollar-dominated international monetary order. This perception has been reinforced by the Chinese government's new support for RMB internationalization and for the calls of European and BRICS countries for a more multipolar currency order. In general, Cohen observes that "in both words and deeds, the Chinese have appeared to underscore a dissatisfaction with the status quo that goes well beyond anything expressed by earlier newcomers." Suggesting an edge to this blade, Walter reports a "popular narrative" in China "in which the United States systemically tries to prevent the emergence of viable challengers to its predominance."

At an ideological level, some analysts, such as Cohen and especially Kirsh-ner, also wonder about the extent to which Chinese leaders have a more transformative agenda. Kirshner argues that the 2008 global financial crisis undermined the legitimacy of the United States–championed, unregulated global financial order, and that Chinese policymakers are now favoring a more regulated approach to economic governance. He also suggests that the Chinese government's recent initiatives to promote the RMB's use in the region are aimed at creating a monetary order more autonomous from the dollar, one that has its own distinct rules and ideas. China's recent support for relaxing the tie between CMI loans and IMF conditionality could be interpreted as further evidence of the new preferences of Chinese officialdom in this respect. It is noteworthy that Chinese officials have long been critical of IMF neoliberal conditionality in developing countries, as Jiang and Walter point out.

Jiang is more skeptical, however, about the strength of Chinese com-mitment to regional initiatives such as the CMI/CMIM. She argues that China's support is largely symbolic and that Chinese officials are resistant to any regional efforts that might dilute their country's sovereignty, such as intrusive surveillance procedures or initiatives to strengthen exchange rate management. China's monetary diplomacy, she argues, is largely bilateral and driven primarily by short-term pragmatic and political interests (many unrelated to monetary issues) rather than a longer-term vision of preparing for either regional or multilateral leadership. Indeed, from her standpoint, it is these features of China's monetary diplomacy that are more likely to pose a challenge to the multilateral postwar international monetary system over time. Other analysts are also critical of how China's persistent accumulation of massive reserves seems to reflect short-term mercantilist objectives at the expense of the long-term interests of multilateral system.

The Sources of China's International Monetary Policy: Domestic, State-Level, External

The Chinese government's choice of international monetary policies, whatever they may be, will be formative—they will support, reshape, or subvert the global monetary order. This raises the issue of how to explain Chinese international monetary policymaking. Analyses of other countries' experiences highlight the importance of domestic, state-level, and external political influences in this area. These remain appropriate entrées into the study of China's policies, but require a sensitivity to those factors and attributes that are distinct to the circumstances of the People's Republic. It should also be stressed that these levels of analysis are not necessarily incompatible or even competing, and this is reflected across (and even within) the contributions to this volume. Such fluidity of analysis is not at all specific to China: as noted above, both specific ideas of policymakers and broader geopolitical interests motivated the United States to make the Bretton Woods system, and domestic economic interests were not shy about making their preferences known and shaping the final outcome.

Analysis of these issues can be particularly challenging in the Chinese context because of the opaque and secretive nature of its policymaking. The contributors to this volume identify some of the key official players that shape its international monetary policy. At the heart of the Chinese government's decisionmaking is the executive branch of the central government—the State Council. As in other countries, both the country's central bank—the People's Bank of China (PBOC)—and the Ministry of Finance play a key role in international monetary policymaking. Other government bodies (including think-tanks associated with them) that become involved in international monetary policy debates discussed in this book include: the Ministry of Commerce, the National Development and Reform Commission (NDRC), the State Asset Supervision and Administration Commission (SASAC), and various local governments, particularly in the coastal regions. And playing a crucial role throughout Chinese policymaking are the Communist Party and its Central Committee, Politburo, and the Politburo's Standing Committee.

If these are some of key players within the Chinese government, what accounts for the preferences of Chinese officials in international monetary decisionmaking? Political scientists have devoted considerable attention to the influence in other countries of various domestic sectoral groups on international monetary policymaking, particularly banks and manufacturing firms in tradable sectors. These groups are motivated to lobby governments because they experience the costs and benefits of international monetary policies in direct ways, and their influence varies according to their ability to assemble domestic coalitions and access policymakers. Although some analysts have tried to model the international monetary preferences of these domestic sectoral groups in the abstract, most have stressed that these preferences are "highly situationally dependent."[23]

The Chinese domestic context is particularly distinctive because some of the most powerful domestic businesses are state-owned and run by Communist Party members.[24] Several contributors to this volume show how these and other Chinese sectoral groups do indeed lobby for specific policies in international monetary relations. David Steinberg highlights the strong preference of the large and geographically concentrated export-oriented manufacturing sector for reserve accumulation to help preserve a competitive exchange rate.[25] Jiang notes that powerful state-owned enterprises and state banks often oppose financial liberalization because it risks undermining their power and the state control of finance that have been core to China's export-oriented, investment-driven development model.

23. Henning 1994, 26; see also McNamara 1998, Helleiner 2006b.
24. Shih 2009, 39.
25. See also Steinberg and Shih 2012, Schwartz 2009, Hung 2009.

Walter and Wang echo these points and stress the way in which the state-owned business elite is closely tied to the Party and various government agencies. They also emphasize the relative lack of influence on Chinese policymaking of broader societal groups whose interests may be quite opposed to those of this business-party-state elite. More generally, several contributors also stress the importance of the interest of the Communist Party itself and its membership in retaining power.

These domestic pressures are not the only sources of international monetary policymaking in China. In countries around the world, such policymaking also often takes place in state agencies with considerable autonomy because of the technical complexity of the issues involved and because their effects are often diffuse at the macroeconomic level.[26] In the Chinese case, the influence of lobbying by domestic groups is also constrained by the authoritarian nature of the government. Andrew Walter and Hongying Wang, in their contributions, stress the relatively weak impact of domestic interests within China, in comparison with many other societies, on macroeconomic policy outcomes. In particular, Walter and Wang cite the political marginalization of the broad mass of domestic society (in contrast with well-placed, entrenched conservative interests) as a key factor in the central government's failure to engage in an aggressive policy of rebalancing toward internal domestic consumption—a path recommended by a broad cross-section of economists.[27]

Given that officials are often relatively autonomous from domestic lobbying pressures, additional factors are needed to explain their preferences in international monetary decisionmaking. Scholars have identified various ideational influences at work in other countries, ranging from technical ideas to broader ideologies and nationalist framings. Rational choice approaches, which emphasize individual egoists pursuing material interests, have focused on the self-interested and careerist goals of policymakers and the ways in which their behavior is shaped by various institutional and bureaucratic contexts.[28] Steinberg argues, for example, that China's reserve

---

26. See for example Krasner 1977.

27. See for example Martin Wolf, "Why China Must Do More to Rebalance Its Economy," *Financial Times,* September 22, 2009; Lardy and Borst 2013; Pettis 2013.

28. For these approaches, see for example Kirshner 2003, Odell 1982, Helleiner 2006b, McNamara 1998, Bernhard, Broz, and Clark 2002.

accumulation cannot be explained by the search for domestic stability or the pursuit of international influence, but by the fact that "it serves the political and economic interests of a small group of powerful elites."

Various contributors highlight ideational frames that influence officials involved in Chinese international monetary policymaking. One very prominent influence has been their development priorities. Helleiner and Momani note that these priorities were in fact central to Chinese international monetary policy as far back as the Bretton Woods negotiations, when China pushed for an international monetary system that would be supportive of its goal of rapid state-led industrialization. Indeed, Helleiner and Momani see a notable ideational continuity in Chinese policy traceable to ideas articulated by Sun Yat-sen early in the twentieth century, recognizable both during the Bretton Woods negotiations and in Deng Xiaoping's market-oriented reforms and development strategy introduced after the late 1970s. And as Jiang notes, the Chinese government continues to position itself today as a representative of developing country interests in international monetary discussions. Many chapters in this volume also emphasize the priority that the contemporary Chinese leadership assigns to the link between international monetary policymaking and its commitment to rapid economic development.

There are clearly sharp divisions among Chinese officials, however, on the question of how those development goals should be met. Jiang points to a division between reform-minded liberals in the PBOC and conservatives in the Ministry of Finance and the NDRC. While the former back RMB internationalization and financial liberalization to lock in domestic market-oriented reforms, the latter seek to preserve state control over Chinese banks and the financial system. Jiang sees China's emphasis on bilateral monetary agreements as reflecting a compromise between these two competing perspectives. In policy battles in this area, she notes, the finance ministry has gained increasing influence vis-à-vis the PBOC in recent years.[29]

Steinberg also draws attention to disagreements among officials from different bureaucratic agencies, but his analysis locates their source in contrasting incentives that each agency faces. He argues that the PBOC

---

29. For the reformism of the PBOC, see also Bell and Feng 2013.

officials oppose reserve accumulation because their career advancement is linked to successful inflation control and management of the bank's balance sheet. By contrast, officials in the Ministry of Commerce and provincial governments in coastal regions support this policy on the grounds that exporters' success will reflect well on them. Because the PBOC has less political clout than the commerce ministry and the coastal governments, he argues, it has consistently lost key policy battles in this area.

Wang echoes both of these sets of arguments in her analysis of China's role in debates concerning global imbalances. The resolution of these imbalances requires China to reorient its economy toward a more domestically driven growth model that gives more emphasis to consumption. Wang notes the reformist tendencies of the PBOC and the National People's Congress in this respect, but argues that more power rests with a number of government agencies that ally with the state-owned enterprises to support the existing export-driven and investment-led growth model that contributes to the perpetuation of imbalances. These agencies include the finance ministry, NDRC, SASAC, and local governments from the coastal regions.

Wang also emphasizes that China's existing growth model stems from the influence of an ideology of statist nationalism among the policy elite (and the broader public) that prioritizes the goals of maximizing state power and national prestige even over those of improving the standard of living of ordinary people.[30] She and Jiang also highlight the growing political salience among Chinese officials of the goal of "financial security" that aims to minimize the risk of crises, protect sovereignty, and promote stability. The emphasis on financial security reinforces the commitment of many Chinese officials to various financial controls and the accumulation of enormous foreign exchange reserves. In his analysis of the internationalization of the RMB, Kirshner also stresses the priority that Chinese officials place on security, regional power, and international status. Helleiner and Momani note, too, that China's quest for a larger IMF voting share has long been linked to the quest for greater international status, even as far back as the Bretton Woods conference.

Kirshner and Chin both stress one other ideational influence on Chinese international monetary policymaking: the growing Chinese frustration

---

30. See also Wang 2002.

with US approaches to economic governance and its management of the
dollar. The 2008 global financial crisis starkly revealed China's macroeconomic exposure to what are increasingly perceived in Chinese official
circles as irresponsible US economic policies. Chin argues that the crisis
spurred Beijing to move to a more activist, interventionist, systemic reform posture. It also prompted what Kirshner calls "buyer's remorse" as
the dangers of China's accumulation of vast holdings of dollar reserves became more apparent. More generally, as noted above, Kirshner argues that
that crisis delegitimized the US model of economic governance in the eyes
of many Chinese officials. These policymakers, as a result, hope to dimin-
ish China's dependence on the United States and the dollar as well as to
force more monetary and fiscal discipline on the United States through
initiatives such as the promotion of RMB internationalization and the encouragement of a multipolar currency order, talking up the SDR, and ad-
vocating strengthened IMF surveillance of reserve-issuing countries.

Chinese international monetary policy is also clearly driven by the more
interest-based desire of Communist Party leadership to maintain its grip
on power at home. Several contributors point out that this concern leads
Chinese officials to evaluate international monetary issues in terms of their
impact on domestic political stability and their domestic legitimacy. Wang,
in particular, stresses legitimacy (and fears of challenges to legitimacy) as
a key motivating factor behind policy choices. Sound stewardship of the
economy, and nationalism—not to be underestimated as a force in China
and in the contemporary hyper-media environment, less easy to control
and manipulate—are the two foundations of the Party's political power.[31]
Resistance to currency appreciation, for example, stems in part from fears
that job losses in the export sector might generate domestic unrest. Some
analysts also link the Chinese leadership's focus on international prestige and status also to this concern; external prestige boosts its reputation
within China.

In studying other countries, political scientists have demonstrated how
international monetary policymaking is influenced by not just domestic
and state-level factors but also external ones. Once again, the contributors
to this volume show that China is no exception. Walter's chapter explores

---

31. Gries 2005, Shirk 2007, Shambaugh 2013; see also Wang 2002.

the role of IMF and US influence over China's exchange rate policy choices. United States pressure for changes in this area first emerged in early 1990s when the US Treasury named China as a currency manipulator until it ended its dual exchange rate system in late 1994. It appeared again after the early 2000s, and Walter argues that China's post-2005 appreciation of the RMB was linked at least in part to a desire to diffuse US demands and limit the risk of foreign—especially US—retaliation. He notes that because of the domestic constraints noted above, the IMF has had less success in encouraging China to address its "internal imbalance" through structural reforms that would encourage more consumption-focused growth.

Broader global economic and geostrategic contexts have also influenced Chinese international monetary policymaking. Wang attributes China's accumulation of reserves to the belief that such reserves are important "in safeguarding national power and national security"—not to mention regime security—lessons she argues were learned in the wake of the Asian financial crisis. After that crisis, she reports, the concept of national "financial security" became an important part of policy discussions. This emphasis on financial stability, security, and sovereignty is also emphasized by Jiang. She notes further that the Chinese government's taste for bilateralism is in accord with these objectives, while at the same time allowing the country to pursue a number of geopolitical goals, such as enhancing its political influence with strategically important partners, building its image as a "responsible great power," and providing a counterweight to the influence of the West.

As the global financial crisis reminded us (yet again), money matters. China is now one of the three great engines of the global economy, it is an emerging great power, and it is assuming a place as a major stakeholder in the international monetary system. Already, China's power in international monetary relations is growing considerably—albeit unevenly—with its provision of balance of payments finance, its significance to the international politics of macroeconomic adjustment, its influence in international financial institutions, and the slow internationalization of its currency. Its preferences and choices in these areas will shape the nature of the international monetary system and affect the course of international relations more generally.

Whether the Chinese state will choose to be a taker, maker, or breaker of the existing international monetary system remains very uncertain. This volume reveals, however, how China's priorities and decisions will be shaped by political influences stemming from the domestic, state, and external levels. By analyzing the distinctive nature of those influences, the contributors pioneer the study of the *politics* of China's international monetary relations. In so doing, they shed new light on Chinese foreign economic policymaking, the future of the international monetary system, and the trajectory of China's continuing emergence as a great power in the coming decades.

1

The China Question

Can Its Rise Be Accommodated?

Benjamin J. Cohen

Whether measured by the size of its reserves, the role of its exchange rate, or the use of its currency, Beijing's growing influence in the international monetary system is unmistakable. The issue to be addressed in this chapter is: Can the proverbial Middle Kingdom be smoothly absorbed into the leadership ranks of the global system, or could it instead become a force for instability or even conflict? Call it the China question.

The answer to the China question depends, in particular, on two critical factors. First is the issue of systemic flexibility. How adaptable are the institutions and procedures of global monetary governance? How easy is it for the monetary system to adjust to significant changes in the distribution of power? And second is the issue of China's intentions. What do the Chinese want? Can Chinese preferences be successfully accommodated? Both factors are essential, and much rides on the outcome.

Happily, historical analysis suggests that there is little problem on the first score. Other emergent powers in the past have been effectively absorbed without lasting disruption or irreparable damage. On the second score, however, there may be more cause for concern, since we know so little about China's strategic priorities. As several contributors to this volume note, Beijing repeatedly sends mixed signals about its intentions. To say the least, its ultimate goals remain shrouded in mystery.

Analytical Framework

The China question confronts us with two analytical challenges. First, how do we know when a newcomer is big enough to challenge the system's status quo? And second, how do we know when the emergence of a big newcomer has been successfully accommodated? Both challenges call for historical interpretation, which is inherently subjective. Each, therefore, is an issue on which reasonable people might reasonably disagree. Interpretation will be more persuasive if it can be grounded in a systematic analytical framework with well-articulated standards to provide an acceptable basis for judgment.

Monetary Power

Begin with the notion of "big." This of course is an issue of power. How do we know when an actor has gained sufficient power to challenge the established order?

Measuring monetary power is notoriously difficult. Until not long ago, the very concept of power in international monetary relations was, as Jonathan Kirshner noted in a seminal work, "a neglected area of study."[1] More recently, considerable progress has been achieved in parsing the meaning and uses of monetary power.[2] Yet for all the insight that has been gained, we still have no easy way to distinguish scales or levels of power in the monetary system.

For the purposes of this chapter, monetary power will be equated with *influence:* an ability to shape the behavior of others. This approach is in keeping with the conventions of mainstream international relations theory, as highlighted in a recent survey by David Baldwin—a tradition

---

1. Kirshner 1995, 3.
2. Lawton et al. 2000, Andrews 2006.

stretching back to the early work of Robert Dahl, who argued that "A has power over B to the extent that he can get B to do something that B would not otherwise do."[3] The focus here is on the effects rather than the sources of power. An actor will be considered "big" if its actions (or inactions) can have systemic consequences, altering or controlling the outcome of events. Influence will be considered synonymous with authority or leadership.

How would we know when monetary influence is at work? The exercise of power is not always self-evident, particularly if it is indirect or passive. Power does not regularly announce itself. The most practical approach is to focus on specific roles—identifiable functions that can be considered as tangible manifestations of power. A "big" actor is one that is seen to act with authority or leadership in monetary affairs.

And what might those roles be? For inspiration, this chapter will look to the work of the late Charles Kindleberger, who wrote a great deal about monetary power. In his justly celebrated book, *A World in Depression,* Kindleberger suggested that a monetary leader would be expected to play three distinct roles: (1) maintaining a relatively open market for distress goods; (2) providing contracyclical, or at least stable, long-term lending; and (3) acting as a lender of last resort at times of crisis.[4] In later work, he added two additional functions: (4) policing a relatively stable system of exchange rates; and (5) ensuring some degree of coordination of macroeconomic policies.[5] All five of these roles clearly imply a measure of influence. Together, they define the *scope* of monetary power.

Accordingly, this chapter will look to these five roles as tangible manifestations of monetary power. A newcomer will be considered big enough to challenge the system if it has become: (1) a major, if not dominant, import market; (2) a sizable capital exporter; (3) a significant influence on exchange rates; (4) a substantial influence on macroeconomic conditions; and/or (5) a potential source of crisis financing. Some combination of these five roles will be considered sufficient to qualify an actor as a major influence on the distribution of monetary power. The greater the number of the roles played, the larger is the scope of the actor's power.

---

3. Dahl 1957, 202–3; Baldwin 2013.
4. Kindleberger 1973.
5. Kindleberger 1981, chap. 21.

Accommodation

So how, then, do we know when the emergence of a big newcomer has been successfully accommodated? That too is a difficult question. The emergence of a new pole of influence is hardly apt to be frictionless and will certainly not occur overnight. Authority in human affairs is not readily shared, and that is particularly true of relations among sovereign states with their distinct and often divergent political and economic interests. Some resistance on the part of incumbents is naturally to be expected, at least initially.

Broadly speaking, three alternative outcomes are possible. At one extreme, resistance to a newcomer might remain adamant, leading to rising tensions and the risk of serious policy conflict—hardly a denouement to be desired. Second, the newcomer might be co-opted by existing powers, persuaded or coerced into aligning its preferences with the prevailing rules of the game—in effect, into acquiescing with the status quo. Or third, opposition could eventually give way to some measure of acceptance of the newcomer's priorities, with space carved out for the rising power to join in playing a leadership role. The last may be considered the meaning of accommodation: a successful transition to a new sharing of authority with due deference to the interests of the newcomer. For the purposes of this chapter, three criteria will be used to judge whether a big new actor has been or can be successfully accommodated in this sense.

The first criterion will focus on the nature of the actor's impact on the overall stability of the system. Effects may be transmitted via the trade balance or the capital account and will be felt in exchange rates, payments balances, and general macroeconomic conditions. The emergence of a new power, determined to assert its own interests, is often destabilizing—at least at the start. The question is: Does its impact remain disturbing, or do priorities eventually come into alignment? A gradual movement toward a new overall balance in the system, while respecting the preferences of the newcomer, will be taken as a sign of successful accommodation.

A second criterion will have to do with crisis financing. Emerging powers usually accumulate a sizable stock of central bank reserves; in time, as well, their currencies may begin to play important international roles in trade, financial markets, or the reserves of other economies. Both ample reserves and an internationalized currency enable a country to act, if it wishes, as a lender of last resort in time of crisis—a source of liquidity for others. Voluntary acceptance of the role of crisis lender may also be seen as a sign of successful accommodation. Has the actor willingly become a recognized credit source when others get in trouble?

The third criterion has to do with governance mechanisms. Has the actor been formally incorporated into prevailing leadership councils? Governance of the global monetary system is famously complex, if not obscure, comprising not only the formal structures and rules of the IMF but also the more informal decision-making procedures of regularized negotiating bodies like the G7 and the G20. A third sign of successful accommodation would be effective inclusion into some or all of these governance mechanisms. In short the newcomer would be accepted, implicitly or explicitly, as a full member of the club.

The Rise of China

Judging by these standards, there seems little doubt that China has now become a big player in monetary affairs. The signs of the country's newfound monetary power are unmistakable, as the editors of this volume emphasize in their introduction. After three decades of double-digit growth, the Middle Kingdom has emerged to become the second largest economy in the world, surpassing the former number two, Japan, in 2010. As a voracious importer of raw materials and energy, China has become the dominant market for a wide swath of commodity producers, from close neighbors in Southeast Asia and Australia to South America and Africa. At the same time, as the "world's workshop" manufacturing or assembling vast amounts of goods for export, the country has enjoyed trade surpluses that have exceeded even those of Japan and Saudi Arabia in their prime. China today sells everything from textiles and apparel to wind turbines and solar panels. In the mid-2000s, the Middle Kingdom's surpluses on current account amounted to as much as 10 percent of GDP.

Correspondingly, these surpluses have cumulatively made China one of the world's greatest creditor nations, with external claims far exceeding liabilities. For many years most foreign earnings went directly into the currency reserves of the People's Bank of China, the Middle Kingdom's central bank, reaching a new high of some $3.5 trillion in mid-2013—the greatest stockpile of reserves for any one country in history. Even today, the PBOC's reserves account for as much as three-quarters of China's international claims. More recently, as Yang Jiang notes in this volume, some of these assets have been deployed in the form of foreign aid, often quite obviously for politico-strategic purposes. Additionally, an increasing emphasis has been put on economically profitable forms of overseas placement. This can be seen in the country's rising level of outward direct investment, led by state-owned enterprises, which since 2005 has accelerated rapidly to as much as $70 billion a year in 2010 and 2011. More than 80 percent of the total involved minerals or energy projects.[6] It can also be seen in the creation of the China Investment Corporation, a sovereign wealth fund, with an initial endowment in 2007 of some $200 billion. By 2012, CIC's assets had more than doubled, to some $440 billion. The value of China's accumulated claims abroad is still small as compared with those of the United States or other mature economies, with their much longer histories of foreign investment. But even with its late start, the Middle Kingdom clearly is well on its way to becoming a major capital exporter.

China's massive reserves have also put the country in a position to act as a key source of crisis financing for others. In this regard, the Middle Kingdom's new capabilities were signaled as early as 2000 when Beijing signed on to the Chiang Mai Initiative (CMI), a regional framework for the provision of emergency liquidity assistance negotiated by the so-called ASEAN + 3 group—the ten members of the Association of Southeast Asian Nations plus the three Northeast Asian countries of China, Japan, and Korea (the "Plus Three" countries). CMI established the basis for a new network of bilateral swap arrangements between the Plus Three countries on the one hand and members of ASEAN on the other hand. The Plus Three countries promised to make dollar resources available to ASEAN members, when needed, in exchange for equivalent amounts of local currency. More recently, in 2010, the network of BSAs was formally transformed into a new common facility dubbed the Chiang Mai Initiative Multilateralization (CMIM), with resources now totaling $240 billion. China's share of commitments to CMIM was set at 32 percent ($76.8 billion). Although Yang Jiang dismisses Beijing's "currency swap diplomacy" in her chapter

6. Scissors 2012.

here as a "shallow form of monetary cooperation," it is nonetheless useful in helping to consolidate Chinese influence in East Asia.

Finally, it is clear that China is beginning to have a noticeable impact on exchange rates and macroeconomic conditions, at least in its immediate neighborhood. Historically most nations in East Asia, like many countries elsewhere, have chosen to shadow the US dollar in targeting their exchange rates, a practice that Ronald McKinnon has long described as an informal "dollar standard."[7] More recently, however, China's yuan—also known as the renminbi (RMB, or "people's currency")—has begun to play a substantially larger role as an anchor for regional currencies. According to econometric estimates by Randall Henning, four of the main economies of Southeast Asia—Malaysia, the Philippines, Singapore, and Thailand—now place more weight on the yuan than the dollar in the management of their exchange rates, forming what amounts to a nascent "renminbi bloc."[8] And through these links to the yuan, local monetary and fiscal policies are being influenced as well.

With all these signs of China's newfound monetary power, it would seem evident that a major new player has burst onto the scene, disrupting the status quo. No one knows, of course, whether the Chinese juggernaut will continue on its course. Debate rages over whether Beijing's economic model can long sustain the momentum of the last three decades.[9] But for now at least, the Middle Kingdom's rise seems real. What is less clear is whether China's emergence can be successfully accommodated. As indicated, the outcome will be determined by two factors in particular—the flexibility of the monetary system in general and the specific intentions of Beijing's leadership.

Systemic Flexibility

This is not the first time in living memory that the entrance of a big newcomer has significantly altered the distribution of power in monetary relations, challenging the system's status quo. At the end of World War II,

---

7. McKinnon 2005.
8. Henning 2014.
9. Beckley 2011/12.

when the Bretton Woods regime was established, the United States bestrode the system like a colossus. The system could fairly be described as unipolar. But in the decades since, several new powers have successively emerged to challenge US dominance, including West Germany, Japan, and most recently Europe's Economic and Monetary Union (EMU) with its euro. To this list some might also add a fourth, Saudi Arabia. New poles of influence have emerged. In each case, the emerging actor achieved a level of capability sufficient to pose a significant challenge to the status quo. But in each case existing institutions ultimately proved flexible enough to absorb the newcomer without undue stress. The modern monetary system has demonstrated a remarkable capacity to accommodate rising powers.

The Starting Lineup

One could go back further, of course—to the interwar period, for instance, when the United States first surpassed Britain as a monetary power; or even further to the nineteenth century, when the British faced emerging rivals in France and Germany. But those freewheeling eras had little in common with the more institutionalized regime that began with Bretton Woods. For serious comparative analysis, it seems best to begin with the system as it existed in 1945.

At that time, the starting lineup was clear. It consisted of one heavy hitter, the United States, and a motley cast of supporting players—Gulliver and the Lilliputians. American leadership was unquestioned. The United States was the world's biggest import market and, through programs like the Anglo-American Loan Agreement of 1946 and the Marshall Plan, the only major source of both long-term lending and crisis liquidity. The US dollar, universally regarded as being "as good as gold"(if not better), was enshrined as the anchor of the new Bretton Woods system of pegged exchange rates, and monetary and fiscal policy in Washington overwhelmingly set the tone for macroeconomic conditions elsewhere. The system was about as unipolar as it could get short of formal empire. Hegemony did not seem an unfair description.

Clearest evidence of America's dominance could be found in the initial allocation of IMF member quotas and seats on the Fund's Board of Executive Directors. Quotas are the main determinant of voting rights at the IMF. Though in principle set according to strictly objective formulas, quotas in practice are intended to be a rough reflection of the monetary pecking order: a measure of each state's relative standing on the scale of monetary power. In 1946, when the IMF formally came into existence, the United States was assigned nearly one-third (31.68 percent) of all member votes. The only other country to come close was Great Britain, with 15.12 percent, and even that was considered rather generous. Though the pound sterling at the time still enjoyed some status as an international currency, at least within the sterling area, Britain itself was plainly a wounded nation, unable to play any of the roles normally associated with monetary leadership. At best, London could be regarded as Washington's feeble junior partner.

For the Board of Executive Directors—originally known simply as the Executive Board—the Fund's Articles of Agreement specify that five seats are to be appointed by the members with the largest quotas, with the remainder, normally, to be elected by diverse constituencies. At the start, the five appointed seats, in addition to the United States and Britain, went to France, China, and India. At best, these additional three could be regarded as not much more than courtesy appointments. None of the three was in any position to exercise much authority in monetary affairs. France had been occupied during World War II and had lost much of its industrial capacity. Its currency was weak and its reserves exhausted. China was in the midst of a debilitating civil war, eventually won by the Communists in 1949. And India, newly independent, was preoccupied with building state institutions after the Great Partition with Pakistan. The distribution of global monetary power was radically skewed in favor of the United States.

West Germany

The first serious challenge to American dominance came, unexpectedly, from a defeated World War II foe. This was the Federal Republic of Germany, otherwise known as West Germany, formally created in 1949 through amalgamation of the US, British, and French zones of occupation. At the end of hostilities in 1945 the former Third Reich lay in ruin, its cities and industries largely destroyed. The Deutsche mark (DM) did not even come into existence until 1948, and even as late as 1950 the reborn country's balance of payments was in severe crisis, requiring outside assistance. But then the German economic miracle began, generating rapid growth

and persistent export surpluses. By the end of the 1950s the Federal Republic was firmly ensconced as the leading economy of Europe and its preeminent monetary power.

The reach of West Germany's newfound influence could be best seen in
its impact on macroeconomic conditions, not only in Europe but even in
the United States. The German public's well known aversion to inflation
was fully reflected in the hardline policies of the Federal Republic's central
bank, the Bundesbank. Across Europe governments felt driven to match
the DM's high interest rates in order to avoid downward pressure on their
own currencies—a pressure only modestly relieved by two small revalu-
ations in 1961 and 1969. In the 1970s, when a common intervention system known as the "snake" was created to bind together exchange rates in
the European Community (succeeded in 1979 by the European Monetary
System), the centrality of the DM was universally acknowledged. Though
West Germany did not actively seek an international role for the DM,
for fear of losing control over its own monetary policy, its well-respected
money soon came to be broadly accepted as the anchor for other European
currencies.

Across the Atlantic, meanwhile, the United States struggled throughout the 1960s to stem the flood of dollars pouring into purchases of the
DM, severely complicating Washington's efforts to cope with swelling external deficits. For domestic reasons tighter monetary policy in the United
States was resisted, giving rise to headline stories about a burgeoning interest rate war with the Germans. I recall a prominent US economist at
the time tartly saying to me that we now imported our cars from Japan
and our interest rates from Germany. Though resisting pressure for a substantial revaluation of the DM, which could have hurt German exports,
the Federal Republic did what it could to help keep the policy conflict
from getting out of hand. As a close ally of the United States in NATO,
West Germany had no wish to ruffle Washington's feathers. Hence in a famous letter from the Bundesbank to the US Federal Reserve, a pledge was
made to keep German reserves in dollars rather than convert them into
gold. Likewise, West Germany agreed to make significant payments to the
United States to "offset" the cost of maintaining American troops in the
Federal Republic. But in the end these and other concessions proved insufficient to forestall the Nixon administration's dramatic decision in August

1971 to suspend the gold convertibility of the dollar, effectively introducing a new era of floating exchange rates.

Already by that time, however, it was clear that West Germany's emergence as a monetary power was being successfully accommodated. As early as 1961 the Federal Republic was given a quota at the IMF equal to that of France and received its own appointed seat on the Executive Board. West Germany took the place of China, whose quota had been frozen following the Communist victory in 1949 (and remained frozen until the mainland government replaced Taiwan in the China seat in 1980). And three years later, when the so-called Group of Ten was named to negotiate the first reform of the IMF since Bretton Woods (leading to the creation of Special Drawing Rights), no one questioned that the Germans should be included. The Federal Republic clearly had become part of the inner circle. This was by no means a co-optation. West Germany's tenacious defense of its tight monetary policy amply demonstrated the extent to which German priorities were now to be part of the international conversation. Rather, this was simply confirmation that the Federal Republic had, in a sense, "arrived."

Indeed, some sources wanted to go even further, to promote West Germany formally to a position of peak leadership in exclusive partnership with the United States in a sort of monetary "bigemony."[10] But that was more than other key players, such as Britain and France, were willing to accept. Instead, the Federal Republic was folded into a new Group of Five or G5 (alongside the United States, Britain, France, and Japan) that was created in 1975, soon expanded with the addition of Canada and Italy to become the G7. For years thereafter the G7, representing nearly half of the world's economy, functioned informally as the center of governance of the monetary system.

Japan

Ironically, the next major challenge also came from a defeated World War II foe—Japan. Like Germany, Japan experienced a postwar economic miracle, an export-led boom starting in the mid-1950s that by the 1960s was generating growth rates in the double digits. In 1968 Japan became the

---

10. Bergsten 1975.

world's second largest economy, enjoying record payments surpluses and a rapidly growing stockpile of international reserves. During the 1970s the yen became one of the most popular currencies in global financial markets. By the 1980s Japan was the world's biggest creditor nation, clearly a monetary force to be reckoned with.

Unlike Germany, though, Japan played a relatively limited role as a direct influence on exchange rates or macroeconomic conditions. For the Federal Republic, fully committed from the start to the project of European integration, a leadership role in monetary affairs came naturally once economic recovery took hold. However much the Germans may have resisted internationalization of the DM, others nearby could not be prevented from following. Japan, by contrast, had made no such commitment to regional reconciliation. Hence Tokyo had no willing followers in its own neighborhood, where memories were still fresh of Japan's wartime atrocities. On monetary matters, most governments in the region preferred to take their cue from Washington.

Nor, prior to the 1990s, did the Japanese show much interest in playing a more direct role. Like Germany, Japan was long inclined to resist internationalization of its currency for fear of losing control over monetary policy. The Japanese did see their successful economy as an exemplary model for Asian neighbors to emulate, an idea popularized as the "flying geese" theory of economic development. But it was not until the bursting of Japan's "bubble" economy in 1989 and then the Asian crisis of 1997–98 that Tokyo began to take a more proactive role in regional finance. Now currency leadership in East Asia became a central element of policy, largely as a defensive measure intended to reduce the domestic economy's exposure to external volatility—what William Grimes has called "internationalization as insulation."[11] Success in creating anything like a "yen bloc," however, has proved elusive. For the most part, the reach of Japanese monetary power continues to be felt primarily in the country's prominence as a capital exporter and secondarily as a potential source of crisis financing.

In any event, postwar Japan had little appetite to challenge the monetary dominance of its political patron, the United States. With Japanese national security directly dependent on American military might, Tokyo

---

11. Grimes 2003, 186.

elected to maintain a passive, low-profile stance in its overall foreign policy. Japan had no wish to make waves and acquiesced frequently, albeit unhappily, to American priorities—such as when Tokyo agreed to engineer a revaluation of the yen in 1971 and again in 1978 and 1987. Accommodation of Japan's monetary ascent, therefore, could take place with comparative ease. In the 1960s the country was welcomed as a member of the Group of Ten and later to the G5/G7. And in 1971 Tokyo gained an appointed seat on the IMF Executive Board, replacing India. Though Japan's share of voting rights at the Fund was not to match Germany's for another twenty years, it was nonetheless clear that by the 1970s the Japanese too had "arrived."

Saudi Arabia

A third challenge, of a quite different order, came from Saudi Arabia after the dramatic oil shock of 1973, when world oil prices quadrupled. The Saudi kingdom was the world's largest exporter of crude petroleum and at the time sat atop nearly a third of known energy reserves. Unexpectedly, a country that had not even become a member of the IMF until 1957 found itself a major player in monetary affairs, with a huge surplus of revenues and a rapidly rising stockpile of foreign assets. With scant resources other than oil and a population under fifteen million, Saudi Arabia could hardly be compared with Germany or Japan in broad economic terms. The country did not even have a national currency until 1961. But in strictly financial terms, the Saudis were now in a position to exercise major influence.

The oil shock was clearly destabilizing. On the one hand, energy importers were forced to scramble to find ways to cope with much higher import bills. The suddenly huge transfers to the Saudis and their partners in the Organization of the Petroleum Exporting Countries had the dual effect of accelerating inflation (through the higher price for oil) and retarding growth (by diverting spending for other purposes), ushering in a new era of prolonged stagflation around the world. On the other hand, energy exporters were now endowed with a mammoth accumulation of wealth, which many feared might become a kind of doomsday "money weapon." Oil revenues were paid in dollars, and in the United States in particular there was much concern that the Arab members of OPEC, led by Saudi Arabia, might be tempted to use their new riches as an instrument of linkage to pressure Washington on Middle East political or military issues.

The Saudis alone were thought to account for anywhere from one-half to three-quarters of Arab holdings of greenbacks.[12]

In practice, however, accommodations were quickly found. In return for critical concessions from Washington—including, in particular, informal security guarantees against possible threats from enemies within or without—Saudi Arabia gave assurances of continued support for the dollar. The kingdom was promised top secret confidentiality for its holdings and was even provided a separate "add-on" facility to handle its purchases of US government securities outside the normal auction process.[13] On a broader scale Saudi Arabia began lending funds to the International Monetary Fund, then strapped for cash, to help support the Fund's recycling of so-called petrodollars to energy importers. By 1979 the kingdom had become the IMF's second largest creditor after the United States, qualifying it for an appointed seat on the Fund's Executive Board alongside the established monetary powers of the G5. Saudi Arabia's quota was also rapidly raised, moving it from fifteenth place among members in the mid-1970s to sixth place in 1981.

Since the 1980s the kingdom's monetary star has dimmed somewhat, despite the fact that it has continued to pile up financial assets. In more recent years, Saudi Arabia's share of Fund quotas has slipped from sixth place to twelfth, falling behind the rising BRIC powers (Brazil, Russia, India, and China) as well as Canada and Italy. Moreover, having lost its position as the IMF's second largest creditor, the kingdom was deprived of its appointed seat on the Executive Board in 1992. In recognition of their continuing importance, however, the Saudis were instead accorded the rare privilege of electing their own exclusive executive director—a de facto equivalent of an appointed seat. Though Saudi Arabia may no longer qualify as a top player, the country clearly remains a member of the world's monetary elite.

The Euro Area

Finally, there is the euro area, Europe's Economic and Monetary Union, which formally came into existence in 1999. From the start EMU was

---

12. Cohen 1986, 126.
13. Spiro 1999.

expected to pose a formidable challenge to the monetary status quo. The birth of the euro, it was thought, would create a new power in international monetary affairs. Even without the participation of Britain and some other European Union members, the euro area would constitute one of the largest economic units in the world, rivaling even the United States in terms of output or share of global trade. Consequences for the monetary system thus promised to be momentous. EMU would become a major rival to the United States. Europe's new money, building on the widespread popularity of Germany's old DM, would pose a serious threat to the long-standing dominance of the greenback. According to one celebrated forecast, the euro might even overtake the dollar as a reserve currency by as early as 2015.[14]

Experience, however, has defied expectations. Unquestionably, the newborn euro did begin life with many of the attributes needed for competitive success, including a large economic base, deeply rooted political stability, and an enviably low rate of inflation, all backed by a joint monetary authority, the European Central Bank, that was fully committed to preserving confidence in the currency's future value. Yet in practice, after a fast early start, cross-border use of the euro for most purposes appears to have leveled off by the middle of its first decade, and under the pressure of Europe's sovereign debt crisis more recently may even have begun to slip back a bit. Overall, the euro has done little more than hold its own as compared with the past aggregate market shares of the DM and EMU's other "legacy" currencies. Moreover, it is well known that while the dollar continues to be used virtually everywhere, the euro's domain is still confined mainly to a limited number of countries with close geographical and/or institutional links to the European Union. Strictly speaking, we would be closer to the mark speaking of a "one-and-a-half currency system" rather than genuine rivalry.[15] The outcome to date has been decidedly anticlimactic.

Partly, this disappointing result has been due to the natural incumbency advantages enjoyed by the greenback; and partly also to the European Central Bank, which has studiously maintained a hands-off policy toward

---

14. Chinn and Frankel 2008.
15. Cohen 2011, chap. 8.

the issue of euro internationalization. But most of all the outcome would seem attributable to inherent defects in EMU's ambiguous and decentralized governance structure, which has left ultimate authority mainly in the hands of its largest members. Germany, France, and Italy continue to participate separately, on their own behalf, in the G7; and there is no unified EMU representation on the Executive Board of the IMF, where the euro area's seventeen members are scattered across no fewer than eight different constituencies. Accommodating to the creation of EMU, therefore, has proved easier than many had anticipated. Business among the major players can go on much as it has done in the past, and the distribution of power in the system remains relatively unaffected.

Lessons

Looking back, what do we learn from this brief history? Admittedly, the sample is small—just three big newcomers to date (Germany, Japan, and Saudi Arabia), plus a more or less inconclusive fourth (EMU). Yet even so, the narrative is instructive. Three lessons stand out.

First, it is clear that when push comes to shove, the monetary system does not lack the flexibility needed to adjust to the emergence of significant new poles of influence. Not surprisingly, the rise of new powers tends, at least initially, to be disruptive. Germany, Japan, and Saudi Arabia, in their time, all started with export surpluses large enough to stress the overall system. The global community had to scramble to find constructive ways of coping with the pressure of counterpart deficits without ignoring the priorities of the newcomers. Could the necessary finance be mobilized? Could interest rate wars or other destabilizing policy conflicts be avoided? Could room be found for a new actor in prevailing leadership councils? In each case accommodations proved possible. Rather than rigidly resist newcomer interests, threatening stalemate or even systemic failure, existing powers managed to carve out space for a new sharing of authority. By adapting, the system endured.

Second, it is clear that accommodations by the newly emergent powers were essential as well. It takes two to tango. Stabilization also required a spirit of compromise on the part of newcomers—a willingness to play within the prevailing rules of the game rather than to fundamentally challenge the existing order. Each had its own ideas about how the system should be governed. But to borrow a phrase long ago coined by John Ruggie, their preferences tended for the most part to be "norm-governed"—that is, consistent with prevailing principles and understandings, not seeking radical transformation.[16] In their time each newcomer was content to accept admission into existing leadership councils rather than to push for new institutional arrangements. All seemed more interested in being accepted into the inner circle than in starting a new club.

Finally, it is difficult not to notice the underlying geopolitics in all this history. In every episode, including the birth of the euro in 1999, there was clearly a strong security dimension to the relationship between the aspiring newcomer and the still dominant incumbent, the United States. Germany and Japan both have long been close political and military allies of the United States, as are the members of EMU today; while the governing elite of Saudi Arabia continues to depend on an American defense umbrella for protection against potential adversaries. Economic and financial interests may for a time have diverged sharply. But in the end, differences were never allowed to jeopardize broader geopolitical relationships. As Kirshner has noted, "conflicts took place exclusively between friends, and beyond that the high politics . . . served as an 'emergency brake' that placed a limit on just how far monetary squabbles . . . could go."[17] In short, politics trumped economics.

China's Intentions

Now, once more, the monetary system faces a major emergent power, so again some manner of adaptation seems called for. Can the Chinese be successfully accommodated, as others were in the past, or is the Middle Kingdom somehow quantitatively or qualitatively different? This time, in contrast to previous experience, absorption of the newcomer may prove to be a far more daunting challenge.

Accommodation

Certainly, the door has been thrown open. As in the past, when faced with a big newcomer, existing powers have looked for accommodation rather

---

16. Ruggie 1983.
17. Kirshner 2009, 196.

than reacted with rigid resistance. Consider China's massive trade surpluses, for example, which have been painful for many countries. As both Andrew Walter and Hongying Wang note in this volume, commercial imbalances have prompted considerable external pressure on Beijing, especially from the United States, to revalue its currency. Yet in practical terms reactions have been restrained. Though the Chinese have obviously long manipulated the yuan's exchange rate to maintain a strong competitive advantage, there have been remarkably few direct retaliatory measures. Responses have been limited primarily to loud, but largely futile, verbal complaints.

China's interests have not been denied. Rather, existing powers have actively sought to make room for the Middle Kingdom in prevailing leadership councils. At the IMF, as Eric Helleiner and Bessma Momani meticulously describe in their chapters, a place was quickly found for the newcomer once the mainland government replaced Taiwan in the China seat in 1980. Chinese voting rights were rapidly increased; and like Saudi Arabia, China was soon allowed to elect its own exclusive executive director. After the latest quota review, anticipated to take effect in 2014, China will have the third largest quota at the Fund, behind only the United States and Japan, and its own appointed seat on the Executive Board. Similarly, China's new global influence was implicitly acknowledged by the decision in 2008, after the start of the worldwide financial crisis, to transfer leadership authority from the G7 to the broader G20, where Beijing plays a prominent role. Some sources, reminiscent of earlier calls for a German-American "bigemony," would go even further, to formalize a newly dominant G2 "partnership of equals" between the United States and China.[18]

Response

But will an open door be enough? Ultimately, the outcome will depend on the attitude of the newcomer, which is not at all certain. Making room for China will not suffice if Beijing is unwilling to play within the prevailing rules of the game. To repeat: it takes two to tango, and it is not at all clear that the Chinese are ready to dance. In the words of this volume's

---

18. Bergsten 2008.

introduction, we do not know whether Beijing wishes to be a "taker," a "maker," or a "breaker" of the existing order.

To date, the signals from China have been mixed. With the country newly embarked on a once-in-a-decade political transition, it is far from clear what Beijing's preferences in coming years may actually turn out to be. Much will depend on the outcome of struggles among key domestic interest groups, as emphasized by several contributors here, including David Steinberg, Andrew Walter, Hongying Wang, and Yang Jiang.

On the one hand, the Chinese seem happy to be accepted into the inner circle both at the IMF and in the G20. Beijing gains face by being seen as a member of the club. Moreover, China has benefited enormously from the prevailing rules. The country would appear to have no interest in undermining a system that has allowed it to achieve such rapid rates of economic growth. This is the view of Helleiner and Momani in their chapters, who see Beijing's efforts to gain a leadership role at the IMF as little more than an effort to garner respect from the international community. It is also the view of Yang Jiang, who views Beijing's monetary diplomacy as notably limited in ambition. Policy initiatives, she contends, tended to be limited in scope and motivated mainly by considerations of political symbolism or pragmatic commercial gain.

But on the other hand, in both words and deeds, the Chinese have appeared to underscore a dissatisfaction with the status quo that goes well beyond anything expressed by earlier newcomers. There are many in the Middle Kingdom, it would appear, who would like to fundamentally change the way the monetary world works. In this volume, both Gregory Chin and Jonathan Kirshner stress Beijing's ambitious agenda for international monetary reform. Both see in recent experience a marked determination to enhance China's structural power at the expense of the United States, the incumbent monetary leader.

Consider, for example, the notorious 2009 essay by Zhou Xiaochuan, governor of the PBOC, which called for a new currency system "that is disconnected from individual nations . . . thus removing the inherent deficiencies caused by using credit-based national currencies."[19] In plain language, this was a frontal assault on the "extraordinary privilege" long

---

19. Zhou 2009, 2.

enjoyed by the United States as a result of the global dominance of the dollar. In the years since, as Chin reports in his chapter, Beijing has actively promoted a wider role for alternatives to the greenback such as the euro and the IMF's Special Drawing Rights.

Beijing appears to be working hard to tilt the global balance of monetary power as much as possible in its favor, quite unlike anything attempted at a comparable stage by Germany, Japan, or Saudi Arabia. For example, in addition to its commitment to the CMI/CMIM, Beijing has also moved quickly since the 2008 financial crisis to negotiate a series of local currency swap agreements designed to provide RMB funding to other central banks, when needed, for use in trade with China. In just under five years, as Yang Jiang notes, pacts were signed with some twenty-three jurisdictions adding up to a total value of more than $450 billion. Ostensibly, the aim of these agreements was to insure against the kind of risks that could come with another financial crisis. But the facilities were also designed to supply yuan, when desired, for use in bilateral trade on a more regular basis—in effect, to provide indirect encouragement for commercial use of the Chinese currency in lieu of the dollar.

More broadly, as Chin and Kirshner both emphasize in their chapters, it is apparent that China has embarked on a deliberate program to promote the widest possible use of the "people's currency" as an alternative to the greenback. The aim, it would appear, is to gain even more influence in monetary affairs. In addition to its growing role as source of crisis financing, Beijing has gradually widened the range of trade transactions that may be settled in yuan, further encouraging the money's internationalization. By 2013 as much as 14 percent of Chinese trade was being settled in RMB, up from essentially zero in earlier years. Meanwhile, in the autonomous region of Hong Kong, new markets have been created for yuan deposit accounts and yuan-denominated securities (so called dim-sum bonds). Most observers agree that it will be a long time before the RMB can truly match the appeal of the greenback as an international currency.[20] Above all, successful internationalization will require the development of a sophisticated and open capital market, which at a minimum could take a decade or more. The Chinese, however, are no strangers to the demanding rigors of a Long March.

---

20. Cohen 2014.

Ultimate Goals

On balance, therefore, we just do not know what to expect. At issue, most fundamentally, are the ultimate goals of China's overall foreign policy. Analysts have long argued about the Middle Kingdom's long-term ambitions in international affairs. Are the Chinese prepared to continue working within a global system still dominated by the United States, or does Beijing aspire to replace Washington in a new "Chinese Century"? Put bluntly, is China a status quo power or a revisionist state? Do the Chinese accept the legitimacy of the existing world order? Are they willing to limit their priorities to "norm-governed" changes? Or, *par contre,* are they looking for a more radical transformation of the international environment? Is their goal fundamental change at the level of basic principle—a new global system, in effect, based on "Chinese characteristics"?

Many analysts dismiss the risk of Chinese revisionism. For Nathan and Scobell, for instance, the main goals of Chinese foreign policy are strictly defensive, driven by multiple and enduring security threats. China, in their words, "is too bogged down in the security challenges within and around its borders to threaten the West."[21] For John Ikenberry, any danger to the status quo is moderated by the very nature of the United States–dominated system, which is more institutionally embedded and functionally articulated than past international orders. China is constrained in two ways. "On the one hand, [the system] will provide attractions, incentives, and opportunities for China—thereby encouraging Beijing to integrate further into the existing order. On the other hand, it is a deeply rooted and expansive order that is difficult to undermine or circumvent—thereby making it difficult for Beijing to oppose it or offer a viable alternative vision of international order."[22] In short, China has every reason to limit its priorities to "norm-governed" change.

The Chinese themselves, however, seem to be of two minds, torn between conflicting goals. As one informed source suggests, there are in fact two Chinas—an "economic China" concentrated on economic development and modernization; and a "political China" determined, above all, "to achieve and maintain power in an asymmetric power relation to

21. Nathan and Scobell 2012, xi.
22. Ikenberry 2013, 55.

Western superpowers."[23] While economic China would be content to continue enjoying the material benefits of the current system, political China would be more inclined to regain the rights and privileges that have long been regarded as the Middle Kingdom's natural due. Deeply rooted in Chinese political culture is the notion of *tianxia,* literally "under heaven," with its sense of power centrality expressed in a traditional tributary system. China has long felt entitled to the mantle of regional, if not global, leadership. The Chinese also still harbor deep resentment over what they perceive as a "century of humiliation" at the hands of the barbarian West. In a society with a very long historical memory, we cannot lightly dismiss the salience of such sentiments.

Moreover, as Thomas Christensen has aptly pointed out, China does not have to be able to mobilize an overwhelming preponderance of force in order to threaten the status quo.[24] The system may be deeply rooted, as Ikenberry contends. But that does not mean that Beijing is without points of leverage, should it choose to use them. Likewise, the material costs of destabilizing the existing order could be considerable, but they are unlikely on their own to be decisive. To argue otherwise is to recall the unfortunate Norman Angell, who shortly before World War I argued that the growth of trade ties in Europe had made war in the region impossible.[25] The risk of Chinese revisionism cannot be dismissed so easily.

In the end, therefore, the China question is likely to hinge on considerations far beyond the realm of monetary affairs alone. As noted, geopolitics has always played an important role in such situations. There is no reason why the same should not be true today. Once again, politics can be expected to trump economics. The difference is that in previous episodes tensions were between friends—all in the family, as it were. China, however, is not a military ally like Germany or Japan, and certainly not a client state like Saudi Arabia; but rather is a global rival and potential strategic adversary. In this sense, the Middle Kingdom is indeed qualitatively different from all the other big newcomers to the monetary system since World War II. A smooth path to accommodation cannot be taken for granted.

---

23. Li Xing 2010, 13.
24. Christensen 2001.
25. Angell 1910.

2

THE HIDDEN HISTORY OF
CHINA AND THE IMF

Eric Helleiner and Bessma Momani

China's growing monetary influence has generated much speculation about the future of the international monetary system. In this volume, Benjamin Cohen recalls how other emerging monetary powers in the postwar period were all successfully accommodated within the existing system. Like many other analysts, however, he is less sure about the consequences of China's rise because of uncertainties about "the attitude of the newcomer." In particular, he wonders about the extent to which Chinese policymakers may be more inclined to challenge both US leadership and the system itself.

This chapter offers a historical perspective on Chinese official attitudes toward the institution at the core of that system: the International

We are very grateful to Odette Lienau, Mui Pong Goh, and two anonymous reviewers for their insights and comments as well as to the Social Sciences and Humanities Research Council of Canada for financial assistance to support this research. This chapter draws on material in Helleiner 2014a.

Monetary Fund.¹ Some observers question China's commitment to the
Fund, often as part of their broader arguments about China's potential role
as a challenger to the status quo in global monetary governance. Drawing
on historical analysis, we offer a different perspective, demonstrating that
China's support for the IMF has deeper and more consistent roots than are
usually acknowledged. If history is any guide to the future, our analysis
suggests that China will continue to back this Bretton Woods institution
and the multilateral order it represents.

To begin with, we examine China's role in the establishment of the IMF,
a subject that has been almost entirely neglected in existing literature. The
Bretton Woods system is widely depicted as an Anglo-American creation,
but the Chinese government—under the leadership of the Kuomintang
(KMT) at the time—was more deeply involved in the negotiations than
is usually recognized. While protective of their policy autonomy, Chinese
officials and analysts saw their role as a founding member of the IMF as
useful to their country's development objectives, China's standing in the
world, and their desire to see greater equality of treatment among countries in monetary affairs. Far from being an outsider to the United States–
led Bretton Woods order, China was present and engaged at the creation
of both the Fund and World Bank.

We then analyze the evolution of the views of the Chinese Communist
Party (CCP) leadership that took power after the 1949 revolution. The CCP
is usually assumed to have been initially hostile to both the Fund and the
World Bank, which the People's Republic did not join until 1980.² However, in the immediate wake of the Bretton Woods Conference, the CCP
leadership appeared to favor China's participation in the Bretton Woods
institutions, linking membership to China's economic development goals
just as had the KMT government. Although its position changed with the
onset of the Cold War, the CCP returned to this initial position after Deng
Xiaoping came to power in the late 1970s. Since China joined the Fund
in 1980, Chinese views toward the institution have revealed a number of
continuities with China's position during the Bretton Woods negotiations.

---

1. Because the focus of this volume is on international monetary relations, the chapter focuses on China's historical engagement with the IMF rather than the World Bank. But as the text
makes clear, Chinese views toward the Bretton Woods order were also strongly influenced by
their interest in the World Bank.

2. Momani 2013.

China's Neglected Role in the Bretton Woods Negotiations

China's role in the creation of the Bretton Woods system has received little attention in existing academic literature. The country does not even appear in the index of Richard Gardner's widely read classic account of the Bretton Woods negotiations.[3] Like other scholars, Gardner portrays those negotiations as primarily involving bilateral "sterling-dollar" diplomacy between the United States and Britain in which the top negotiators of these two countries, Harry Dexter White and John Maynard Keynes, were the central players.

This perspective is much too narrow. Forty-two other delegations were present alongside those of the United States and Britain at the July 1944 meeting and many of them were active participants in the preconference and conference negotiations.[4] China was among the most prominent of these countries. It was included in an inner core of seven countries that US officials decided in July 1942 to consult with on early drafts of plans for the postwar international monetary order.[5] After White and Keynes released their respective initial plans in early 1943, China was also one of the few governments—along with those of Canada, France, and Norway—to prepare a formal alternative plan that they "hoped may contribute toward the reaching of general agreement."[6] At the Bretton Woods Conference itself in July 1944, China also brought a delegation whose size (thirty-three

---

3. Gardner 1980. The most detailed discussion we have found of China's role is Young 1963, 377–81.

4. Helleiner 2014a. For details on China's role, see Helleiner 2014a, chap. 7.

5. White to Morgenthau, July 21, 1942, Box 8, Chron. 38, Chronological File of Harry Dexter White, November 1934–April 1946, Record Group 66 (General Records of the Dept of Treasury), US National Archives, Washington, DC. The other six countries were Australia, Brazil, Britain, Canada, Mexico, and the USSR.

6. "Memorandum As Submitted by Chinese Experts Giving General Observations on American and British Plans for International Monetary Organization" June 9, 1943, p. 6, Box 8, Folder 1, Harry Dexter White Papers (hereafter HDWP), Public Policy Papers, Department of Rare Books and Special Collections, Princeton University Library, Princeton, NJ. The archival records also suggest that US officials initially hoped that China and the USSR would be signatories of the April 1944 Anglo-American Joint Statement, but it appears as though there was not enough time for consultations to take place. See for example "Meeting in Mr. White's Office, March 13, 1944," "Meeting in Mr. White's Office, April 5, 1944," Box 11/5, Bretton Woods Conference Collection (hereafter BWCC), Archives of the International Monetary Fund, Washington, DC (hereafter IMF Archives).

people) was second only to that of the United States itself (forty-five) and more than double that of Britain (fifteen).[7]

China's policy toward postwar international monetary issues was shaped by a small circle of officials in Chiang Kai-shek's government. After retreating in the face of the Japanese invasion, the KMT government had established a provisional capital of the country in Chongqing where H. H. Kung played the key role in coordinating Chinese policy toward the Bretton Woods negotiations. A longtime close associate of Chiang (as well as his brother-in-law), Kung was at this time in powerful positions as both minister of finance and head of the central bank.

Sun Yat-sen and the KMT's Development Goals

Throughout the negotiations, Kung and other Chinese officials were very supportive of the goal of creating both the Fund and the Bank. Their support for the creation of new multilateral financial institutions had deep historical roots. As Kung explained to the Bretton Woods delegates, Chinese policy toward postwar international monetary planning drew direct inspiration from the ideas of Sun Yat-sen, the founder of Chiang Kai-shek's KMT party (and another brother-in-law of Kung)[8]. Particularly important was a book that Sun had written in 1918 titled *The International Development of China.*[9]

In this work, Sun had proposed the creation of a public international financial institution that could mobilize foreign capital, technology, and expertise to foster state-owned development projects in China aimed at boosting the country's standard of living. He had long been deeply committed to the economic modernization and strengthening of China as part of his broader philosophy of supporting the "people's livelihood." In historian Margherita Zanasi's words, the "people's livelihood" principle was "ultimately a socialist goal which implied state intervention, restriction of private capital, and the building of state capital."[10]

---

7. These numbers come from Schuler and Rosenberg 2012, appendix A. They include not just the official delegates but also all the secretaries, advisers, experts, consultants, and assistants associated with the various country delegations.

8. Kung, Chiang, and Sun had all married daughters of Charlie Soong.

9. Sun 1922.

10. Zanasi 2006, 34.

Sun argued that the modernization of China could not be achieved without international assistance because of the magnitude of the task. By channeling foreign assistance through his proposed "International Development Organization," he hoped to avoid the kinds of interimperialist rivalries and spheres of influence that had afflicted China in the past. Indeed, Sun suggested to Western powers that his "international development scheme" would help prevent a future war from breaking out over China and thus would promote world peace and become "the keystone in the arch of the League of Nations."[11] Through their support of China's development, Sun argued, Western countries would also find an outlet for their surplus capital as well as a growing market for their products as their war industries were converted to peacetime purposes.

Sun's highly innovative advocacy of a public international development institution was ahead of its time. When he circulated his plans to the 1919 Paris Peace Conference and various Western government officials, the foreign help that he sought for China was not forthcoming.[12] But the plan garnered much attention abroad, including among US analysts in the early 1940s who favored the inclusion of international development goals within the UN system.[13] It also remained an inspiration for the KMT, particularly when discussions of postwar plans arose in the early 1940s. At an important September 1943 meeting of the KMT's Central Executive Committee, the government formally committed itself to international collaboration to realize Sun's economic program.[14]

At the Bretton Woods Conference, Kung highlighted this commitment. In a prominent speech, he reminded the delegates of Sun's 1918 proposal and stated that "Dr. Sun's teaching constituted the basis of China's national policy. America and others of the United Nations, I hope, will take an active part in aiding the post-war development of China." Echoing Sun's arguments, he proclaimed: "China is looking forward to a period of great economic development and expansion after the war. This includes a large-scale program of industrialization, besides the development and modernization of agriculture. It is my firm conviction that an economically strong

---

11. Quotes from Sun 1922, 219, 231, 9.
12. Sun 1922, 233, appendixes 2–5; Wilbur 1976.
13. Ekbladh 2010, 74; Borgwardt 2005, 133–34.
14. Li 1943, 221. See also Wu 1943.

China is an indispensible condition to the maintenance of peace and the improvement of well-being of the world."[15]

Given these goals, it was not surprising that the Chinese government had been a strong supporter of the Bretton Woods negotiations from the start. But when they saw the initial White and Keynes plans, Chinese officials were also concerned that "neither plan gives sufficient consideration to the development of industrially weak nations."[16] For this reason, they developed a formal plan to be considered alongside the British and US proposals. Because the plan has been ignored in histories of the Bretton Woods negotiations, it deserves some attention.[17]

The Chinese Plan

The ten-page plan, dated June 9, 1943. was developed by Chinese technical experts as part of preparations for four officials to attend consultations in Washington that White had organized.[18] An accompanying memo to the plan noted that the Chinese government was "not necessarily committed" to it, but the proposal laid out clearly the positions that the government subsequently took toward the negotiations.[19] The plan was sent formally to the United States in early September and US Treasury Secretary Henry Morgenthau told Kung that US technical experts had "indicated considerable interest in the views expressed in these proposals, particularly with regard to the desirability of giving special consideration to the needs of China and countries in a similar position."[20]

15. US State Department 1948, 1156.

16. Quote is a summary of "Memorandum from the Ministry of Finance, April 21, 1943" from "Summary of Comments on International Monetary Plans," Chongqing, May 25, 1943, p. 7, in Arthur N. Young Papers, Hoover Institution Archives, Stanford University, Stanford, CA, Box 78.

17. Even Horsefield's (1969) classic documentary volume, which reproduces the original Bretton Woods plans of the US, British, Canadian, and French governments, neglects to include that of the Chinese government (Norway's is also ignored).

18. For the Chinese plan, see "Preliminary Draft of a Proposal for a United and Associated Nations Fund for Monetary Rehabilitation and Stabilization," June 9, 1943, Box 8, Folder 1, HDWP.

19. "Memorandum As Submitted by Chinese Experts," p. 6.

20. Morgenthau to Kung, September 14, 1943, p. 1, Box 8, Folder 1, HDWP.

The Chinese plan effectively highlighted the link that Chinese officials drew between their development goals and the US and UK plans for the postwar international monetary system. Neither White's proposed Fund nor Keynes's plan had focused on international development lending, but they had each mentioned its importance and White was known to be developing a proposal for an international bank to work alongside his proposed "Stabilization Fund." In their covering letter, the Chinese experts stressed the priority that China placed on development lending:

> The provision of capital for development of nations' resources although not directly a part of the monetary plans, is still very closely related to them, and is of special interest to China. Both the American and British monetary proposals refer to this subject . . . . The Chinese Government recognizes that medium and long term provision of capital may well be discussed separately from monetary arrangements; but would stress the very great importance to China of provision of capital and its close bearing upon the satisfactory working of any plan for monetary rehabilitation and stabilization.[21]

In another memo written at this same time, Chinese officials reiterated this point, noting that they hoped for international arrangements to be created for the "provision of long-term capital to aid in developing the resources and raising the standard of living of undeveloped regions."[22] When they met for a bilateral meeting with White on June 18, 1943, Chinese officials reported that "Dr Kung felt that discussions on the International Bank and the International Fund should be held simultaneously. This would give some assurance that the matter of long-term capital needs were being taken care of as well as short-term needs for current account."[23] In subsequent meetings and correspondence with White in the fall of 1943 and spring 1944, Chinese officials continued to show great interest in the progress of the US proposal for the International Bank for Reconstruction and Development.[24]

---

21. "Memorandum As Submitted by Chinese Experts," p. 3.
22. "Postwar International Monetary Arrangements," June 9, 1943, p. 1, Box 8, Folder 1, HDWP.
23. "Conference in Mr. White's Office, June 18, 1943," Box 69, File Stabilization Fund (April–July 1943), Papers of Adolfe Berle, Franklin D. Roosevelt Library, Hyde Park, NY.
24. A. Lipsman, "Meeting in Mr. Friedman's Office, April 20, 1944," and "Memorandum, Proposal for a United Nations Bank, April 17, 1944," p. 1, Box 11/5, BWCC.

Following White's lead, the Chinese plan itself outlined a formal draft of an international fund focused on monetary issues which they titled a "United and Associated Nations Fund for Monetary Rehabilitation and Stabilization."[25] The fund had two central purposes. The first was "to achieve post-war rehabilitation of the monetary systems of member nations and establishment of sound and definitive rates of foreign exchange." This objective reflected China's urgent need for external financial help to stabilize its currency given its domestic inflationary conditions. The other purpose of the fund was more similar to that of White's Stabilization Fund and Keynes's International Clearing Union: "To promote long-term stability of national monetary systems and rates of foreign exchange through a system of adequate central reserves and multilateral clearing of international balances of payments, thus contributing to the sound recovery and growth of international trade and the mutually advantageous international flow of capital."[26]

Many other aspects of the Chinese plan drew upon or slightly modified key components of the Keynes and White plans. Indeed, in their covering memo, the Chinese technical experts stated that their plan "does not pretend to originality, since it embodies ideas from the American and British plans and from other sources."[27] For example, a central role of the fund was to finance balance of payments deficits. Chinese analysts saw this feature of White's and Keynes's plans as helpful to China's development goals. As one editorial writer in a Chongqing newspaper put it in April 1944, "as a country long suffering from the disequilibrium in her balance of payments, China will be greatly facilitated in her task of national reconstruction by the assistance of the Fund."[28] Another Chinese editorial writer put the argument in more political terms: "the worst tragedy in the history of mankind was the oppression of the economically weaker countries by the strong, as the odds were always against the backward countries (in their attempts) to maintain equilibrium in the balance of payments. Fortunately, outmoded economic theories will find no place in the future structure of world peace—a peace built on economic equality among all

---

25. "Preliminary Draft of a Proposal."
26. Ibid., p. 1.
27. Ibid., p. 6.
28. "The Establishment of an International Monetary Fund—Another Step Towards Peace Taken by the United Nations," *Sao Tang Pao* (Chongqing), April 24, 1944, p. 3, HDWP, Box 8, Folder 1.

nations."[29] Foreign observers also highlighted how the Fund might allow China to avoid the kind of exploitation it had experienced with past foreign loans: "the process of obtaining short-term foreign exchange credits directly through the Fund . . . will not entail political subservience on the part of the borrowing country."[30]

This interest in the more equal treatment of all nations found its way into another feature of the Chinese plan. Echoing Keynes's proposals, the Chinese experts hoped that the fund could ensure that adjustment burdens were imposed not just on deficit countries but also on surplus countries such as the United States. Countries that had large debit balances in the international fund (measured as a certain percentage of their quotas) would be forced to pay a charge and adopt measures recommended by the fund's board for restoring equilibrium. Countries with net credit balances would also face a charge and have to undertake discussions with the board about measures to reduce their surpluses.[31]

Under the Chinese plan, currency values were also to be fixed and defined in terms of gold. Chinese officials also linked their support for fixed exchange rates to their development goals. Here, for example, is how an official with the Chinese central bank explained the government's attitude to the local press in April 1944:

> The most acute problem for an industrially backward country in its economic relations with the industrially advanced countries is found in the fact that the former is invariably used as a dumping ground for the products of the latter through their policy of depreciating the exchanges. The situation will be improved with the establishment of the Fund, the purpose of which is to stabilize the value of exchanges and to stop the old practice of depreciation. Thus assured of a stabilization of her foreign exchanges, China will be in a position to proceed on the one hand with her program of national reconstruction through the utilization of foreign investments of capital, and on the other with the increase of her imports of raw materials on the basis of self-regeneration. Moreover, in adopting a monetary standard which is the

---

29. "A Managed International Gold Standard System," *Commercial Daily News,* April 24, 1944, p. 2, HDWP, Box 8, Folder 1.
    30. Grey 1944, 166.
    31. "Preliminary Draft of a Proposal," p. 6.

same as that of other countries, she will be saved the pains she experienced in the past ensuing from monetary discrepancies.[32]

Chinese officials seemed rather ambivalent about how much power to give the fund in approving exchange rate changes. Their formal proposal followed White's lead in noting that exchange rates could be adjusted only with the agreement of the fund's board. But they also allowed countries to do a one-off devaluation without fund approval if they experienced a large net debit balance over a two-year period. In a memo of June 9, 1943 commenting on White's Stabilization Fund, Chinese officials also noted critically that "the Fund has wide and far reaching powers such as to fix rate of exchange of member nations; to recommend measures for correct-ing disequilibrium; for example: devaluation of currency. Such powers would affect the sovereign rights of member nations. We submit that in carrying out any such measures the Fund should receive the approval of the member nation in question."[33] Indeed, Chinese officials subsequently told White that their country would need special treatment in the imme-diate postwar period vis-à-vis its exchange rate obligations because of its unstable monetary situation.[34]

Chinese officials also stated that while they agreed with the general goal of removing exchange restrictions, they were not sure how quickly China could establish free exchange markets. For this reason, they pushed successfully for the inclusion of a "transitional period" under which countries—with the fund's approval—would not yet need to commit to currency convertibility at a fixed exchange rate.[35] They were also very supportive of provisions for control of capital movements that were in-cluded in the Keynes and White plans. To increase the effectiveness of these provisions, the Chinese plan followed the lead of Keynes and White in encouraging cooperation in this field. Each member of the fund would

---

32. "Establishment of International Monetary Fund Favourably Commented on by Chinese Experts," *Central Daily News* (Chongqing), April 26, 1944, p. 3, HDWP, Box 8, Folder 1.
33. "Memorandum: American Plan on Post-War Currency Stabilization," June 9, 1943, p. 1, HDWP, Box 8, Folder 1.
34. Friedman, "Meeting in Mr. White's Office, Sept 17, 1943," Box 21, File: D4-28, Intra-Treasury Memoranda of Harry Dexter White, 1934–45, Record Group 56 (General Records of the Department of the Treasury), US National Archives.
35. "Memorandum As Submitted by Chinese Experts," p. 1.

be required "upon request, to cooperate with any other member nation that may regulate international capital movements." Echoing provisions in White's 1943 plans, each member could be asked "(1) to prohibit in its jurisdiction acquisition of deposits or other assets by nationals of any member nation imposing restrictions of capital transfers except upon authorization of the latter nation; (2) to furnish the Government of any member nation on request full information regarding such deposits and other assets; and (3) to consider such other measures as the Board may recommend."[36] More generally, the Chinese plan also mentioned that the fund's board "in conjunction with the governments of member nations, shall study the feasibility of national and international measures to regulate international capital transfers, and the adoption by a member nation of measures appropriate to this end shall not be deemed to be contrary" to other commitments in the plan.[37]

Because of opposition from the New York financial community, these provisions for cooperative controls on cross-border capital flows largely disappeared from the subsequent US and British proposals. But Chinese interest in the provisions remained, particularly as public concern grew in the country about those who had sent money abroad during the war. This concern culminated in a resolution being passed at the May 1945 Sixth Kuomintang Congress asking the US government to provide the names of Chinese citizens holding capital in the United States and the amounts involved. The request was refused.[38]

Governance and China's Standing in the World

Finally, the governance of the fund was structured in a similar way as under the White plan. On the fund's board, some large countries would have a single representative, while others would be organized into groups and be represented collectively by one director. The number of a country's votes would be determined by a combination of basic votes allocated to all members and its quota size. The determination of the latter would take

---

36. "Preliminary Draft of a Proposal," p. 9. See also "Memorandum as Submitted by Chinese experts," p. 4.
37. "Preliminary Draft of a Proposal," p. 10.
38. Young 1963, 387–88.

into consideration the value of its imports and exports, its gold and foreign asset holdings, its money and bank credit, and its national income "and importance in the world economy."[39]

United States officials noted that their Chinese counterparts were "very anxious" to ensure that China be among the leading four countries in the fund, in keeping with their political status in the wartime alliance with the United States, the USSR, and the UK.[40] But assigning China a quota size that would give it this high standing was very difficult to justify on the basis of economic criteria. For this reason, Chinese officials argued in discussions with the United States that more political factors might need to be introduced into the quota calculations. As they put it in June 1943, "countries who have suffered most [in the war] should have a larger voice than those that did not suffer at all even though they have a greater economic strength."[41] In the end, US officials assigned China the fourth largest quota only through some very arbitrary adjustments of the quotas behind closed doors, a move that left countries such as France extremely annoyed.[42] Even then, the Chinese hoped for a larger share, asking— ironically, in light of postwar political developments—whether US officials had considered including Formosa (or Taiwan) in the economic calculations of China's quota.[43]

The emphasis that Chinese officials placed on their quota size highlighted the high symbolic value assigned by the Chinese government to their participation in the fund. China's role at Bretton Woods represented a high point for the country in terms of its influence in international monetary affairs. During the era of the international gold standard of the late nineteenth and early twentieth centuries, China had been a marginal player in international monetary discussions, as one of a dwindling number of countries that maintained silver-based monetary standards.

39. "Preliminary Draft of a Proposal," p. 4.

40. Friedman, "Meeting in Mr. White's Office, Sept 17, 1943," p. 2.

41. John Deutsch, "International Stabilization of Currencies—Informal expert discussions, US Treasury, June 15–17, 1943," p. 18, National Archives of Canada, Record Group 19 vol. 3981. For Chinese lobbying on this issue, see for example, Friedman, "Meeting in Mr. White's Office, Sept 17, 1943."

42. Mikesell 1994, 22–23, 36–7. For China's appreciation of this result, see Young 1963: 381. For White reiterating the promise of fourth place, see "Meeting in Mr. White's Office, April 5, 1944," Box 11/5, BWCC.

43. A. Lipsman, "Meeting in Mr. Bernstein's Office, May 8, 1944," HDWP, Box 8, Folder 4.

Its international influence was also undermined by the fact that the Chinese government did not create a central bank—or even a consolidated homogenous currency within the country—until the mid-1930s.[44] From a Chinese standpoint, their government's prominent involvement in the Bretton Woods negotiations signaled an important shift in the country's international status.

China's status in the negotiations largely hinged on the fact that Roosevelt viewed China as one of four major world powers, along with the United States, Britain, and the USSR, that would help to govern the postwar world.[45] Representatives of other countries were often dismissive of this notion. At the Bretton Woods Conference, the British delegate Lionel Robbins opined in his diary that "the Chinese position at the conference is, of course, largely bogus, and the high place they are assigned to generally by American diplomacy rests on illusion—at any rate as regards our day, whatever may be the case in fifty years' time."[46]

Foreign observers recognized, however, how important the symbolism was to the Chinese themselves. Writing in the United States–based *Far Eastern Survey* just after the conference, Austin Grey noted that the Bretton Woods were primarily significant for China in this symbolic sense: "First and foremost, is the assumption of a political status for China which the West had been most reluctant to grant it in the past. China is accepted as one of the Big Four economically and financially as well as politically and militarily." In a reference to Sun's 1918 proposals, Grey also pointed out that it would be "a particular source of pride" to the Chinese people that the design of the proposed Bank for International Reconstruction and Development "should follow the lines laid down by the Father of the Chinese Republic."[47] The Chinese press also proudly reported that Chinese officials had contributed to the discussions and that China's membership in the International Monetary Fund would contribute to its growing status in the world. Here is how one editorial writer for a Chongqing paper put it in April 1944: "In spite of her vast territories and abundant natural resources,

---

44. See for example Shiroyama 2009. In the centuries before that, China had often played a very significant role in global bullion flows, but it had done so in a context where the Chinese state did not control the domestic monetary system effectively (Von Glahn 1996).

45. See for example Bagby 1992.

46. Howson and Moggridge 1990, 171.

47. Grey 1944, 166–67.

China used to play an insignificant part in world economies as she lacked the technical instruments necessary for the industrial development of the country. Assured of aid from the Fund which will greatly facilitate her task of national reconstruction, China shall endeavor to make herself one of the Big Four in fact as well as in name."[48]

Changing Views of the Chinese Communist Party Leadership

In the early postwar years, the political context surrounding China's participation in the IMF rapidly changed. Within China, the revolution of 1949 brought Mao Zedong and the Chinese Communist Party to power, while Chiang's KMT retreated to Taiwan. Despite the establishment of the Peoples' Republic of China (PRC) on the mainland, the United Nations continued to recognize the KMT and its Republic of China (ROC) as the official government of China. The IMF adopted the same approach and China's seat on the Fund's executive board remained filled by ROC representatives from Taipei.

The PRC quickly challenged this IMF policy. In August 1950, Zhou Enlai formally asked the IMF's managing director to expel the ROC representative from the Fund on the grounds that the PRC was the sole legal government of China. The next month, Czechoslovakia proposed a resolution within the IMF calling for this move, supported by India and Yugoslavia. After the resolution did not find adequate support, the Czech representative to the IMF continued to raise the issue until his own country's membership in the Fund was revoked in 1954.[49] Despite these challenges, ROC officials continued to represent China.

When Zhou Enlai asked for the ROC's expulsion, he did not include a request that the PRC assume China's seat in the Fund.[50] That omission was hardly surprising given the political context of the time. Few in the CCP leadership would have been enthused about joining the United

---

48. "A Managed International Gold Standard System," *Commercial Daily News* (Chongqing), pp. 2–3. For Chinese reports on China's contribution to the discussion, see for example "The Establishment of an International Monetary Fund," *Sao Tang Pao* (Chongqing).

49. Jacobson and Oksenberg 1990, 59–60.

50. Boughton 2001, 968.

States—controlled Fund, given the outbreak of Korean War a few months earlier and the United States' active support for the ROC. Tensions with the United States and other Western powers only grew with the PRC's intervention in the Korean War a few months later. The PRC's relations with the West were largely severed over the next few years, not to be resumed until the early 1970s.[51]

Initial Interest from the Communist Leadership

Interestingly, however, CCP perspectives on the IMF had been much more positive in the immediate wake of the Bretton Woods conference. These views emerged as part of an initiative by the Communist Party in 1944 to develop a foreign policy for the first time ever. As Odd Arne Westad has shown, the motivation for developing a foreign policy was both the CCP's growing influence within the country and the recognition of the new geopolitical context of the postwar world. The party's first major foreign policy document was released in August 1944, one month after the Bretton Woods Conference.[52]

The document went out of its way to praise Roosevelt's policies toward China such as his opposition to Japan, disapproval of the Chinese civil war, and support for democratic reforms. At this time, the CCP had decided to cultivate relations with the United States, making its first official contact through a group of US military advisers who traveled to its headquarters in Yan'an in July 1944. Mao recognized that the United States would play a major postwar role in the region and he hoped to cultivate its trust in ways that might help check the KMT's power.[53] Mao also felt that Roosevelt represented progressive forces in the US government; indeed, after Roosevelt died in April 1945, Mao even compared his progressive role to that of the revered Sun Yat-sen.[54]

From our standpoint, what is important is that Mao also expressed interest in postwar economic cooperation with the United States. A US official who spoke with him on August 23, 1944 summarized Mao's comments as

51. Jacobson and Oksenberg 1990, 44.
52. Westad 1993, chap. 3.
53. Jian 2001, 23–24.
54. Westad 1993, 69.

follows: "China *must* industrialize. This can be done—in China—only by free enterprise and with the aid of foreign capital. Chinese and American interests are correlated and similar . . . . We can and must work together."[55] A few months later in November, Zhou Enlai made a similar point to another US official: "with regard to China's post-war position, her greatest economic need would be for foreign capital . . . . Moreover, China had to participate in international economic and financial organizations if she was to overcome her present backward state."[56] Zhou's statement appeared to be confirmation of the Communist Party's approval of membership in the Bretton Woods institutions at the very moment that the party was first developing a perspective on foreign policy issues. The statement revealed the very wide consensus that existed across the Chinese political spectrum at the time in favor of China's participation in the Bretton Woods system. The rationale for this participation echoed the development objectives expressed by the KMT leadership at the Bretton Woods Conference as well as Sun's earlier pioneering ideas.

From the Cold War to the Early 1970s

The CCP's initiatives to cultivate US backing, however, fell flat. Although many US officials (including White) were increasingly critical of Chiang and the KMT at this time, the US government refused to support Mao, who soon became more skeptical of US policy toward China.[57] As anticommunist sentiments grew within the United States with the onset of the Cold War, the Truman administration's backing for the KMT intensified (despite Truman's dislike of Chiang). When Mao took power in 1949, his revolutionary ideas also discouraged him from seeking a new accommodation with the United States. The Korean War then ended all prospects of a positive United States–China relationship.[58]

---

55. Summary of Mao's comments in Morgenthau Diary (hereafter MD), The Papers of Henry Morgenthau Jr., 1866–1960, Franklin D. Roosevelt Library, Hyde Park, NY, Book 796, p. 253.

56. Irving Friedman summarizing Zhou's comments in MD, Book 801, p. 272.

57. For White's views on China, see Craig 2004, chap. 8. For broader US skepticism of the KMT, see US State Department 1966, 1059–60. For the US refusal to support Mao and Mao's views at the time, see Jacobson and Ocksenberg 1990, 44; Jian 2001.

58. See for example Jian 2001, chap. 2; Cumings 1999, 154.

Throughout the 1950s and 1960s, China's seat in the IMF thus continued to be held by the ROC, despite the fact that it delayed reporting a par value and refused to pay more than a token amount of its quota until 1970. Because the USSR chose not to join the Fund, the ROC's quota was initially the third largest in the Fund, behind that of the United States and Britain. That situation lasted until the first general quota increase in 1959. By 1971, however, China's quota had fallen to twelfth largest because it was not raised when other countries' quotas were increased.[59] As the relative size of the quota dropped, Taiwan lost its right to appoint an executive director and then eventually in 1972 was unable to find enough other countries to support the election of its director to the board.[60]

The more significant challenge to the ROC's position in the Fund came in the wake of the UN General Assembly vote in October 1971 to give the Beijing government the right to represent China at the UN. The UN vote left the IMF and the World Bank in a predicament, one that was aptly labeled the "China problem" in their internal correspondence. Their legal teams quickly met with the UN secretary general's representatives to discuss the issue, and the meeting reaffirmed long-standing views in the Bretton Woods organizations that they were free to decide internally on the issue of membership, but that they were required to consider UN decisions and deliberations. The World Bank's general counsel, Aron Broches, suggested that the two organizations "let the dust settle down a little first" before making a decision.[61]

The IMF staff privately made comparisons of IMF quota weights to UN voting patterns on the matter to see how the "dust would settle" on voting for Chinese membership in its Executive Board and found that support for continued ROC representation of China would prevail.[62] On a number of occasions, Taiwan's Ambassador Martin Wong also met with management to reaffirm his country's desire to stay in the Fund. Ambassador Wong said that the ROC's membership was important for both "prestige and psychological impact." While the Taiwanese were prepared to forgo membership

---

59. Boughton 2001, 970.

60. Jacobson and Oksenberg 1990, 63.

61. Deputy General Counsel Gerstein, "Representation of China," October 29, 1971, p. 1.

62. W. L. Hebbard (IMF secretary) to Managing Director, "Hypothetical Fund Voting Base on Pattern of UN Voting on China Representation," October 29, 1971, p. 1, IMF Archives.

in the World Bank, the government in Taiwan would concentrate its fight on keeping Fund membership.[63]

The Fund also could not revoke Taiwan's membership because it was meeting its obligations at the IMF. Potentially even more controversial was the issue of quotas. If the PRC applied for a new membership, its quota might be as large as the fifth biggest at the Fund, outranking Japan. Moreover, if the Fund accepted the legitimacy of the PRC, then Taiwan could not continue with its present quota which was calculated based on mainland assumptions. But the Fund had no legal mechanism to unilaterally decrease a member's quota. These and other financial and technical considerations worried Fund management. Ultimately, however, the IMF's executive directors "stressed that the decision was likely to be taken by Foreign Offices and not Treasuries or Central Banks, and it would be difficult for the Foreign Offices to distinguish between the UN and the Fund."[64]

Renewed Chinese Interest in Membership

After receiving a letter from Beijing requesting that Taiwan be stripped of its representation at the Fund, IMF management agreed on January 17, 1972 to "not acknowledge it and that we take no action to response [*sic*] to it."[65] In September 1973, however, the PRC's foreign minister, Chi Peng-Fei, wrote again to the IMFs managing director, Johannes Witteveen, noting: "China is one of the founding members of the IMF, but for more than 20 years China's seat at the IMF has been illegally usurped by the Chiang Kai-shek clique." He stated that "this wrong state of affairs must be put right" as agreed to by the United Nations members.[66] According to Jacobson and Oksenberg, this message was personally approved by Mao, "indicating that he countenanced Chinese participation in the IMF."[67]

---

63. Frank Southard, "Meeting with Mr. Hau and Ambassador Wong," December 9, 1971, p. 1, IMF Archives.

64. Joseph Gold, "Memorandum for Files," November 10, 1971, p. 3, IMF Archives.

65. Managing Director Gordon Williams, "Kittani Telegraph re China," January 17, 1972, p. 1, IMF Archives.

66. Chi Peng-Fei, "Letter to Mr. H. Johannes Witteveen, Managing Director," September 24, 1973, p. 1, IMF Archives.

67. Jacobson and Oksenberg 1990, 63.

During the previous two decades, Jacobson and Oksenberg note, "in spite of the rhetoric of the Mao era, several Chinese leaders, a number of middle-level officials, and various institutions had retained a keen interest in reclaiming China's seat in the World Bank, IMF and GATT."[68] These figures appear to have gained the upper hand at this time. Beginning in 1970–71, under the guidance of none other than Zhou Enlai, Chinese government policy had moved slowly away from the focus on national economic self-reliance of the 1960s. When the economic reformer Deng Xiaoping was politically rehabilitated and rejoined the leadership in 1973, China's opening to the world economy accelerated.[69]

In June 1974, however, some of the reformist momentum was stalled when the ministries of Finance and Foreign Affairs recommended in a report against joining IMF. They had a number of concerns including the fact that China's existing voting share was too small to give the country much influence. Particularly worrying was the fact that membership would impose constraints that were not compatible with China's socialist and self-reliance policies. The report's recommendations were backed by the top leadership.[70]

The PRC did not contact the Fund again until January 1976 when it was prompted by a very practical concern arising from an IMF decision at the time to return a portion of all members' gold to fund credits to poor countries. The PRC insisted that the gold should not go to the Taipei regime.[71] Another cable, sent in September to the IMF managing director, nearly mirrored the letter to Witteveen three years earlier and went out of its way to state that if Taiwan were to use any IMF quota belonging to China proper, then the PRC would "reserve the right to recover the losses arising from any illegal disposal."[72] The PRC circulated the contents of the cable to Fund member governments in hopes of stirring the pot at the upcoming annual IMF meetings in Manila in October. The PRC also attempted to pressure the Philippine government to deny visas to Taiwanese officials attending the meetings, pressure that was resisted when

---

68. Jacobson and Oksenberg 1990, 59.
69. Lardy 1999.
70. Jacobson and Oksenberg 1990, 64–65.
71. Jacobson and Oksenberg 1990, 65.
72. Chen Hsi-Yu, "Cable to Mr. H. Johannes Witteveen, Managing Director," September 30, 1976, p. 5, IMF Archives.

IMF management threatened to move the meeting elsewhere if visas were not granted.[73] But the cable did not reflect any new consensus in the PRC leadership to join the IMF; indeed, it was sent at a time of enormous political turmoil in China that followed the death of Mao a few weeks earlier.

In a restricted session of the Executive Board in early December 1976, a number of directors called for the immediate expulsion of Taiwan and for the managing director to invite the PRC to assume its place at the board. They also felt that the technical matters impeding PRC membership should be overlooked for the time being and that perhaps discussions should move from the finance ministries and central banks to the foreign ministries. These arguments were put forward by the Nordic constituency and supported by France and the constituencies led by Zambia, the Netherlands, Egypt, and India. The United States, however, favored the IMF management's position that PRC membership in the Fund could not be accepted until the new member assumed all of the rights and obligations of membership. In response to a request from the United States, the board agreed to postpone a vote on the issues in order to allow directors time to consult with their capitals.[74]

After some further inconclusive discussions between Fund staff and PRC representatives, the situation changed dramatically when Deng Xiaoping emerged as China's key leader in late 1978. Deng was committed to market-oriented economic reforms and a development strategy that would promote Chinese growth and industrialization by cultivating economic linkages with the West.[75] The outward-oriented nature of strategy was reminiscent of Sun's thinking as well as that of the Communist Party in 1944–45.

As part of his new strategy, Deng was keen to see China join the Fund and the Bank.[76] While the expulsion of Taiwan achieved a diplomatic victory, membership would provide the government with valuable information about international finance and economics as well as access to Fund

73. Cesar Virata, "Letter to Johannes Witteveen," September 13, 1976, p. 1; Johannes Witteveen, "Letter to Chen Hsi-Mu, President of the People's Bank of China," September 30, 1976, p. 1; IMF Archives.

74. Executive Board Minutes, "China—Relations with the Fund—EBM 76/159," December 3, 1976, pp. 1–14, IMF Archives.

75. Vogel 2011.

76. Vogel 2011, 808 n. 16.

and Bank loans and expertise. More generally, membership in these multilateral institutions would encourage China's new efforts to cultivate more open relations with the rest of the world.[77] After a December 1978 meeting of the Central Committee of the Communist Party approved the new economic policy direction, the Chinese leadership agreed in early 1979 that China would request membership in the two institutions.

The fact that the United States and the PRC had finally entered diplomatic relations on January 1, 1979 cleared the way for a positive reception of the request. After various preliminary discussions, the PRC's formal request for membership was finally sent to the IMF managing director in the spring of 1980. On April 17, the IMF Executive Board decided unanimously that the PRC would become China's official representative in the Fund with a quota of 550 million Special Drawing Rights (SDR). The question of what to do with China's gold was also settled by a more controversial and divisive United States–led board decision three days later allowing Taiwan to receive 40 percent of the profit proceeds of the gold restitution while the remainder went to the PRC. Because of the political sensitivities involved, the Executive Board, in an unusual step, asked that the Fund not issue a press release on the latter decision.[78]

China in the Fund: Continuities with the Past

The consequences of the PRC's entry into the Bretton Woods institutions have been much less dramatic than many anticipated. As Ezra Vogel notes, "before China joined institutions like the World Bank and IMF, some participants worried that China's participation would be so disruptive that they would have trouble functioning." He argues that the results have been rather different: "China's participation has strengthened those organizations even as it has represented its own interests; it has abided by the rules of the organizations."[79] A number of the motives for China's support for the Fund have been similar to those expressed at the time of the Bretton Woods negotiations.

---

77. Jacobson and Oksenberg 1990, 66–70.
78. Executive Board Meeting "China," EBM/80/72, April 14, 1980, pp. 1–13, IMF Archives.
79. Vogel 2011, 697.

To begin with, echoing the view of Chinese officials in 1943–44, the PRC's policy toward the Fund has been partly related to its interest in the World Bank. Under the Bretton Woods Articles of Agreement, membership in the Bank requires membership in the Fund; White and other officials in the early 1940s had insisted on this linkage as way of encouraging countries to accept the Fund membership obligations.[80] The PRC's membership in the Bank was approved one month after it joined the Fund and China quickly developed a close relationship with the Bank, drawing on the latter's expertise and loans in ways that would no doubt have met with Sun Yat-sen's full approval. Indeed, China soon became the Bank's largest client.

In the early years of its membership, China also drew in limited ways on the Fund's resources to cover balance of payments deficits. Loans were drawn from the IMF in 1981 and 1986 for this purpose. Again, the Chinese negotiators at Bretton Woods would have applauded the Fund's usefulness in these episodes. They might also have appreciated the fact that the Fund offered technical assistance and expertise in areas such as banking, monetary and fiscal policy, and statistics. As Boughton notes, "this activity was particularly important for broadening and deepening the awareness in China of Western economic thought and of the best financial and accounting practices in other countries."[81]

Boughton also notes more generally that a key benefit of Fund membership for China has been "the general one of acceptance and recognition in the world community."[82] As during the Bretton Woods negotiations, the Chinese government has shown a particularly strong interest in the size of its quota and voting share in the institution. Even before it was admitted to the Fund, the Chinese government made clear that it would immediately request an increase in the country's existing quota allocation of SDR 550 million which had remained unchanged since the Fund's establishment in the 1940s.[83] As in the past, the symbolism was important; Jacobson and Oksenberg note that Chinese officials were driven by "a desire to

---

80. Helleiner 2014a, chap. 4.
81. Boughton 2001, 780.
82. Boughton 2001, 780. See also Jacobson and Oksenberg 1990, 121–26.
83. "Memorandum—China," April 4, 1980, pp. 1–5, IMF Archives.

attain a quota larger than India's and one that would enable it to elect an executive director with a single country constituency."[84]

On May 28, 1980 the Chinese government formally requested a reconsideration of its quota, and an ad hoc increase to SDR 1.2 billion was quickly approved in September 1980. China's quota was then increased further in November to SDR 1.8 billion by applying retroactively the terms of the 1978 Seventh General Review. Its new quota was ahead of India's in size and eighth largest in the Fund, behind those of the G7 countries. China was also granted a single-country seat by expanding the size of the executive board from twenty-one to twenty-two.[85]

As China's economic significance in the world has rapidly grown, China has continued to press for greater quota size to reflect its rising global economic status. Reforms have been slower and more modest than many Chinese policymakers would prefer, but under the latest set of reforms, China's voting power will increase from 3.81 percent to 6.07 percent, vaulting it into third place in the pecking order of the institution behind the United States and Japan. China has also petitioned for and gained a prominent seat in IMF management. Zhu Min was appointed a special adviser to the IMF managing director in February 2010 and then became deputy managing director in July 2011.

Interestingly, China has also become a leading advocate of governance reform to enhance the influence of other developing countries in the decision making of both the Fund and Bank. At the 2007 IMF–World Bank governors' annual meetings, China's IMF governor reiterated China's long-standing view of the issues: "BWIs should actively reform their own governance, reflect the improvement of the economic positions of the developing countries, and demonstrate in a balanced manner the interests of the different members so as to design policies in the interest of the developing countries and long-term global development."[86]

As part of their desire for greater "balance" and more equal treatment of nations, Chinese officials have also reiterated a view their KMT predecessors expressed in their 1943 Fund draft: that the IMF can play a useful role in encouraging adjustments in the behavior of the United States. In 1943,

84. Jacobson and Oksenberg 1990, 76.
85. Boughton 2001, 979.
86. http://www.imf.org/external/am/2007/speeches/pr34e.pdf.

Chinese policymakers—like Keynes—hoped the Fund could help prompt the United States to address its large balance of payments surpluses. Now, the concern is more about excessive US payments deficits and undisciplined US macroeconomic policy. As Gregory Chin notes in his chapter in this volume, Chinese officials have since the late 1990s consistently urged stricter IMF surveillance over the "reserve-issuing countries" as a means of trying to minimize negative spillovers on the rest of the world from poor policymaking in those countries.

The perspective of the Chinese government toward the constraints imposed by Fund membership has also displayed some continuity with the views expressed during the Bretton Woods negotiations. For example, Chinese officials waited a full sixteen years after joining the Fund before they accepted Article VIII obligations and introduced full current account convertibility.[87] They have also taken full advantage of the fact that the IMF does not require capital account convertibility. Indeed, Chinese policymakers have been skeptics of the efforts of some IMF staff and Western policymakers to champion financial liberalization, and they have defended countries' right to use capital controls under IMF rules. In the wake of the East Asian financial crisis, Chinese officials also called on the IMF to "effectively monitor and regulate international capital flows."[88] In these stances, they have been important defenders of the content of the original IMF Articles of Agreement.

As at Bretton Woods, the Chinese government has also shown some sensitivities about its exchange rate policy choices. Since the IMF's acceptance of floating exchange rates in the 1970s, the constraints imposed by IMF membership in this area of national policymaking have been much weaker than during the era of the adjustable peg exchange rate system. But the issue has still generated some tension. Indeed, it arose almost immediately after China's entry into the IMF when the government created an internal settlement rate on foreign exchange in late 1980 without informing the Fund. Because the Fund considered this a dual exchange rate, the move required its approval. But China declared it an internal matter and the issue was dropped by 1985 when the rate itself was discontinued.[89]

---

87. Lardy 1999.
88. http://www.imf.org/external/am/2002/imfc/state/eng/chn.htm.
89. Jacobson and Oksenberg 1990, 123.

Exchange rate policy was also at the center of the most significant tension to have emerged between the Fund and China in recent years: that surrounding the 2007 United States–led initiative to strengthen the IMF's surveillance role vis-à-vis exchange rate policy (see Andrew Walter's chapter).

What is the likely to be the attitude of China—Cohen's "newcomer" power—toward the IMF in the coming years? Some question the level of its commitment to this institution at the center of the United States–led international monetary order. We offer a different perspective, stressing the long historical roots of China's commitment to the Fund. As we have shown, it is often forgotten that Chinese officials were very involved in, and supportive of, the creation of the Bretton Woods institutions. Even the Communist Party leadership in Yan'an appeared to favor China's participation in these bodies in the immediate wake of the conference. While the Cold War temporarily changed the party's perspectives, support for the Fund reemerged among the PRC's leadership after the late 1970s, and many of the reasons were similar to those expressed during the Bretton Woods era.

Building on Sun Yat-sen's pioneering ideas a century ago, Chinese analysts have long seen their relationship with public international financial institutions as fostering an outward-oriented development strategy. Their desire for China to be an active member of the Fund has also been linked to broader symbolic goals relating to the country's standing in the world. In addition, Chinese policymakers have held out hope that the Fund might play a role in encouraging greater equality of treatment of nations in international monetary affairs. To reap these benefits, Chinese officials have also acknowledged the need to accept the obligations of membership, while seeking to minimize limitations on their policy autonomy in areas such as exchange rate policymaking and the use of capital controls.

These deep continuities with the past suggest to us that China is likely to remain engaged with the Fund, even as the country's power in international monetary affairs grows in the coming years. Of course, the past may be a limited guide for interpreting the future. Other contributors to this volume detect a new assertiveness in China's international monetary policy after the 2008 financial crisis that is charting new directions. In contrast to our focus on the country's past commitment to multilateralism, Yang Jiang's chapter illuminates a growing preference for bilateralism in China's international monetary policymaking. It is possible, thus, that discontinuity may become an increasingly important feature of Chinese policymaking in this area in the coming years.

But we are struck by how Chinese officials have retained their support for the Fund in the context of some prominent new Chinese initiatives in international monetary affairs. For example, while working for stronger regional financial cooperation in East Asia, the Chinese government has insisted on the retention of a link between the CMIM and the IMF. In this context, their country's newfound creditor status has given Chinese officials a new appreciation of its surveillance role and loan conditionality. Governor Zhou's famous 2009 essay on international monetary reform was also centered around a proposal to strengthen the SDR. Indeed, it drew explicit inspiration from Keynes's ideas during the Bretton Woods negotiations. These developments reinforce our belief that China's commitment to the institution at the center of the multilateral financial order is more durable than many anticipate.

3

Why Has China Accumulated Such Large Foreign Reserves?

David A. Steinberg

China currently holds an unprecedented quantity of foreign exchange reserves. Figure 3.1 shows that China held over $3 trillion of foreign reserves by 2011, which was equivalent to almost half of the country's entire gross domestic product.[1] Although numerous countries have acquired large volumes of foreign reserves in recent decades, China holds far more foreign reserves than any other country. Its arsenal of foreign reserves is more than two and a half times larger than any other country's—the second largest

This research benefited from financial support provided by the Graduate School and the Buffett Center for International and Comparative Studies at Northwestern University. I thank Jerry Cohen, Eric Helleiner, Jonathan Kirshner, Karrie Koesel, Wendy Leutert, Philip Lipscy, and the participants in the Cornell workshop for comments on earlier drafts, and Haiyan Duan and Kai Kang for their research assistance. I am especially grateful to Victor Shih for his extensive guidance and support on this research.

1. Data on foreign reserves are obtained from World Bank 2012. The data refer to nongold reserves.

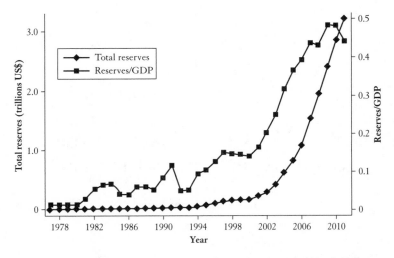

Figure 3.1. Foreign exchange reserves in China, 1978–2011. World Bank 2012.

reserve holder, Japan, had $1.3 trillion in reserves in 2011—and more than fifty times bigger than those of the average country.

China's reserve purchases have had profound effects on the global political economy. Chinese foreign exchange policies have spilled over to China's East Asian neighbors, several of which have hoarded reserves to "keep up with the [Chinese] Joneses."[2] Since a large portion of China's reserves consists of US assets, Chinese reserve purchases lowered borrowing costs in the United States and helped inflate America's housing bubble.[3] China's reserve purchases also suppress the value of China's currency, which makes China's exports highly competitive on world markets, and produce global imbalances. For these reasons, China's large purchases of foreign reserves are widely viewed as an important cause of the 2008 global financial crisis.[4] The myriad ways in which China's reserve policies have affected the global economy indicate that, at least in this regard, China's role in the international monetary system is one of "system maker." Here I aim

2. Cheung and Qian 2009, 826.
3. Roubini and Setser 2005.
4. Chinn and Frieden 2011, Eichengreen 2011, Helleiner 2011, Obstfeld and Rogoff 2009, Roubini and Mihm 2010.

to explain why China has rapidly accumulated foreign exchange reserves and greatly influenced the evolution of the international monetary system in the process.

The main argument of this chapter is that domestic political considerations drive Chinese foreign reserve policy. Although reserve accumulation may have increased China's international monetary power, as Benjamin Cohen and Hongying Wang suggest in this volume, the pursuit of external power and influence has not been the main reason why China has accumulated foreign reserves. Similarly, while reserve accumulation may have improved China's economic performance by generating rapid export-led growth, Chinese policymakers did not choose to accumulate foreign reserves in order to improve the welfare of the average Chinese citizen.[5] Rather, China has accumulated foreign reserves because it serves the political and economic interests of a small group of powerful elites. The presence of a powerful political faction that benefits from reserve accumulation is an important necessary precondition for the accumulation of large quantities of foreign reserves. To be sure, domestic political coalitions are not the only factor that influences foreign reserve holdings in China or elsewhere. Nevertheless, rapid reserve accumulation is unlikely to occur in the absence of strong domestic political support.[6]

In this chapter, I present case studies of two different periods in which China rapidly accumulated foreign reserves: 1994–97 and 2003–8. Chinese foreign reserve policy in the latter period has received a great deal of scrutiny, but little attention has been paid to the sharp rise in foreign reserves that took place in China between 1994 and 1997. Although the total size of China's reserve holdings was far smaller during the 1990s, figure 3.2 reveals that the annual rate of growth of foreign reserves was even more rapid between 1994 and 1997 than between 2003 and 2008.[7] Here I examine

---

5. For discussions of how Chinese foreign exchange policies have contributed to the country's economic success, see Herrerias and Orts 2011 and Rodrik 2010.

6. In other words, the distribution of political power within a country is not a sufficient condition for reserve accumulation. Other factors, such as international capital flows, determine whether foreign reserve accumulation is feasible at any given moment in time.

7. The average annual growth of reserves was 64 percent between 1994 and 97 compared to 38 percent for the 2003–8 period. Even if one excludes the extremely rapid reserve accumulation in 1994, the average annual growth in the 1995–97 period is still slightly greater (39 percent) than in the 2003–8 period. The average annual growth in the reserve-to-GDP ratio was also slightly faster in 1995–97 (17 percent) than in 2003–8 (14 percent).

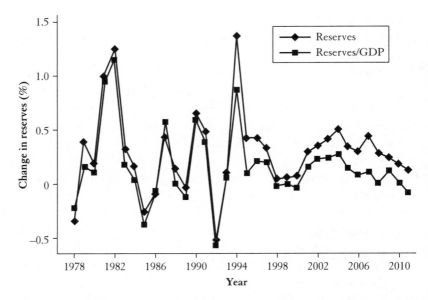

Figure 3.2. Annual percentage changes in foreign exchange reserves in China, 1978–2011. World Bank 2012.

both periods in which China rapidly accumulated foreign reserves in order to establish stronger and more robust conclusions about the causes of Chinese reserve accumulation.[8]

The key question here is why China decided to increase its holdings of foreign exchange reserves in both of these periods even though it had a number of other policy options available. The government could have intervened less in the foreign exchange market and allowed market forces to set the renminbi's value. China also could have altered its trade and financial policies to reduce exports and capital inflows, which would have reduced the country's net foreign exchange earnings. In fact, some Chinese

---

8. China experienced slower reserve growth in the late 1990s because capital was flowing away from East Asia at the time, but the balance of political power was little changed. This chapter focuses on periods with large reserve accumulation because my goal is to show that certain domestic political conditions are necessary causes of rapid reserve accumulation. Several previous studies have shown that the types of domestic political considerations highlighted in this chapter also influenced China's external monetary policies in the late 1990s (Bowles and Wang 2006, Liew 2004, Steinberg and Shih 2012).

government officials lobbied for these policies. Thus we need to understand why the Chinese government chose to accumulate foreign reserves instead of following any of these alternative policies.[9]

The case studies show that Chinese reserve accumulation in 1994–97 and 2003–8 was driven by the political calculations of Chinese government officials. Both periods witnessed high-profile political conflicts over foreign reserve policy. China's central bank has consistently opposed the accumulation of foreign reserves because its officials are the ones who are held responsible for the negative effects of reserve accumulation, such as inflation and poor financial returns. On the other hand, senior bureaucrats who are responsible for financial stability, and whose career advancement hinges on the avoidance of financial crisis, were the main advocates of reserve accumulation in the 1990s. Likewise, officials responsible for the well-being of export-oriented industries lobbied for reserve accumulation in both periods, and did so with particular force during the 2000s. The balance of power between these competing political forces drove Chinese foreign reserve policy in the two periods. In China, government officials who oppose reserve accumulation have less political clout than those who favor it. It is unlikely that China would have accumulated foreign reserves if the central bank or other opponents of this policy had been more influential within the Chinese political system.

This chapter contributes to our understanding of China's international monetary relations in three important ways. First, the evidence presented here demonstrates that China is not a monolithic entity with a single set of international monetary objectives, but one where different actors hold opposing views about how the country should engage with the international monetary system. The importance of domestic political divisions echoes the findings of some of the contributors in this volume, including Andrew Walter on economic rebalancing and Yang Jiang on Chinese monetary diplomacy. Second, the evidence presented here suggests that Chinese policymakers' parochial political interests are the primary determinant of their international monetary preferences. In contrast

---

9. The concern here, therefore, is the quantity of foreign reserves, not their asset or currency composition. On the latter question, see Bowles and Wang 2008, Drezner 2010, Helleiner and Kirshner 2009, and Shih and Steinberg 2012.

to the arguments put forth by Hongying Wang and by Eric Helleiner and Bessma Momani in this volume, I find little evidence that ideational frames influence Chinese policymakers' positions on foreign reserve policy. A third important implication of this chapter is that, due to some distinctive features of China's domestic politics, China's future international monetary policies are likely to differ substantially from those of previous rising powers.

My argument proceeds as follows. To begin with, I describe the economic effects of foreign reserve accumulation and explain why the leading economic theories of reserve accumulation do not convincingly account for China's reserve accumulation. Next, I develop a domestic political explanation of reserve accumulation, which argues that foreign reserve policy is characterized by political conflict between different government factions, and the outcome of such conflict is determined by the balance of power between these competing groups. Finally, the case studies of Chinese reserve accumulation in 1994–97 and 2003–8 are presented. I conclude by discussing what these findings suggest about China's evolving role in the international monetary system and their implications for theories of international monetary policymaking.

The Economics of Reserve Accumulation

Economists have put forth two main explanations for why countries hoard foreign exchange reserves: the "precautionary" theory and the "mercantilist" theory. Each theory highlights an important economic benefit that reserve accumulation delivers and is supposedly responsible for the adoption of this policy. The precautionary and mercantilist theories are useful for drawing attention to these benefits, but these "economic" theories do not provide a satisfactory explanation of reserve accumulation in general and they do not adequately explain the Chinese case.

The precautionary theory, also known as the "self-insurance" theory, asserts that countries accumulate reserves because this enhances financial stability. Influential economic models of financial crises maintain that central banks that hold large reserves can more easily defend against a speculative attack when one occurs, and this ability also deters speculators from attacking the currency in the first place.[10] The evidence strongly supports the notion that large reserve holdings reduce the risk of a financial crisis.[11] In light of the large economic and social costs associated with financial crises, many economists have concluded that countries rapidly accumulate foreign reserves in order to prevent such crises. The self-insurance logic suggests that variables that increase the "precautionary demand" for foreign reserves should be associated with larger reserve holdings. Exponents of this theory have hypothesized that an open capital account and a recent history of financial crises should increase foreign reserve holdings.[12]

A second popular theory asserts that countries accumulate reserves as a means to promote exports.[13] According to this mercantilist argument, countries purchase foreign reserves because of its effects on international trade to prevent their exchange rates from appreciating, and thus promote exports.[14] Dooley, Folkerts-Landau, and Garber, the most forceful proponents of this view, suggest that reserve accumulation is a "sensible" development strategy because it encourages investment in export-oriented industries, which results in a "superior" domestic capital stock.[15] This logic suggests that countries that are highly reliant upon exports should have the strongest demand for foreign reserves.

Economic theories of reserve accumulation are useful for highlighting two economic benefits of reserve accumulation—financial stability and export-led growth—but they tend to downplay the economic costs of holding large volumes of foreign reserves. These costs can be quite large, and include low financial returns, increased inflationary pressures, and reduced purchasing power. First, foreign reserves are an unprofitable asset for central banks to hold. Most such reserves are held in the form of US Treasury

---

10. Krugman 1979, Obstfeld 1996.

11. Frankel and Saravelos 2012, Gourinchas and Obstfeld 2012.

12. Aizenman and Marion 2003b. Aizenman and Lee 2007, Bernanke 2005, Obstfeld et al. 2010, Rodrik 2006.

13. Dooley et al. 2003.

14. Purchasing foreign currency reduces the supply of foreign currency, which bolsters the value of foreign currency relative to local currency—i.e., prevents the local currency from appreciating in value. A weak exchange rate promotes exports because it reduces the price of domestic goods relative to foreign goods.

15. Dooley et al. 2004, 2. See also Rodrik 2008.

securities, which yield a very low rate of interest.[16] Rodrik estimates that the low returns earned on foreign reserves reduce many countries' income by as much as 1 percent of GDP.[17] Second, large-scale reserve accumulation can increase inflationary pressures in the economy.[18] Foreign reserve accumulation can increase inflation because it increases the amount of liquid assets in the economy. While central banks can reduce the inflationary effects of foreign reserve accumulation via "sterilized" interventions—selling bonds to offset the increase in liquidity—their ability to effectively sterilize foreign currency inflows is often limited.[19] Third, the exchange rate effects of reserve accumulation are not unambiguously beneficial. By keeping the exchange rate weak, reserve accumulation makes it more expensive for local businesses and consumers to purchase imports, thus reducing individuals' purchasing power.[20] While reserve accumulation undoubtedly has a number of positive economic effects, it also has many negative ones.

Purely economic explanations are, at best, incomplete. First, when one takes the costs of reserve accumulation into consideration, it is not at all clear whether reserve accumulation increases or decreases aggregate welfare. To put it differently, there is no consensus on the optimal level of reserves. As with many other areas of financial policy, the economics of reserve accumulation are ambiguous.[21] Even within a single country, different individuals, sectors, and classes are likely to have very different perspectives on the

---

16. During the 2000s, approximately two-thirds of allocated reserves were dollar-denominated (IMF Cofer Database). Holding dollar-denominated foreign reserves during this period was additionally costly because the dollar's depreciation for much of the period led to valuation losses on central banks' foreign reserve holdings.

17. Rodrik 2006.

18. Pineau et al. 2006, Roubini and Setser 2005.

19. Calvo 1991. For example, large-scale sterilization often increases interest rates on domestic bonds, which tends to draw in more capital inflows, and increases the required amount of sterilization. Higher interest rates also exacerbate the fiscal costs of reserve accumulation as they drive a larger wedge between the interest that central banks earn on foreign reserves and the interest that they must pay holders of government bonds (Reinhart and Reinhart 1998). Capital controls partially mitigate these problems in China. The country has also used "financial repression" to spread the costs of sterilization to commercial banks and households, but this, too, obviously involves a number of important costs. See Zhang 2012 and the discussion of China's 2003–8 policies later in this chapter.

20. Broz and Frieden 2001.

21. Kirshner 2003.

optimal level. This leads to the second problem with economic theories of reserve accumulation: they pay insufficient attention to the distributional effects of foreign reserve policies.[22] Not everyone benefits from export-led growth, for example. For many actors, the costs of reserve accumulation are likely to far exceed the benefits. Economic models of reserve accumulation are incomplete because they do not explain why policymakers prioritize the benefits of such accumulation over the many costs.

Economic theories also have difficulty explaining why China has accumulated far more reserves than any other nation. It is unlikely that the economic benefits are any larger in China than in other countries. The precautionary demand for reserves should be relatively low there: unlike many of its neighbors, China did not suffer a currency crisis in the late 1990s, and it retains stringent controls on international capital flows that greatly limit speculators' ability to attack the renminbi. China also has a much larger domestic market and is less reliant upon exports than many countries, making its mercantilist demand for reserves equally puzzling. In sum, it seems implausible that the economic benefits can explain why China has accumulated over \$3 trillion in foreign exchange reserves. Political factors must be considered to understand this ravenous demand.

A Domestic Political Explanation of Chinese Reserve Accumulation

In order to understand why China or any other country accumulates foreign reserves, policymakers' political incentives must be considered. My core argument here is that foreign reserve accumulation only occurs when politicians who benefit from this policy are more powerful than politicians who are harmed by it. To develop this argument, I first explain why policymakers care more about how foreign reserve policies affect their political careers than about how it affects the average citizen's well-being. Next, I describe the main protagonists involved in political conflict over foreign reserve policy. Government officials charged with financial stability and

---

22. On this point, see also Helleiner and Malkin 2012, Shih and Steinberg 2012.

export performance favor reserve accumulation while officials responsible for price stability and nontradable industries oppose it. Finally, the balance of power between these competing interests determines foreign reserve policy. Thus, China has accumulated a massive volume of reserves because the advocates of reserve accumulation have more political clout than its opponents.

Policymakers are political creatures who care, first and foremost, about their political careers. They therefore tend to favor whichever policies improve their chances of remaining in office or getting promoted to higher office.[23] These political considerations are as relevant for foreign reserve policies as for any other issue. Policymakers favor reserve accumulation when it benefits their constituents or makes it easier for them to fulfill their ministry's mandated objectives. Conversely, policymakers oppose reserve accumulation when this policy harms their constituents or compromises their ability to accomplish the goals with which they have been tasked. In China, where government officials are evaluated based upon the performance of the region or sector that they represent, Chinese politicians have incentives to advocate for policies that benefit their constituents or their ministry, regardless of that policy's broader impact.[24] In short, decisions about foreign reserve holdings are highly politicized.

Two different types of political actors are likely to advocate for reserve accumulation: those whose careers depend upon financial stability and those with stakes in export-oriented industries. Policymakers often lack strong incentives to implement policies that prevent financial crises: implementing prudent policies often yields limited political dividends because it is extremely difficult for policymakers to claim credit for preventing a catastrophic nonevent.[25] Only political elites whose tenures are highly vulnerable to a financial crisis should push for large precautionary reserve holdings.[26] In China, high-ranking bureaucrats in the central financial

---

23. Bueno de Mesquita et al. 2003.

24. Cai and Treisman 2006, Mertha 2009, Shih 2008, Shirk 1993.

25. Keefer 2007, Healy and Malhotra 2009.

26. All Communist Party officials would be concerned about a financial crisis if there was a high likelihood that a financial crisis would end the Party's rule. This seems unlikely, however: more often than not, authoritarian regimes survive in power during economic crises. Such regimes are especially likely to retain power if they are single-party regimes (rather than military

ministries are one group that favors reserve accumulation for precaution-ary reasons. According to Shih, economic problems threaten the career prospects of China's senior economic officials, and their ability to prevent financial catastrophes boosts their political fortunes.[27] Since senior eco-nomic officials are likely to take the blame for a financial crisis, they should favor large reserve holdings to avoid such a fate. Chinese technocrats also favor reserve accumulation because they can use foreign reserves to solve other pressing economic problems, such as recapitalizing insolvent banks, which boosts their political prestige.[28] The precautionary demand for re-serves should emanate primarily from a small group of senior officials in the economic ministries who have the largest stake in financial stability.

Similarly, export-led growth does not benefit all sectors of the economy and thus is not attractive to all policymakers. The mercantilist benefits of reserve accumulation are highly attractive to policymakers whose political fortunes are tied to the well-being of export-oriented industries. There are two main representatives of such industries within China that should de-mand reserve accumulation for mercantilist reasons: the Ministry of Com-merce (MOFCOM), which is the central government ministry responsible for international trade and for the welfare of domestic industries; and of-ficials from China's coastal provinces, the region where most of China's export-oriented industries are located.[29] Since they are accountable for the well-being of export-oriented industries, these officials benefit politically when these industries are successful and they face a greater risk of losing their jobs or being demoted when export-oriented industries suffer. As a result, these policymakers are likely to advocate for a weak exchange rate and reserve accumulation on behalf of their constituents. To be sure, this group—unlike the technocrats in the central financial bureaucracies—does not have a direct interest in the level of foreign reserves; however,

---

regimes) (Geddes 1999, Haggard and Kaufman 1995), and if they maintain capital controls (Pepinsky 2009), both of which are true in China's case. Indeed, the Communist Party did not ex-perience any serious threat to its rule during the large currency devaluation in 1994 or in the midst of severe banking difficulties in the late 1990s. As a result, it is likely that only the subset of Chinese government officials who have direct responsibility for the performance of the financial system are likely to prioritize financial stability over other objectives.

27. Shih 2008.
28. Shih 2008, 28–29, 189.
29. Freeman and Wen 2011, Steinberg and Shih 2012.

their preference for an undervalued exchange rate causes them to support foreign reserve accumulation.

On the other hand, many policymakers fight against the accumulation of foreign reserves. Policymakers who are charged with maintaining price stability are likely to oppose reserve accumulation to avoid increases in liquidity and inflationary pressures. In China, as in most countries, the central bank is mandated with controlling inflation. Officials at the central bank, the People's Bank of China (PBOC), are likely to take the blame when inflation exceeds targeted levels. Central bank officials should oppose reserve accumulation because it contributes to an outcome—inflation—that threatens their political careers.

Central bankers should also favor small reserve stockpiles for a second reason: the poor financial performance of foreign reserves.[30] Since these are an asset on the central bank's balance sheet and are low-yielding, the central bank is the institution that is most directly harmed by holding them. Central bank officials should oppose reserve accumulation because it directly weakens the financial position of their institution. Even though central bankers do not seek to maximize profits as if they were private investors, they may reasonably worry that poor financial performance leaves them vulnerable to the criticism that they have failed to deliver higher returns for Chinese taxpayers.[31] Thus, one reason why central bank officials oppose holding large quantities of foreign reserves is to avoid blame for these assets' dismal returns. As a result, they are likely to lobby the government to adopt a less interventionist foreign exchange policy that allows them to avoid acquiring large volumes of foreign reserves.

Finally, policymakers who are responsible for the welfare of nontradable industries should oppose reserve accumulation. Nontradable industries benefit when the exchange rate appreciates because this makes it cheaper for them to purchase imported inputs.[32] As a result, political elites that represent nontradable industries should push for foreign reserve policies that are compatible with a stronger currency. Officials in China's inland provinces, which are less dependent upon trade, are likely to advocate for small reserve stockpiles.

---

30. Shih and Steinberg 2012.
31. Chin and Helleiner 2008, 95.
32. Frieden 1991.

Foreign reserve policy is characterized by a conflict between different political factions. This conflict pits central technocrats and the representatives of exporting firms, who favor reserve accumulation, against the central bank and representatives of nontradable firms, who oppose reserve accumulation. The relative political clout of these competing groups determines the outcome of this dispute, and thus whether a policy of reserve accumulation is adopted. Countries are only likely to accumulate foreign reserves when political elites with a direct personal stake in reserve accumulation are able to defeat opponents of reserve accumulation.

In China, final decisions about foreign exchange reserve policy are made by individuals at the very top of the Communist Party hierarchy, principally the secretary general, the premier, and other members of the Politburo Standing Committee. Officials at the upper level of China's political system consider two main factors when making decisions about economic policy. The first is ensuring the survival of Communist Party rule. However, this concern is not likely to play an overriding role in decisions about foreign reserve policy because no particular foreign reserve policy has a clear advantage in this regard. On one hand, large foreign reserve holdings may enhance the Party's survival because this promotes export-led growth and reduces the risk of future banking crises. On the other hand, large foreign reserve holdings may undermine the Party by increasing inflation in the short term. Thus, the level of foreign reserves does not have an unambiguous effect on the survival prospects of the Communist Party rule in China.

Top Party officials, therefore, pay close attention to a second set of concerns: the preferences of bureaucrats, local government officials, and other lower-level Party officials who sit on the Central Committee, the body that selects China's top leaders. These leaders seek to adopt policies favored by these lower-level officials in order to maintain their support and ensure that Central Committee members do not switch their allegiance to rival leaders.[33] Thus, when choosing the desirable quantity of foreign reserves, China's top political decisionmakers have strong incentives to adhere to the wishes of the Party's most powerful factions.

---

33. Shih 2008, Shirk 1993.

The balance of power within the Chinese political system is heavily tilted toward the beneficiaries of reserve accumulation. It is difficult to assess political power independently of political outcomes, but one can do so by comparing political actors' resources, representation in important decisionmaking bodies, and administrative rankings. Such a comparison indicates that proponents of reserve accumulation are better positioned than opponents to influence foreign reserve policy. The main opponent, the PBOC, is politically weak. It is one of the least independent central banks in the world today, and it does not even have the authority to alter interest rates without the approval of its political masters.[34] The central bank is also one of the lowest-ranked ministries in China—lower, for example, than the Ministry of Commerce.[35] China's coastal provinces also have considerable clout within the Chinese political system, and have been overrepresented in the Politburo and its Standing Committee, the most powerful decisionmaking bodies in the country.[36] In addition, central technocrats who are preoccupied with the danger of financial crisis have been delegated considerable authority over Chinese financial policy at certain junctures.[37] For instance, Zhu Rongji, the leader of China's technocratic faction in the late 1990s, had more influence over financial policy than any other individual in that period.[38] Thus, the balance of power within the Chinese political system tilts heavily toward supporters of foreign reserve accumulation. These power imbalances are an important reason why China has accumulated such large foreign reserves. I now examine how these domestic political considerations influenced foreign reserve policy in China in 1994–97 and 2003–8.

Chinese Foreign Reserve Accumulation, 1994–1997

On January 1, 1994, China devalued its exchange rate from 5.8 to 8.7 renminbi per dollar.[39] In order to prevent the RMB from appreciating

---

34. Gilley and Murphy 2001, Chung and Tongzon 2004.
35. Wright 2009, 187.
36. Li 2005.
37. Shih 2008.
38. Brahm 2002, Liew 2004.
39. China also unified its multiple exchange rate system at this time.

away from its newly undervalued rate, the central bank began purchasing foreign currency reserves at a rapid clip.[40] As a result, foreign reserves increased from $22 billion to over $50 billion in 1994. Within the Chinese government, this rapid reserve growth "started a debate over whether it was suitable to have foreign exchange reserves on such a scale."[41] This debate, which raged over the next two years, featured the PBOC squaring off against two opposing groups: senior technocrats, and government officials that were sympathetic to exporters' concerns. In the end, the weaker political actor, the PBOC, lost this debate, and China continued to purchase large volumes of foreign reserves over the next three years.

The central bank loudly protested the growth of foreign reserves in the mid-1990s. It provided three main arguments against reserve accumulation. First, it pointed out that reserve accumulation exacerbated inflation, and that reducing inflation ought to be the nation's top priority. Inflation reached 24 percent in 1994, its highest level during China's reform era. According to economists at the central bank and elsewhere, foreign reserve accumulation contributed to rapid growth in the money supply, which was one of the main causes of high inflation at the time.[42] A second and related concern expressed by the central bank was that the need to accumulate reserves reduced its ability to manage

---

40. Many contemporary Chinese observers considered the exchange rate to be undervalued after the 1994 devaluation: Liu Fei, "Correlation between RMB New Exchange Rate System and Domestic Money Supply," *Caimao Jingji* [Finance and Economics], no. 12 (December 11, 1995): 31–33, Foreign Broadcast Information Service (hereafter FBIS), January 31, 1996; Sun Mingchun, "Adjustment in Management of Renminbi Exchange Rates and Related Policies," *Guanli Shijie* [Management World], no. 2 (March 24, 1995): 72–78, FBIS, June 9, 1995; Yang Fan, "Several Issues Concerning Renminbi Exchange Rate," *Guanli Shijie* [Management World], no. 2 (March 24, 1994): 35–39, FBIS, July 17, 1996; Xiong 1995; Yang Fan, "Several Issues Concerning Renminbi Exchange Rate," *Guanli Shijie* [Management World], no. 2 (March 24, 1994): 35–39, FBIS, July 17, 1996.

41. Chen Bingcai, "Foreign Exchange Reserve Growth Needed," *Jingji Cankao Bao* [Economic Information Daily], June 27, 1995, p. 4, FBIS, August 28, 1995.

42. Hua Erchang, "An Analysis of China's Macroeconomic Situation." *People's Daily,* March 2, 1995, p. 9, FBIS, March 30, 1995; Liu Xiaoxi, "On Whether the Inflow of Foreign Capital Produces an Inflationary Effect," *Gaige* [Reform], no. 3 (May 20, 1995): 75–79, FBIS, July 28, 1995; Su Yunqin and Lin Sen, "A Synthesis of Views on Inflation," *Caimao Jingji* [Finance and Economics], no. 6 (June 11, 1995): 35–40, FBIS, September 19, 1995; Jing Xuecheng, "Foreign Exchange Reserves Increase; Renminbi Exchange Rate Remains Firm," *Caimao Jingji* [Finance and Economics], no. 10 (October 11, 1995): 17–22, FBIS, December 26, 1995; People's Bank of China, Wuhan Branch 1996, Xiong 1995, Yu 2001.

the macroeconomy.[43] Jing Xuecheng of the PBOC's Policy Research Office, for example, argued that a large increase in reserves "has a serious affect on monetary policy formulation and implementation . . . [that] overwhelms all else . . . [and] creates a certain amount of difficulty for central bank macroeconomic regulation and control."[44] Third, central bankers opposed reserve accumulation because foreign reserves earned a low rate of return.[45] One official from the PBOC's Financial Research Institute, for instance, wrote the following: "Foreign exchange reserve assets are low-interest or interest-free foreign currency creditors' rights with very little interest income and very high risk in exchange rates . . . . Therefore, it is not the case that the more foreign exchange reserves the better."[46] One official published an article in the *People's Daily,* the official mouthpiece of the Communist Party, which reiterated the central bank's arguments and concluded: "China now has ample reserves of foreign exchange."[47]

The PBOC and other opponents of reserve accumulation proposed several specific policy changes that would help achieve the objective of reducing foreign exchange reserves. Some government officials suggested that the central bank should spend its foreign reserves to pay for imported goods.[48] Opponents of reserve accumulation also lobbied the government to encourage capital outflows and to slash export tax rebates, measures that would reduce China's reserve accumulation in the future.[49] The central bankers also advocated for the adoption of a more flexible exchange rate system.[50] In the context of the mid-1990s, a more flexible exchange rate had a number of advantages for the central bank. It would allow the RMB to appreciate in value, which would make imports cheaper and reduce

---

43. Sun 1995, Xiong 1995.

44. Jing, "Foreign Exchange Reserves Increase."

45. Lin Zhiyuan, "Conditions and Policies for the Reform of Convertibility of the Renminbi," *Jingji Yanjiu* [Economic Research], no. 2 (February 20, 1994): 33–38, FBIS, May 11, 1994; Jing, "Foreign Exchange Reserves Increase"; Sun 1995.

46. Lin, "Conditions and Policies for the Reform of Convertibility of the Renminbi."

47. Hua, "An Analysis of China's Macroeconomic Situation."

48. Liu, "On Whether the Inflow of Foreign Capital Produces an Inflationary Effect"; Su and Lin, "A Synthesis of Views on Inflation"; Wang 1995.

49. Jing, "Foreign Exchange Reserves Increase"; Su and Lin, "A Synthesis of Views on Inflation."

50. Su and Lin, "A Synthesis of Views on Inflation"; Jing 1995, Sun 1995.

inflationary pressures. It would also reduce exports, which would in turn reduce foreign reserve accumulation and lower inflationary pressures. Finally, central bankers were attracted to a flexible regime because it would enhance their monetary policy autonomy. In short, Chinese central bankers lobbied the government to adopt measures that would relieve them of the burden of accumulating foreign exchange reserves.

A number of powerful groups, however, defended accumulation and pressured the government to continue the practice. Export-oriented industries and their political patrons were one such group. The exporter coalition did not care about the level of reserves per se, but they insisted that the exchange rate must not appreciate—an objective whose fulfillment required the government to purchase more foreign reserves. The 1994 devaluation was strongly supported by Chinese government officials responsible for the export sector: Minister of Trade Wu Yi called the 1994 exchange rate reform a "dream come true for her ministry"; and officials from the coastal province of Guangdong praised it as "very favorable to the expansion of foreign trade and exports."[51] Even though China's exchange rate was highly stable following the January 1994 devaluation—it appreciated a mere 4.6 percent between January 1994 and June 1995—exporters nevertheless started to complain about the harmful effects of exchange rate appreciation in the summer of 1995.[52] The state-owned foreign trade sector was "shout[ing] loudly" that the exchange rate was no longer undervalued and they warned the government that "without a devaluation of the RMB, second half of the year [1995] exports will suffer."[53]

Sympathetic government agencies echoed the exporters' arguments. For instance, the State Economic and Trade Commission published a report on China's export environment in May 1995 that argued: "If the exchange rate continues to rise, it will have a negative impact on exports . . . we should not underestimate the possible appearance of problems in the

---

51. "New Unified Rate Will Help Boost Exports," *China Daily,* December 12, 1993, FBIS, December 13, 1993; Wen Pei Wo, "Unification of Renminbi Exchange Rates Well Received in Various Localities," ibid., December 31, 1993, FBIS, January 3, 1994.

52. Author Interview 1. I cite these interviews numerically to preserve the interviewees' anonymity. All cited interviews took place during summer 2008 and spring 2009.

53. Yang Fan, "China's Export Tariff Rebates and Foreign Exchange Rate Stabilization Problems," *Caimao Jingji* [Finance and Economics], no. 12 (December 11, 1995): 28–30, FBIS, January 31, 1996.

1995 foreign export environment. We must deal with it seriously and take firm and decisive action."[54] According to another central government official, "the central bank should strive for a rate level which promotes long-term expansion of import-export industries and maintains export-industry competitiveness."[55] Liu Fei of the Chinese Academy of Social Sciences, a government-run think tank, echoed this view: "Exchange policy must do all possible to maintain the country's competitiveness abroad."[56] Export industries and their political allies lobbied hard against exchange rate appreciation—and by extension, in support of foreign reserve accumulation—in the mid-1990s.

The "technocratic faction," consisting of Vice Premier Zhu Rongji and his followers in the central government bureaucracy, was a second important group that favored reserve accumulation at this juncture.[57] Their reason for doing so, however, was rather different from those of the exporters. These senior technocratic officials were obsessed with China's financial stability. Their top concern was the potential for exchange rate volatility, a concern that they often justified in light of rising international capital mobility.[58] This coalition insisted that it was imperative for China to do everything possible to avoid the types of currency crises that afflicted Britain and Italy in 1991 and Mexico in 1995.[59] In the opinion of Zhu Rongji, China was exposed to the "same kinds of risks that had already been witnessed with the meltdown of the Peso in Mexico, and in other parts of the world."[60]

During the mid-1990s, the Zhu Rongji faction frequently argued that China needed to amass a major reserve stockpile to reduce the risk of a

---

54. Economic Information Center of the State Economic and Trade Commission, "Analysis of China's Current Export Environment," *Jingji Gongzuo Tongxun* [Economic Work Newsletter], no. 10 (May 31): 21–22, FBIS, August 10, 1995.

55. Sun, "Adjustment in Management of Renminbi Exchange Rates and Related Policies.".

56. Liu, "Correlation between RMB New Exchange Rate System and Domestic Money Supply," pp. 31–33.

57. The description of this political faction is based upon Shih 2008.

58. Brahm 2002, 31; Chen Yuan, "China's Present Financial Reform and Development." *Guanli Shijie* [Management World], no.4 (July 24, 1995): 8–9, FBIS, September 25, 1995; Liu, "Correlation between RMB New Exchange Rate System and Domestic Money Supply."

59. Liu, "Correlation between RMB New Exchange Rate System and Domestic Money Supply"; Yang, "Several Issues Concerning Renminbi Exchange Rate."

60. Brahm 2002, 32.

financial crisis. According to a former adviser to Zhu, "It seems apparent that as early as 1995, Zhu was already firmly convinced that the Renminbi exchange rate would need to be kept stable. For this to happen, China's foreign-exchange reserves would have to be beefed up."[61] Chen Yuan, whom Zhu appointed to be the vice governor of the PBOC, echoed these views, arguing that it is "extremely important for China to ensure an appropriate level of foreign exchange reserve" because this "ensures a stable RMB exchange rate."[62] Some officials at the State Planning Commission shared this view: "the effort to stabilize the foreign exchange rate . . . call[s] for increased foreign exchange reserves," wrote one official.[63] Zhu and his allies also justified the large and growing reserve stockpile as necessary for safeguarding the financial stability of Hong Kong, which was scheduled to return to China in 1997.[64] For example, the state-run *China Daily* newspaper argued that "a huge foreign reserve is desirable to keep the financial stability of Hong Kong when it returns to the sovereignty of China in two years."[65] Thus, self-insurance arguments featured prominently in China's lively debate over foreign reserve policy in the mid-1990s. The precautionary demand for foreign reserves emanated primarily from high-ranking individuals whose ability to win further promotion depended upon their ability to prevent financial turmoil.

In light of these opposing policy preferences, it was not possible for China's leadership to please everyone. The central bank was the one that lost this political battle. As Figures 3.1 and 3.2 show, Chinese reserves continued to grow rapidly between 1995 and 1997, and by the end of 1997, they were more than five times larger than in 1993. The central bank's opposition was therefore unable to put a stop to reserve accumulation in this period. The PBOC's failure likely reflected its relatively weak political position within China's party-state. The central bank was no match for their various powerful opponents, particularly Zhu Rongji and his technocratic coalition.

61. Brahm 2002, 31–32.

62. Chen, "China's Present Financial Reform and Development." On Chen's relation with Zhu, see Shih 2008, 154.

63. Chen, "Foreign Exchange Reserve Growth Needed."

64. Ibid.; Brahm 2002, 31; Wang 2003.

65. "Strong RMB May Spell Trade Deficit," *China Daily,* July 9, 1995, FBIS, July 10, 1995.

This episode has several important implications for our understanding of the politics of foreign exchange reserves. First, the evidence indicates that foreign reserve policy is rife with political conflict. Second, the positions that policymakers adopt reflect their own parochial concerns. In this case, the strongest opposition to reserve accumulation came from the central bank, the one agency that was responsible for dealing with the economic risks of this policy, such as low returns and inflationary pressures. By contrast, the main supporters of reserve accumulation were policymakers who personally benefited from this policy, because it either increased their constituents' profits or helped them avoid a career-destroying financial calamity. Between 1994 and 1997, bureaucratic interests had a much stronger effect on policymakers' preferences than did other factors, such as ideology. Third, foreign reserve policy decisions reflect the balance of political power between different groups. In sum, this case study demonstrates that domestic political factors were responsible for the rapid accumulation of foreign reserves in China from 1994 to 1997. More generally, the case study reveals that domestic politics can impact foreign reserve policy in important ways.

Chinese Foreign Reserve Accumulation, 2003–2008

The Asian financial crisis, which began in 1997, reduced China's growth and exports, and therefore its reserve accumulation. However, the country experienced a much milder economic slowdown than most other Asian nations. Unlike many of its neighbors, China did not see its foreign reserves drained or its currency devalued in the late 1990s. After a half-decade lull in reserve accumulation, China's foreign reserve holdings started to grow rapidly again starting around 2002–3. When China's new leaders, President Hu Jintao and Premier Wen Jiabao, were appointed in 2003, they faced the same dilemma as their predecessors: Should China accumulate more foreign reserves or should China adopt measures to avoid further accumulation? As Figures 3.1 and 3.2 show, the Hu-Wen administration chose the former course. Between 2003 and 2008, Chinese foreign reserves increased at a rate comparable to the 1994–97 period, and

China's absolute holdings of reserve holdings reached an unprecedented level.[66] This section explores why.

The political underpinnings of foreign reserve policy in the 2003–8 period were similar in many ways to the political dynamics that drove reserve accumulation between 1994 and 1997. As in the 1990s, the PBOC consistently lobbied against reserve accumulation, whereas the strongest demands for reserve accumulation in this period emerged from the Ministry of Commerce and the coastal provinces, which reflected their interest in export-led growth. However, the precautionary demand for foreign reserves was far more limited in this period than it was in the 1990s. To the extent that policymakers were concerned with financial stability, this led them to oppose—not support—further reserve accumulation in the 2000s.

Since 2003, the PBOC has resumed its role as the main opponent of reserve accumulation. One of the PBOC's main concerns and arguments was that this policy contributed to inflation. Many PBOC officials were of the belief that the rapid buildup of foreign reserves was contributing to inflation.[67] Central bankers, including PBOC governor Zhou Xiaochuan, and Yu Yongding, a prominent former member of China's Monetary Policy Committee, frequently complained about the inflationary effects of China's foreign currency policies.[68] The PBOC also opposed reserve accumulation because it had negative effects on the central bank's balance sheet.[69] United States Treasury securities took up a large portion of China's foreign reserves—a problem for the PBOC because these securities yielded it a very low rate of return.[70] Even worse, the dollar was depreciating against the renminbi during this period, which reduced the local currency value of the PBOC's dollar-denominated reserves. Stephen Green estimates that dollar depreciation led to valuation losses of $19 billion in the year 2006 alone, an amount large enough that it "threatens [the PBOC with]

---

66. Here, I focus on the overarching decision in this period to accumulate reserves. There were some brief and partial departures from this trend at certain moments, such as in July 2005 and during the winter of 2007–8. For a more detailed analysis of these temporary fluctuations between 2003 and 2008, see Steinberg and Shih 2012.

67. Interviews 32 and 40. This view was also widely held outside the central bank (see for example Pettis 2007, 2008).

68. Green and Mann 2004, Wright 2009, Yu 2003.

69. Interview 32.

70. Zhang 2012.

technical insolvency."[71] Ljungwall and colleagues calculate that, when these currency valuation losses are taken into account, the central bank experienced negative profits from 2007 onwards.[72] These losses worried the central bankers because officials from other ministries became highly critical of the PBOC for its failure to effectively manage the nation's foreign reserves.[73] The negative financial effects of reserve accumulation were one of the major reasons that the PBOC pushed for changes to the country's foreign currency policy: "one of the PBoC's big concerns . . . is that an appreciating CNY [Chinese yuan] devalues its FX [foreign exchange] assets vis-à-vis its liabilities."[74] The central bank opposed reserve accumulation because it went against their institutional interests as the holders of foreign reserves and the guardians of price stability.

As a result of these concerns, the central bank and its allies argued that China must stop accumulating reserves. For example, in a recent editorial, Yu Yongding has argued that China "must stop policies that result in further accumulation of foreign exchange reserves... . The People's Bank of China must stop buying US dollars . . . China should have done so a long time ago. There should be no more hesitating and dithering."[75] The central bankers urged China's leadership to change its exchange rate policies in order to reduce reserve accumulation and its damaging effects. They frequently argued that the RMB should be revalued because this would reduce the need to accumulate foreign reserves. The PBOC also advocated for the adoption of a more flexible, market-based exchange rate system, which would improve its ability to control monetary conditions and achieve its anti-inflationary objectives.[76] The rigid and fixed exchange rate regime, which required rapid reserve accumulation, was anathema for the central bank.

Unlike during the earlier period, the precautionary demand for reserve accumulation was virtually nonexistent during the 2000s. Once Chinese reserves

---

71. Green 2007a.

72. Ljungwall et al. 2013.

73. These attacks ultimately resulted in transferring some foreign reserves from the PBOC to a sovereign wealth fund that was not managed by the PBOC—a shift that reduced the central bank's prestige and clout (Wright 2009, Walter and Howie 2011).

74. Green 2007a.

75. Yu Yongding, "China Can Break Free of the Dollar Trap." *Financial Times,* August 4, 2011.

76. Interview 2; Freeman and Wen 2011, Wright 2009, Green 2007c.

exceeded one trillion US dollars in value in 2006, most Chinese leaders no longer believed that additional reserves contributed to financial stability.[77]

My view that Chinese officials did not desire to increase foreign reserves for their own sake during this period contrasts somewhat with the argument put forth by Hongying Wang in this volume. Wang argues that many Chinese commentators believe that China's large national holdings serve the national interest because they increase China's leverage in world politics. In one sense, Wang's argument is not inconsistent with my relatively narrow point that Chinese policymakers no longer advocated for reserve accumulation as a means of enhancing financial stability. However, even if one accepts that Chinese reserve accumulation has had the effect of enhancing national power and autonomy—a point that some observers both inside and outside China find doubtful—this does not imply that the grasp for national power actually contributed to the adoption of this policy in the first place.[78] Rather, "it is unlikely that even the Chinese expected the accumulation [of reserves] . . . to propel them into the heightened global status" when this policy was originally adopted.[79] National security–based arguments do not appear to have featured prominently in debates over foreign reserve policy in China. The key players involved in debates over international monetary policies were political elites in charge of economic portfolios, not those responsible for foreign policy. In short, there is little evidence that self-insurance or national security considerations contributed to reserve accumulation in China during this period.

Rather than viewing foreign reserves as a form of self-insurance, many officials believed that further reserve accumulation posed a threat to China's financial stability in this period. Reserve accumulation harmed China's financial sector because, in order to address its detrimental effects, the PBOC implemented several domestic financial policies that squeezed the profits of China's commercial banks.[80] As part of its efforts to remove money from

---

77. Interviews 21, 33; Wright 2009, 256; Bowles and Wang 2008, 346.

78. Drezner 2009 and Wang 2007 call into question the impact of China's foreign reserve holdings on its power.

79. Nicole E. Lewis, "China's Foreign Exchange Reserves: Unintentional Means to a Strategic End." Huffington Post, January 12, 2010, http://www.huffingtonpost.com/nicole-e-lewis/chinas-foreign-exchange-r_b_420115.html.

80. Green 2007a, 2007b, Lardy 2012, Ljungwall et al. 2013, Walter and Howie 2011, Wright 2009, Zhang 2012.

circulation and prevent inflation, the PBOC raised the "required reserve ratio"—the portion of a commercial bank's deposits that it is required hold in reserve at the central bank—to 17.5 percent in 2008; as recently as 2003, the required reserve ratio was only 6 percent. A high required reserve ratio was extremely painful for China's banks because the interest rate that they earned on required reserves was less than 2 percent—far lower than the 7–8 percent interest that they would have earned lending out these funds.[81] In addition to the required reserve ratio, the PBOC also forced commercial banks to purchase low-interest central bank bills, which further reduced their earnings. Zhang Ming of the Chinese Academy of Social Sciences estimates that these policies reduced the profits of China's commercial banks by RMB 1.3 trillion between 2003 and 2010, which was even larger than the profit decline experienced by the PBOC in that period.[82] In the 2003–8 period, concerns with financial stability led some Chinese officials to oppose, not support, reserve accumulation.

Export-oriented industries and their patrons in the Ministry of Commerce and provincial governments were the only group that strongly supported reserve accumulation between 2003 and 2008. The export coalition wanted China to accumulate foreign reserves because this was the means to achieve its ultimate objectives: the maintenance of a weak exchange rate and a highly competitive export sector. The Ministry of Commerce was the central government agency that pushed most strongly for an undervalued exchange rate and, by extension, for reserve accumulation.[83] For example, Minister of Commerce Bo Xilai was the strongest opponent of foreign exchange reform in interministerial debates on this question between 2003 and 2005.[84] Similarly, MOFCOM made a concerted, and ultimately successful push for pro-export policies, including slower exchange rate appreciation, in early 2008.[85] MOFCOM argued that a stronger exchange rate would be detrimental for Chinese businesses. To bolster this case, the MOFCOM and its allies in China's think tanks conducted stress

---

81. Green 2007b.

82. Zhang 2012.

83. Freeman and Wen 2011, Steinberg and Shih 2012, Yi 2007.

84. Wright 2009, 183.

85. Eadie Chen, "China's MOFCOM Calls for Slower Yuan Rise," Reuters, July 14, 2008, http://in.reuters.com/article/2008/07/14/china-economy-policy-idINPEK15048620080714; Green 2008.

tests that demonstrated that appreciation would have devastating effects on export firms.[86]

Local governments in southeastern China have also pushed for the continuation of export-friendly foreign exchange policies since 2003. Officials in the coastal provinces reiterated the same arguments as MOFCOM, that pro-export policies are necessary to prevent mass bankruptcies and social unrest.[87] For instance, a 2010 report by the Shenzen municipal government made the case for an undervalued exchange rate by arguing that a 3 percent appreciation would reduce the city's exports by $9 billion.[88] Local officials also lobbied for export-oriented foreign exchange policies by inviting high-level officials from the Politburo Standing Committee to come visit local factories and understand their circumstances. During 2008, coastal officials arranged for Premier Wen Jiabao and Vice President Xi Jinping to meet business owners, where they listened to exporters' complaints and felt compelled to support policies that would assist coastal industries.[89] According to one customs official in the export-oriented province of Zhejiang, due to their desire to ensure that local export industries remain profitable, some local officials knowingly allowed export firms to overreport their export revenues so that these firms received a larger tax rebate from the central government.[90] Since coastal China is "the machine that has created the huge foreign-exchange reserves," it is unsurprising that coastal officials have dedicated themselves to ensuring the continuation of export-promoting foreign reserve policies.[91]

China's accumulation of a historically unprecedented quantity of reserves has primarily benefited a small group of export-oriented industries. Many other groups in China have paid a steep price for this policy: consumers' purchasing power has suffered as a result of the weak exchange rate; Chinese commercial banks have experienced punitive domestic monetary

---

86. Lardy 2012; Interview 6.
87. Steinberg and Shih 2012.
88. Freeman and Wen 2011, 6.
89. "Premier Wen Jiabao Inspects Jiangsu." Xinhua, July 7, 2008, http:// cpc.people.com. cn/GB/64093/64094/7476043.html; Xu L., "Push Forward Scientific Development in the Midst of Liberalizing Thinking—A True Account of Xi Jinping's Inspection of Guangdong," *Guangzhou Ribao* (Guangzhou Daily), July 7, 2008.
90. Interview 12.
91. Walter and Howie 2011, 8.

policies; and the central bank, and ultimately Chinese taxpayers, have suffered large valuation losses on these reserves. As Andrew Walter points out in this volume, most of these groups that have been harmed by reserve accumulation are politically marginalized. The Chinese government did not choose to accumulate reserves because this enhanced aggregate welfare. Rather, China acquired a massive stockpile of foreign reserves because this provided large economic benefits to a narrow group of exporters, and it improved the political prospects of powerful officials who are responsible for export performance. The opponents of reserve accumulation were hardly altruists either: central bankers were more concerned with how reserve accumulation affected their own careers than how it affected the Chinese public. China would not have rapidly accumulated foreign reserves if the central bank and other opponents of reserve accumulation were more powerful. The balance of political power is the key variable that explains the explosive growth of foreign reserves in China during the 2000s.

China has been purchasing large quantities of foreign exchange reserves for most of the past twenty years. As a result, China's central bank now holds a record $3 trillion of foreign reserves. There is, however, no consensus within China that reserve accumulation has served the country's interests. Political conflict has been a ubiquitous feature of Chinese foreign reserve policy. Actors that have benefited from reserve accumulation have constantly had to battle against groups that are harmed by it and reserve accumulation has depended on the fact that its supporters were able to triumph over its opponents. It is unlikely that China would have acquired such large foreign exchange reserves if some of the groups that are harmed by reserve accumulation had more political influence. Domestic political factors, and the interests of China's political elites in particular, best explain why China rapidly accumulated foreign reserves.

However, the nature of domestic political cleavages over reserve accumulation was somewhat different in each period examined here. In both periods, the central bank was the main opponent of reserve accumulation, but the coalition that advocated for increased foreign exchange reserves differed in the two periods. Between 2003 and 2008, few influential groups argued that China needed more foreign reserves. The reserve accumulation that took place merely reflected certain groups' insistence that China maintain an undervalued exchange rate. This mercantilist motive for reserve accumulation was also important in the 1994–97 period, but in the 1990s there was also a group of prominent central government technocrats that favored accumulating more foreign reserves for precautionary reasons. In other words, reserve accumulation was a deliberate policy goal in the first period, but it was largely a by-product of other policy objectives in the latter period. For our purposes, however, the exact reason why officials pushed for reserve accumulation matters less than the fact that both periods witnessed powerful groups pushing for this policy.

Even though China's massive stockpile of foreign reserve holdings is atypical, one important implication of this chapter is that conventional theories of international monetary relations help explain why China's behavior is so unusual. The political cleavages in China surrounding foreign exchange policies bear many resemblances to those found in other countries.[92] China's exceptionally rapid reserve accumulation reflects the exceptional political strength of groups that favor large holdings of foreign reserves, which in turn is likely a function of China's unique domestic political and economic characteristics. These include an authoritarian political system that disenfranchises consumers who would fare better under a more consumption-oriented growth strategy; a large and geographically concentrated export-oriented manufacturing sector; a weak and politically dependent central bank; and a state-dominated financial system that makes it easier for the government to sterilize its foreign reserves.[93] Although China's foreign reserve policies are different from those of most states, the political dynamics that drive these policies are not. Prevailing domestic political theories of international monetary relations, which emphasize the importance of domestic groups' preferences and the ways that national institutions aggregate these preferences, apply well to the case of China.[94]

---

92. See, for example, Henning's (1994) study of the United States, Germany, and Japan; Kessler (1998) on Mexico; Pepinsky's (2009) analysis of Malaysia and Indonesia; and Walter's (2008) research on Hong Kong, Korea, Thailand, and the Philippines.

93. The role of the authoritarian regime type is discussed by Walter in this volume. On China's manufacturing sector, see Kaplan 2006 and Steinberg and Shih 2012. Shih and Steinberg 2012 discuss the role of central bank independence. On the role of China's financial structure, see Chin and Helleiner 2008, 94; Lardy 2012, Zhang 2012.

94. Lake 2009 provides a useful overview of this general "open-economy politics" approach to international political economy.

One final implication of this study is that the impact of China's rise on the evolution of the international monetary system will continue to depend upon Chinese domestic politics. Jonathan Kirshner's chapter suggests that the "logic of international politics" will drive China to follow similar international monetary policies to those of previous rising powers. By way of contrast, this chapter implies that the distinctive logic of Chinese domestic politics may cause China to adopt different international monetary policies from those of its predecessors. For instance, China's authoritarian regime and its illiberal financial system may make it less likely to implement the same types of external monetary policies, such as currency internationalization, that were adopted by rising powers such as the United States and Japan. Whether China will act as a force for stability or instability in international monetary affairs—the answer to what Benjamin Cohen refers to in this volume as the "China Question"—depends primarily upon whether Chinese leaders expect disruptive policies would improve or threaten their domestic political standing. China is likely to continue to influence the international monetary system, but the way it will do so will depend primarily upon its internal developments.

4

GLOBAL IMBALANCES AND THE LIMITS OF THE EXCHANGE RATE WEAPON

Hongying Wang

In the first decade of the twenty-first century, large and growing current account imbalances emerged among the major economies in the world. The United States saw its deficit balloon while oil-producing countries, Germany, Japan, and China accumulated large surpluses. Many economists worried that such imbalances would not be sustainable; at some point the correction would come in a way that would disrupt the international financial system and lead to economic recession.[1] After 2004 China became especially salient in the global imbalance because of the dramatic increase in its current account surplus. In the late 1990s, China's surplus

I thank the editors of this volume, Eric Helleiner and Jonathan Kirshner, and other participants in the workshop at Cornell University in November 2012, as well as Robert Cox and J. David Richardson for their comments on earlier drafts of the chapter. I also thank two anonymous reviewers for their useful critiques and suggestions.

1. See, e.g., Obstfeld and Rogoff 2005.

was 2–5 percent of its GDP. By 2007, the figure had reached an alarming 10 percent. More and more analysts as well as politicians pointed their fingers at China as a major contributor to the worsening deficits of many of its trading partners. This issue has been especially acrimonious in Sino-American relations.[2]

Although the financial crisis of 2007–8 did not actually result from a disorderly unwinding of current account imbalances, but rather from the proliferation of subprime mortgages in the United States under poor financial regulation, China's critics continued to stress the country's role in the crisis. Echoing a speech given by Chairman of the Federal Reserve Ben Bernanke in 2005, some of the most influential voices in American economic policy circles argued that by investing their trade surpluses in the American financial market, China and other developing countries created a "saving glut" that encouraged excessive and substandard lending in the United States, which ultimately led to the American subprime crisis and the global financial crisis.[3] In other words, even though the current account imbalances did not directly cause the financial crisis, they did so indirectly, and China was a chief culprit.

Chinese officials and diplomats have tried hard to ease the tension with other countries caused by this perception. In late 2011, the Information Office of the State Council published the first White Paper on China's foreign trade, which sought to explain the complexity of China's trade surplus and to assure the world that China was not pursuing a policy of unfair trade. But attempts like this have not alleviated the problem. Politicians and influential economists continue to condemn China for its mercantilist policy.[4]

Moreover, policymakers and the public in the United States and elsewhere shared a consensus that China's large current account surplus, the bulk of which was trade surplus, was mainly due to its controlled exchange rate regime. By keeping the value of the RMB artificially low, they believed, China gained an unfair advantage in its exports to the world market. By implication, liberalizing the exchange rate regime would reduce

---

2. For a concise discussion that situates this issue in the larger context of Sino-American relations, see Lieberthal and Wang 2011.

3. Besides Bernanke 2005 and 2007, also see Bergsten 2008; Paul Krugman, "The Chinese Disconnect," and "Chinese New Year," *New York Times,* October 23, 2009, January 1, 2010.

4. See e.g. Rodrik 2013.

China's current account surplus to a normal level and help rebalance the global economy.[5]

The focus on China's exchange rate in addressing its role in the global imbalance is not surprising. The current cycle of global imbalance is one of several since World War II. Previous episodes include the periods of 1971–73, 1977–78, the mid-1980s, and the mid-1990s. In each episode, the United States was the main deficit country, with European countries and Japan running persistent current account surpluses. In those earlier cycles of imbalance, the exchange rate was an important part of US policy toward rebalancing. As Eric Helleiner and Jonathan Kirshner point out in the introduction to this volume, the United States used the "dollar weapon" quite effectively vis-à-vis the surpluses of Europe and Japan.

In this chapter, I provide an alternative analysis of China's role in this round of global imbalance and the utility of the exchange rate weapon. I argue that China's contribution to the global imbalance has been exaggerated. Furthermore, to the extent China has been part of the problem, the solution does not only or even mainly lie with the exchange rate regime. China's urge to export is rooted in its development model, which is characterized by high savings and low consumption. The Chinese government has tried to modify the model in recent years, but its efforts have been half-hearted and have thus far produced limited effects.

To begin with, I critique the popular diagnosis of China's role in the global imbalance and the prescription of liberalizing China's exchange rate regime. China's trade surplus with Europe and the United States is substantially the collective trade surplus of East Asian economies. To reduce China's trade surplus one should not focus mainly on the exchange rate because China's export propensity is an integral part of its development model. I then examine the efforts made by the Chinese government in recent years to reform the development model, particularly as regards increasing household income and reducing household savings. The reason that these policy initiatives have not been effective in expanding domestic consumption is that they have not

---

5. A report by the Peterson Institute for International Economics predicts that if the Chinese government keeps the exchange rate of the RMB unchanged, China's current account surplus will rebound to 4–5 percent of GDP by 2017. On the other hand, if the RMB is allowed to appreciate in real terms at 3 percent a year, China's current account will be approximately in balance by 2017 (Cline 2012).

dealt with the high and growing rates of corporate and government savings. Finally, I analyze three sets of political obstacles that have kept the pace of reform slow—ideology, institutions, and interests. The reigning ideology of statist nationalism values national power, national security, and national prestige over the welfare of ordinary people. The institutions of state capitalism privilege the state and its corporations at the expense of labor and the general public. The interest groups benefiting from the current development model are powerful in the Chinese political system, and their resistance to change has played an important role in the continuation of the existing model.

China's Contribution to the Global Imbalance

To correctly assess China's contribution to the global imbalance, it is important to understand the peculiar structure of China's foreign trade. It consists of ordinary trade and processing trade. Processing trade involves processing imported parts and intermediate products (known as processing imports) and exporting the final products (known as processing exports). The processing imports used by China to make final products come mainly from neighboring economies in Asia—Taiwan, Japan, South Korea, Malaysia, Thailand, and Singapore—whereas the processing exports are mostly sold to the United States, European countries and Japan. According to a recent study, in 2008 East Asian economies account for 77 percent of China's processing imports and only 29 percent of its processing exports. What may seem to be China's contribution to the global imbalance has in fact been the collective contribution of East Asian economies. This general pattern also applies to China's role in the trade imbalance with the United States. In 2008, for example, the United States had a deficit of $285 billion with China, of which 60 percent was due to processing trade.[6]

Just as the description of China as a main source of the global imbalance is inaccurate, the focus on China's exchange rate policy is also misplaced. While the Chinese government has indeed frequently intervened in the foreign exchange market to influence the value of the RMB, the impact of the exchange rate on trade is not as great as many expect it to be. In fact,

---

6. This and other examples are discussed in Xing 2012.

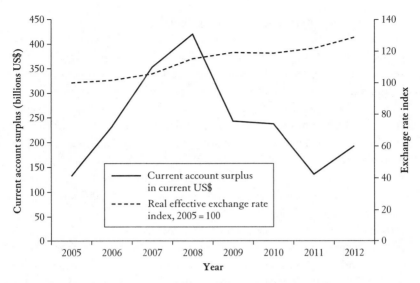

Figure 4.1. China's current account surplus and exchange rate, 2005–2012. Based on data from the World Bank, http://databank.worldbank.org/.

since 2005 the Chinese government has allowed the RMB to appreciate by about 25 percent in nominal terms or 30 percent in real terms against the dollar, but such a significant appreciation of the Chinese currency has not produced a corresponding effect. From 2005 to 2008, China's current account surplus continued to grow strongly (see figure 4.1). Although the appreciation of the RMB no doubt cut into the price competitiveness of China's exports, the country was able to ameliorate its impact, perhaps by relocating production to inland areas with lower labor cost and by moving up the technology ladder in exports. Moreover, as noted above, China's processing exports depend heavily on imported parts and intermediate products. When the RMB got stronger, the cost of the processing imports became less for China, which reduced the price impact of RMB appreciation on the final products exported by China.

From 2007 to 2011 the ratio of China's current account surplus to its GDP dropped from 10.1 percent to 1.9 percent.[7] But this was not mainly

7. World Bank, http://data.worldbank.org/indicator/BN.CAB.XOKA.GD.ZS.

due to the effect of the appreciation of the RMB. Two other factors have been more important. First, in response to the global financial crisis, China adopted a stimulus plan that involved massive investment. High investment in fixed assets fueled domestic demand for imported commodities, machinery, and energy. Second, the economic recession in Europe and the United States greatly reduced global demand, and protectionist measures introduced by a number of governments further shrank the export market for China. The IMF predicts that after the economic downturn, China's current account surplus will rise again—to 4.3 percent of its GDP by 2017.[8] With regard to the bilateral trade balance with the United States, China's surplus already rebounded in 2010 and 2011 to above its 2007 level despite the appreciation of the RMB.[9]

Indeed, a number of studies on the responsiveness of China's trade balance to exchange rates have produced mixed results. Summarizing earlier research and using data on China's trade with eighteen trading partners from 2005 to 2009, a recent study concludes that a real appreciation of the RMB reduces China's trade balance with some partners but increases its balance with some others and that it has no overall long-term impact on China's trade balance.[10]

Although China's role in the global imbalance and the global financial crisis has often been overstated and the fixation on exchanges rates is unwarranted, there is no question that China's trade surplus grew rapidly and that it worsened the current account imbalances among the major economies in the years leading up to the global financial crisis. How do we understand China's strong propensity to export? What should be done to modify China's external imbalance? To answer these questions, it is important to look at the bigger picture of China's development model, which is a major source of both the external and the internal imbalance of the Chinese economy.[11]

---

8. IMF, http://www.imf.org/external/pubs/ft/weo/2012/01/pdf/tables.pdf.

9. See data from the US Trade Representative, http://www.ustr.gov/countries-regions/china-mongolia-taiwan/peoples-republic-china.

10. See Wang et al. 2012. As noted above, China's trade surplus with Europe and the United States has been in large part a manifestation of East Asia's collective trade surplus with those regions. Not surprisingly, some economists argue that a joint appreciation of East Asian currencies would be more effective than RMB appreciation alone in reducing China's exports (Thorbecke and Smith 2010).

11. Interestingly, in the last couple of years, the IMF has shifted its attention from China's exchange rate to its internal imbalance. In the 2012 and 2013 Article IV consultations, it argued that the Chinese currency was moderately undervalued, in contrast to its assessment of "substantial

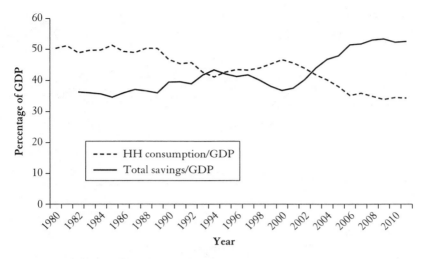

Figure 4.2. China's household consumption and total savings, 1980–2010. Based on data from the World Bank, http://databank.worldbank.org/.

With the beginning of China's reform and opening in the late 1970s and the early 1980s, national savings rose gradually as a share of China's GDP while consumption dropped precipitously (see figure 4.2). China's investment has been high, but its savings have been even higher, and this has resulted in strong exports for many years.[12] To reduce China's external surplus without pushing internal investment even higher, it is imperative to reduce national savings and increase household consumption.

There are many reasons why savings tend to be high and consumption tends to be low in developing countries,[13] but China has gone too far in that direction. Figure 4.3 compares the consumption/GDP ratio in China with

---

undervaluation" in 2011. And in both years' reports the IMF mission urged China to increase domestic household consumption (http://www.imf.org/external/pubs/ft/scr/2012/cr12195.pdf and http://www.imf.org/external/pubs/ft/scr/2013/cr13211.pdf).

12. According to the identity CA = S − I, the gap between savings and investment is the amount of current account balance. Scholars agree that excessive savings rather than insufficient investment has been the main factor behind high current account surpluses in Asian economies, including the Chinese economy (Morgan 2012).

13. For example, savings enable investment and exports, both of which are important in the initial stages of industrialization. Savings also tend to be high because the welfare state is rudimentary and families face high economic uncertainties. In addition, high savings could be the result of underdeveloped financial systems.

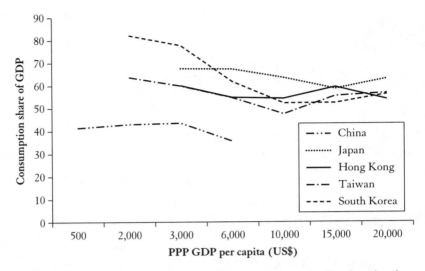

Figure 4.3. Consumption-GDP ratio in selected East Asian economies. Based on data from Alan Heston, Robert Summers, and Bettina Aten, Penn World Table Version 7.1, Center for International Comparisons of Production, Income and Prices at the University of Pennsylvania, July 2012, https://pwt.sas.upenn.edu/php_site/pwt71/pwt71_form.php.

those of its neighboring countries in comparable stages of development. It shows clearly that even in the East Asian region, which has a reputation for high savings and low consumption, the level of consumption in China has been exceptionally low.

The model of high savings and low consumption has worked well in expanding China's GDP, but it has been problematic in other ways. Not only has it led to external imbalance with China's trading partners, it has created serious imbalance inside China as well.

First, the high level of investment has often led to misallocation of resources and inefficiency. China's financial reform lags far behind the liberalization of the real economy.[14] Chinese banks routinely favor state-owned enterprises (SOEs) through lower interest rates and easier debt forgiveness while starving nonstate enterprises, which are the most innovative and dynamic actors in the Chinese economy.[15] Research indicates that the investment share of GDP has risen to an unsustainable level while the

---

14. See detailed discussions in Lardy 1998.
15. This is the central argument of Huang 2008. Also see Martin 2012 for a similar perspective.

investment-to-output ratio has increased to an outlier's position, implying overinvestment and decreasing efficiency.[16] Second, the low-consumption model has failed to improve the living standards of the population at a pace comparable with economic growth. This trend has become increasingly salient in the last decade. In 2000, household consumption accounted for 47 percent of the GDP (down from 51 percent in 1990), but by 2006 it had dropped to 35 percent and has remained around that level since.[17]

To summarize, the popular view of China's role in the global imbalance exaggerates China's contribution and the focus on exchange rates is misplaced. To the extent that China's trade surplus has been part of the global imbalance, it is a result of the country's overall development model, and the suppression of private consumption has led to internal as well as external imbalance. The Chinese government has been aware of this dual imbalance for some time, but the initiatives taken by the Chinese government in response to it have had only limited effect.

Policy Initiatives and Limitations

Repeated criticisms by foreign governments of Chinese mercantilism in the 1990s became a constant irritant to China's leaders, but it was the Asian financial crisis in 1997–98 that caused them to become alarmed about the uncertainty of the international market. In the first few months of 1998, Jiang Zemin and other officials began to emphasize the need to expand domestic demand (*kuo da nei xu*), including developing the western regions of China. When Hu Jintao and Wen Jiabao took over the leadership in 2003, they continued to be alert to China's external imbalance. Hu pointed out that "with a large trade surplus, China was overly dependent on the international market. This would not only lead to trade frictions but also would make Chinese economic development vulnerable."[18] On the other

---

16. See Lee et al. 2012.

17. World Bank, http://data.worldbank.org/indicator/NE.CON.PETC.ZS?page=2. According to the same data bank, the world's average is over 60 percent.

18. Cited in Qi Yiming, "Gaige kaifang yilai kuoda neixu zhanlue fangzhen de xingcheng he fazhan" [The formation and development of the strategy of expanding domestic demand since the beginning of reform and opening], Xinhua, July 14, 2009, http://news/xinhuanet.com/theory/2009-07/14/content_11706896.htm.

hand, unlike their predecessors, they also began to pay attention to the imbalance inside China.

The internal imbalance, especially the slowdown of living standard improvement, became a concern for the leaders of China because it could pose a threat to the fragile legitimacy of the communist regime. Although the CCP has managed to remain the ruling party of China for decades, its legitimacy has faced multiple challenges. The Cultural Revolution and the economic reforms in the 1980s each generated severe political crises that threatened the survival of the party-state.[19] The Cultural Revolution (1966–1976), launched by Mao Zedong toward the end of his life, halted economic development and brought the country to political chaos. By the time it ended, the CCP had lost much of its appeal based on its historical role as the leader of the Chinese revolution. The economic reforms initiated by Deng Xiaoping in the late 1970s were in large part an effort to end this disaster and thus relegitimize the Party's rule. But the contradictions embedded in the reforms gave rise to a new crisis. The combination of partial market liberalization and continued political authoritarianism brewed corruption and unmet expectations. In the late 1980s, the government faced public protests in many parts of the country and ultimately resorted to force to save itself. Since then, the party-state has tried to rebuild its legitimacy through economic growth, ideological reform, and institutional innovation.[20]

More than anything else, the Chinese government has relied on delivering rising living standards to buy political conformity and compliance. As long as they experience better living conditions, the vast majority of Chinese people have been acquiescent toward the regime despite their discontent with issues such as political control, inequality, and corruption. However, if the improvement of their living standards lags farther and farther behind the country's economic growth, their disappointment with other aspects of the regime may well loom large and turn them into a force of political agitation. The so-called "scientific outlook on development" (*ke xue fa zhan guan*) proposed by the Hu-Wen administration emphasized that economic growth must lead to better living standards for ordinary people. Since the global financial crisis in 2007–8, the Chinese government has intensified its call for "changing the development model" and expanding domestic consumption.

19. Ding 1994 provides a good analysis of these challenges to the legitimacy of the CCP regime.
20. These efforts are discussed at length in Holbig and Gilley 2010, Fewsmith 2008, and Shambaugh 2008.

Alongside such rhetoric, the Chinese government has taken some initiatives to increase household income. Early on during his tenure, Hu called for raising the share of household income in the country's GDP. In 2004, the government began to draft a plan for income distribution reform aimed at helping low-income groups. In 2006, the government eliminated agricultural taxes on farmers, which had been in place since 1958, which increased household incomes in rural China. From 2004 to 2011, the government raised pensions for enterprise employees by 10 percent a year. During the Eleventh Five Year Plan period (2005–10), local governments increased minimum wages three times, by an average of 13 percent each time. The government has also raised the income tax threshold for individuals, from 800 yuan a month to 1,600 yuan in 2005, to 2,000 yuan in 2007, and again to 3,000 yuan in 2011. In late 2012, the Eighteenth Party Congress promised to double urban and rural household income (with 2010 as the base year) by 2020. In February 2013, after years of study and consultation, the State Council issued an opinion on income distribution reform, calling for increasing the share of household income in the country's GDP and for wealth redistribution among groups and regions in the country.[21]

The government has also adopted policy measures to reduce household savings. One reason for the high household savings is the broken welfare system. The reform era has seen the dismantlement of the old socialist system, but a new system has been slow in emerging. Households are compelled to save for education, unemployment, old age, and housing, as well as healthcare expenses. In the last decade, the government has gradually expanded the scope and depth of welfare programs. A new Social Insurance Law went into effect in 2011. Health insurance has been greatly expanded, including in the rural areas. Pension plans have been extended to cover groups previously excluded, such as the urban unemployed and rural residents. The government has also invested in affordable housing for the poor. But overall, the welfare provision available for the Chinese population is still quite rudimentary. So far it has not led to a significant decline in precautionary savings.[22]

Another reason for high household savings is the serious inequality in Chinese society. By the early 2000s, China's Gini coefficient had surpassed that of the United States. The concentration of disposable income in the hands

---

21. The text can be found at http://news.xinhuanet.com/politics/2013-02/05/c_114625358_2.htm.
22. Cristadoro and Marconi 2012.

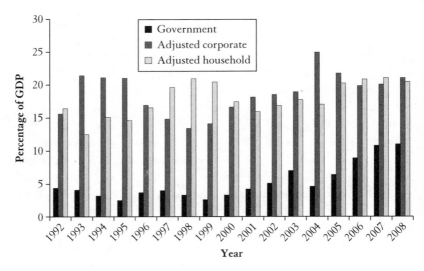

Figure 4.4. China's national savings, 1992–2008. Based on data in Ma and Wang 2010.

of the rich has dampened consumption because the rich tend to have a low marginal propensity for consumption.[23] The more wealth stays in the hands of the rich, the higher are household savings. Because of the government's steps to increase the income of the low and middle classes, in recent years, the overall inequality in China has not increased, but it has hardly decreased.[24]

In the last couple of years, these policy initiatives—along with other factors, such as demographic change—seem to have halted the rise in the household savings rate. However, overall national savings remain high and have continued to rise. The answer to this puzzle lies in the composition of national savings. Household savings are only part of the China's high savings. Corporate savings (essentially corporate profits) and government savings (capital transfer from government for corporate investment and government investment) are also major components. What sets China above other countries in national savings is that all three components are near the global top. Moreover, the growth in the latter two kinds of savings has been chiefly responsible for the rapid growth of national savings in the last fifteen years,[25] as shown in figure 4.4. It is no wonder that focusing only

23. Indeed, as researchers have shown, richer families in China have higher savings rates than poorer families (Yang et al. 2011).

24. This point is made in an OECD study (Herd 2010).

25. For a detailed analysis and comparison, see Ma and Wang 2010. Also see Prasad 2011.

on households has not reduced national savings. To address the imbalance of Chinese economy effectively, it is imperative to reduce the high savings of all three sectors—government and corporations as well as households.

Political Obstacles to Change

Why have the efforts to change China's economic growth model been half-hearted and slow? To be sure, there are economic factors that make it difficult to successfully change the development strategy.[26] But the most crucial factors are political: in particular, three types of political obstacles have hindered the necessary reform of the development model—ideology, institutions, and interests.

Ideology

Besides keeping the economy growing, the CCP has sought to meet the serious challenges to its legitimacy in the post-Mao period by making nationalism another major source of regime legitimation. It is perhaps no exaggeration to say that nationalism has replaced communism as the reigning ideology of the country. This ideology, encouraged by the government and shared by much of the public, is marked by a preoccupation with China's national power and national prestige in the world.[27] There is a prevailing view in China that national power and prestige can only be achieved by a strong state. This is not only politically expedient rhetoric, it is also a deeply held belief rooted in the history of Chinese nationalism.

For much of its history, China was the dominant political power in East Asia, surrounded by weaker entities that seldom posed a threat to Chinese superiority. International politics and nationalism were not part of the traditional Chinese world order.[28] But this changed drastically in the nineteenth century. The Opium War in the 1840s gave China a rude introduction to the modern international system, and for the next hundred

---

26. Paul Bowles argues that China's economic structure makes it a profit-led growth regime rather than a wage-led one. The introduction of wage-led policies to a profit-led regime is not likely to succeed in promoting economic growth (Bowles 2012).

27. Most scholars of Chinese nationalism recognize this feature implicitly or explicitly. See, e.g., Zhao 2004 and Gries 2005.

28. A pioneering analysis of the traditional Chinese worldview can be found in Fairbank 1968.

years or so China faced invasion and coercion by foreign powers. As China went through the "century of humiliation," its elite was consumed by the problem of national survival and standing in the world of nations. Many of them believed that the fate of the Chinese nation was closely tied with the strength of the Chinese state. Revolutionary leaders from Sun Yat-sen to Mao Zedong called for the establishment of a powerful state to unify and modernize China and to ensure China's place in the competitive international system. Unlike Western traditions of nationalism, which have deep roots in the notions of freedom and popular sovereignty, Chinese nationalism was born with a heavy emphasis on state power and state sovereignty.[29] In contemporary China, patriotism has become synonymous with support of the party-state.[30]

This kind of statist nationalism prioritized building up state capacity over improving the living standard of ordinary people. A recent article in the official newspaper, *China Daily,* captures this perspective well. It glorifies the accomplishments of the decade under Hu-Wen leadership with three sets of numbers. First, China's GDP has risen to number two in the world. Second, Chinese government revenues have exceeded 10 trillion yuan. Third, total exports and imports have reached the second highest position in the world. "These three rising lines [on an accompanying graph] are the contours of our country's rapid economic development in the last ten years. They are the tracks of the massive increase of our comprehensive national power." The same article further points out that the rising government revenues and foreign reserves have accumulated large volumes of "real gold and silver for the country. . . . China's overall power, competitiveness and resilience in the face of crises, and its role as a new engine of growth for the world economy has won international recognition and respect."[31] Clearly, the size of the economy, government revenues, and the

---

29. On this point, see Wang Gungwu 1995 and Zheng 1999.

30. Indeed, the Chinese expression of patriotism (*ai guo zhu yi*), where "guo" could mean nation or state, does not distinguish between love for the nation and love for the state. As CCP General Secretary Jiang Zemin put it in 1990, "in China today, patriotism and socialism are unified in essence" (cited in Zhao 2004).

31. See "Shushuo shinian: sanzu shuju gouhua chu zonghe guoli shangsheng guiji" [A Decade Told by Numbers: Three Sets of Statistics Trace Increased Comprehensive National Power], *China Daily,* June 4, 2012, http://www.chinadaily.com.cn/dfpd/18da/2012-06/04/content_15782287.htm.

foreign reserves are highly valued in the official version of the national interest. This mentality goes a long way in shaping the government's attitude
toward China's international balance, industrial policy, and fiscal policy.

First, it has shaped China's approach to its international balance of payments. From 2001 to 2012, China's official reserves rose rapidly from about
$200 billion to over $3 trillion. For the first few years in this period, this
trend met with unreserved enthusiasm. In a report on China's balance of
payment in 2003, the State Administration of Foreign Exchange (SAFE)
stated that "a good state of the balance of payments is a result of healthy
national economic growth and fruitful foreign economic relations. In the
meantime, it has played a positive role in ensuring national economic and
financial security."[32] By the end of 2006, China's foreign reserves had exceeded the symbolic threshold of $1 trillion. For many inside and outside
the government this was a historic accomplishment. They argued that
"foreign reserves are a manifestation of the accumulation of a country's
wealth and the improvement of its comprehensive power. The huge reserves of over $1 trillion mean that our country has abundant international
payment capacity. To some degree this highlights China's economic power,
which is strong enough to influence the world."[33]

Chinese policymakers' belief in the crucial role of large foreign reserves
in safeguarding national power and national security was intensified by the
international environment, especially the effect of the Asian financial crisis
on China's neighbors. The dramatic fall of the Suharto regime during the
crisis and the concessions made by various Asian countries in exchange for
rescue by the IMF drove home the serious damage international financial
turmoil could do to countries without strong foreign reserves. In the aftermath of the Asian financial crisis, national "financial security" became a
leading concept in the Chinese discourse and the size of the official reserves
became a chief indicator of such security.[34]

It is important to note, however, that the discourse on national interest in this area is not monolithic. While the Chinese elite and public are

---

32. See State Administration of Foreign Exchange 2003.

33. See "Zhongguo waihui chubei yu'e tupo wanyi meiyuan" [China's Foreign Reserves Surpass One Trillion Dollars], Xinhua, http://news.xinhuanet.com/fortune/2007-01/15/
content_5609476.htm.

34. Perhaps following the same logic, other countries in East and Southeast Asia have also
increased their official reserves since the crisis (Aizenman and Marion 2003a).

generally proud of the country's foreign reserves, some have become ambivalent about the effect of this development. For example, in 2007 the head of SAFE noted that the sustained huge trade surplus had made macroeconomic management complex and difficult and increased the pressure for RMB appreciation. He argued that China should gradually achieve a more balanced international payment structure.[35] From time to time, China's top leaders have expressed concern over maintaining the value of the reserves, which are mostly invested in dollar-denominated assets.[36]

However, the dominant view still equates a favorable balance of payments with China's comprehensive national power, national competitiveness, and ability to ensure financial stability. The recent global financial crisis has further hardened China's resolve to maintain a strong balance of payments position. The annual report of SAFE often emphasizes the importance of China's large foreign reserves in ensuring the country's ability to manage foreign debt.[37] Faced with the vulnerability of foreign reserves to currency fluctuations and the low returns on holdings of US treasury bills, the Chinese government has not chosen to reduce the reserves, but instead has diversified its holdings by encouraging direct investment overseas. New policies have simplified and eased the procedures for Chinese companies to invest abroad, and the government has also set up a number of national wealth funds to look for overseas investment opportunities. Indeed, China's foreign direct investment outflow has risen dramatically since 2004, around the same time as its trade surplus surged.

Second, statist nationalism also has implications for the government's industrial policy. In the early 1990s, the SOEs, which had been largely left untouched in the 1980s, became subject to reform. Following a strategy of "grasping the big and letting go the small," the government stopped supporting a large number of small and medium-sized SOEs. Meanwhile, using political and economic resources at its disposal, the government has

---

35. See speech by the head of SAFE (Hu 2007).

36. See, e.g., "Wen Jiaobao: Meiguo yao xinshou chengnuo, baozheng zhongguo zichan anquan" [Wen Jiabao: The United States Must Keep Its Promise and Guarantee the Safety of Chinese Assets], http://finance.qq.com/a/20090313/002599.htm.

37. Furthermore, some commentators note that China's strategic reserves of oil and other resources are low, which means it will need large quantities of foreign currencies to purchase materials of vital importance for national security (Yin Chengde, "Zhengque renshi zhongguo de jingji shili" [Correctly understand China's economic power], June 15, 2007, http://theory.people.com.cn/GB/49154/49155/5869454.html).

helped a small number of large SOEs in strategic sectors become highly profitable national champions.[38] In 2012, of the seventy Chinese companies on the Fortune Global 500, sixty-five were state-owned.[39] Many SOEs have gained monopolistic or oligopolistic positions in key sectors of China's economy, such as energy, transportation, communications, and finance. In the last few years, some economists and policy analysts have noted the advancement of the state sector and the retreat of the private sector (*guo jin min tui*), with SOEs acquiring large numbers of non–state-owned enterprises.[40]

A highly touted rationale for this policy is to promote national competitiveness and defend national "economic security" (defined as the safeguarding of the country's natural resources, its market, its control over major industries, its sovereignty in economic policymaking, and its ability to maintain economic stability) in a globalized world. Many among Chinese policymakers and analysts equate SOEs with national interest and national security. Unlike private capital (domestic or foreign), which seeks profits for private owners, they argue, state capital serves the interest of the state and thus the country. It can be counted on to support the government and the people with its wealth and to help the country in times of crises. Therefore, China's national security and prosperity depend on strong SOEs.[41]

Finally, statist nationalism has been used as justification of the growing government revenues. In the 1980s, fiscal decentralization was a hallmark of the early stage of China's economic reform. It brought dramatic economic growth by giving incentives to local governments and entrepreneurs.[42] In the early 1990s, the revenue of the Chinese government, especially of the central government, declined to an alarmingly low level. Policy analysts called for a recentralization of fiscal power and—more generally—for enhanced capacity of the state.[43] The focus on state capacity became especially urgent in light of the collapse of the Soviet Union and

---

38. On SASAC's industrial policy, see Lin and Milhaupt 2011.

39. This was reported in the *New York Times,* October 17, 2012.

40. For a summary of the various perspectives on this phenomenon, see Leng 2013.

41. This position is stated forcefully in an article on the website of SASAC: Ji Xiaonan, "Zhengque renshi he fenxi dangqian 'guo jin min tui' de taolun" [Correctly understand and analyze the current debate over "guo jin min tui"], http://www.sasac.gov.cn/n1180/n6881559/n6987010/10317970.html. Also see Jiang 2011.

42. A widely cited study making this argument is Montinola et al. 1995.

43. An influential report making this plea was Hu and Wang 1993.

the apparent weakness of its successor states. Since then, the official discourse in China has emphasized the importance of government revenues for national interest and national security. Indeed, in the last dozen years, Chinese government revenues have skyrocketed. From 1999 to 2011, government revenues grew from 1 trillion to over 10 trillion yuan, showing an average annual growth rate of about 20 percent. In response to widespread criticism of the accumulation of so much wealth in the government's coffers, officials claim that the government needs to have adequate fiscal power to implement macroeconomic policy, redistribute wealth, and build up national defense.[44]

The ideology of statist nationalism constitutes a major obstacle for changing the existing development model. As long as the government and China's elite remain obsessed with national security, national power, and national prestige, the well-being of ordinary citizens will remain of secondary importance. The existing development strategy that focuses on promoting export competitiveness, strengthening SOEs, and accumulating wealth in the hands of the state will only be subject to minor tinkering at the edges.

Institutions

Another obstacle to changing the current development model is that many of its features have been institutionalized. More than thirty years of economic reforms have not created a market economy in China, but a system of mixed economy best described as state capitalism. This system is characterized by limited use of market mechanisms combined with state ownership of the largest corporations and state control of the most strategic and profitable sectors of the economy. It is also characterized by a symbiotic relationship between the government and businesses at every level. An "entrepreneurial state," "local state corporatism," and "capitalism with Chinese characteristics" are a few labels scholars have used to capture the nature of this phenomenon.[45]

---

44. See, for example, a statement by the Minister of Finance, Xiang Huaicheng (Xiang 2011).
45. These concepts are proposed and elaborated in Duckett 1998, Oi 1999, and Huang 2008, respectively.

One prominent institutional feature of state capitalism is its state-controlled financial system. Admittedly, the Chinese government has gradually introduced liberalizing measures such as equitizing the big state-owned banks, creating local banks and joint stock banks, allowing foreign banks to enter the Chinese market in limited ways, and introducing some flexibility in interest rates and exchange rates, but, it has not changed state domination of the financial system. As of 2010, state-owned banks and banks in which the national governments held controlling shares accounted for 57 percent of total banking assets.[46] Indeed, the government enjoys significant influence over the operation of all types of banks. Here, too, it privileges SOEs at the expense of other types of enterprises, and furthermore, banks exploit depositors by keeping interest rates low. Since 2003, interest rates have been below inflation rates, in effect transferring wealth from households to enterprises.[47] One estimate puts the transfer in the neighborhood of 5–7 percent of GDP each year.[48] Such a system gives a huge competitive advantage to the SOEs. It has been a major source of their high investments and extraordinary profits. As long as the state controls the financial institutions and refuses to liberalize the financial system, it is difficult to change the imbalance.

Another institutional feature of China's state capitalism is the large and bureaucratically dominated public finance system. As noted above, government revenues have grown rapidly in recent years, and government savings make up a large portion of the national savings. With so much wealth in the hands of the government, how it is allocated and spent is an important political issue.

The public finance system in China has been strictly controlled by government bureaucracies. At the national level, the main actors are the National Development and Reform Commission (NDRC) and the Ministry of Finance (MOF). Although the National People's Congress (NPC) is authorized to approve each year's budget, its function has been little more than that of a rubber stamp. The budget submitted by the government tends to be vague, lumping different types of spending under a few broad categories without detailed information or explanation. Members of the NPC are

---

46. Martin 2012.
47. Lardy 2012.
48. Pettis 2011.

hard-pressed to understand the budget, let alone monitor its implementation. Moreover, China's public finance is highly fragmented. The central government accounts for about 30 percent of government spending while the remaining 70 percent is that of the provincial and local governments. Compared to the central government, most local government spending is even less transparent with large amounts of "extra-budget" items, such as fees and levies collected by government agencies and spent outside the budget.[49]

The dominance of government bureaucracies and the lack of public input in the public finance system have created an investment and infrastructure bias in public spending. Although government spending on public goods has increased over time in absolute terms, it tends to favor projects in transportation, communication, and energy. Spending on social programs improving people's quality of life, such as environmental protection, healthcare, education, and social assistance, has lagged behind. This tendency is built into the system, since infrastructure is essential for attracting investment and promoting local economic development. Given the emphasis on GDP growth rate as a major criterion for their political advancement, officials are highly motivated to pour money into various infrastructure projects. Besides, these projects also offer ample opportunities for personal economic gains through corruption.[50] In contrast, social welfare programs are not likely to produce as many political and economic benefits in the near term. Without accountability to the public, government officials have few incentives to increase such spending.

The allocation of the government's four-trillion-yuan stimulus package after the global financial crisis offers a good illustration of how public money is spent in China. As Table 4.1 shows, according to the plan drawn up by the NDRC, the vast majority of the funds went to infrastructure. In contrast, social welfare spending only constituted 8 percent of the package.

---

49. For details of China's public finance system, see Wong 2007.

50. Rampant corruption in infrastructure development has been widely reported, including in the Chinese press. For example, a report by the official Xinhua news agency cites estimates that bribes amount to 5–10 percent of the total cost of a project. It also reports that a nationwide campaign from September 2009 to March 2010 uncovered graft cases in infrastructure projects involving more than 2.99 billion yuan. See "China Fights Rampant Graft in Infrastructure Projects," http://news.xinhuanet.com/english2010/china/2011-10/18/c_131198485.htm.

TABLE 4.1. Breakdown of the RMB 4 trillion stimulus package, 2008

Categories	%
Railway, roads, airports, electric grid	45
Reconstruction of Sichuan earthquake area	25
Rural area infrastructure	9
Technology and structural adjustment	4
Environment	9
Affordable housing	7
Healthcare and education	1

Source: *Caijing* magazine, November 27, 2008, http://www.caijing.com.cn/2008–11–27/110032337. html.

These institutional characteristics of China's state capitalism support the existing development model, so that reform of the model requires institutional changes that involve liberalizing the financial system and democratizing public finance. However, these measures would greatly reduce state control of the economy and undermine the interests of those who have benefited handsomely from the current financial and fiscal systems. The pace and extent of reform have been constrained by the power balance between the relevant interest groups.

Interests

The existing model of development and its underlying institutions have created winners and losers. The winners include powerful government and corporate actors, such as the NDRC, the MOF, the State Asset Supervision and Administration Commission (SASAC), large SOEs, and local governments in the coastal provinces. The NDRC and the MOF derive their power from the allocation of state-controlled resources through planning, guidance, and budgeting, which in turn depends on state control of the financial system and public finance. SASAC and large SOEs owe their resources and influence to the dominant position of the state sector in China's economy.[51] Local governments in the coastal region have

---

51. As Steinberg and Walter point out in their chapters, the Ministry of Commerce (MOF-COM) is a major player in the making of Chinese foreign economic policy. Like its predecessor, the Ministry of Foreign Trade and Economic Cooperation, MOFCOM represents the interests of exporting companies. It has aggressively lobbied for policies that favor Chinese exports, including currency policy and other forms of subsidies, but its role in addressing the domestic imbalance has not been as prominent.

long benefited from the export-oriented development strategy. The jobs, revenues, and economic upgrading provided by the exports have brought wealth and political advancement. Therefore, the local governments have strong incentives to continue an export-oriented development strategy. As the richer provinces, they are also strongly opposed to policies of distribution across regions.[52] All of these winners have significant political clout in China.

The dominant position of the NDRC and its predecessor the State Planning Commission, and of the MOF goes back to the beginning of the People's Republic. As the central planners of the socialist economy, they were extremely powerful. In the reform era, the Chinese economy has become subject to a mixture of plan and market forces, but the government continues to play an important role in guiding the economy and allocating key resources. The NDRC and the MOF have retained authority in the making of industrial policy, extracting and distributing fiscal resources, and even approving or rejecting individual economic projects above a certain scale.[53]

In contrast to the NDRC and the MOF, SASAC is a relatively new government organization. Established in 2002 to take charge of the largest SOEs under the direct leadership of the State Council, its mission is to "fully realize the government's role as the investor and owner of these enterprises." It has the functions of supervising and managing state assets in enterprises, ensuring their safety and growth. It is a powerful agency that has absorbed some of the authority of a number of Party and government

52. A good illustration is their attitude regarding pension policy. The pension system in China is highly fragmented, with surpluses for many provinces and cities in the coastal regions but deficits in inland provinces and cities (Frazier 2010). The central government has for some years called for national pooling of pensions in order to address this imbalance and improve the consumption capability of inland areas. But this has not materialized because of strong resistance by the coastal governments.

53. As an indication of the power of these bureaucracies, when provincial governors go to Beijing, in theory they should meet with the head of the NDRC, who is at the same bureaucratic rank as they are. But this is hardly possible in reality. Instead, they have to line up in the hallways of the NDRC to meet with division-level officials whose bureaucratic rank is two levels below theirs. When former Premier Zhu Rongji was the mayor of Shanghai and met with the minister of finance, he stood throughout the meeting while the minister was seated. Similarly, when the NPC drafts laws, it often requests consultation with relevant government ministries. Most ministries send a bureau chief, but the NDRC and the MOF often send an ordinary staff member below the rank of division chief, which is itself below that of bureau chief.

organizations, including the industrial ministries, the State Economic and Trade Commission, the MOF, and the CCP Department of Organization.[54] The leaders of SASAC are members of the powerful Central Disciplinary Committee of the CCP.[55]

The political influence of coastal provinces in national policymaking has been rising in the reform era. The most prosperous provinces and provincial-level cities in coastal China have produced many of the national political leaders in recent decades, including the influential "Shanghai Gang," which counted as its members former Party Secretary General Jiang Zemin and Premier Zhu Rongji. Many of China's top leaders today have strong ties with coastal areas.[56] Studies of the political mobility of provincial political leaders demonstrate that their political positions are closely linked with the economic performance and fiscal contributions of their provinces.[57] As a result, the interests and preferences of coastal regions are well represented in the central government and its policy choices.

The influence of major SOEs in the policymaking process is in many ways exercised through SASAC, but the symbiotic relationship between the SOEs and the government also provides other channels of influence. In 2006, the CCP issued a cadre exchange policy that stipulated circulation of leaders among SOEs, Party organizations, and government departments. Since then, it has become increasingly common for high-level Party and government officials to become managers of large SOEs and vice versa. The new government that began in March 2013 appointed former chief executive officers of SOEs to such important positions as Minister of Finance, Minister of Public Security, Minister of Industry and Information Technology, SASAC, and the China Securities Regulatory Commission.[58] Beyond these formal channels of interest representation, large SOEs often use their informal patronage networks and other political resources to lobby for policies in favor of their interests.[59]

---

54. See Naughton 2008b.
55. Information comes from the official website of SASAC (www.sasac.gov.cn). Similar to the situation in NDRC and the MOF, provincial officials often line up in the hallways of SASAC, seeking a chance to meet with its staff.
56. For an analysis of the personal and career background of these leaders, see Li 2012.
57. See analysis in Bo 2002 and Sheng 2010.
58. Reported by Xinhua, http://news.xinhuanet.com/politics/2013-03/25/c_124497411.htm.
59. Kennedy 2008 provides details of the lobbying strategies and activities of different types of Chinese companies, including SOEs.

The current development model has created not only winners but also losers. Private entrepreneurs, labor, and the general population as savers and consumers have all suffered from the financial and public finance systems that have deprived them of their fair share of the national wealth. They would all benefit from a change of the existing institutions. Financial liberalization would improve the access to capital of private businesses and give ordinary people higher returns on their savings. More public input into and oversight of public finance would put pressure on the government to implement its promise to increase spending on social programs and thus improve the living standard of ordinary people.

In the current political framework, these groups are extremely weak. In contrast to the supporters of the existing development model, they are largely excluded from the policymaking process and have few channels to effectively voice their preferences and push for their interests.

There have been many studies of the organization and political efficacy of the emerging private businesses in contemporary China. Most of them seek to understand whether such businesses constitute a new political force that would promote China's democratization. The general consensus thus far has been negative. Research finds that the CCP has effectively kept its control over private businesses, rendering them weak and dependent on the state. Economically, the government has restricted the growth of the private sector by adopting policies favoring foreign enterprises and SOEs.[60] Politically, the CCP has managed to co-opt private entrepreneurs through patron-client relationships, control of business associations, and recruitment of the business elite into the Party.[61]

Labor is even more powerless politically. Chinese peasants have always been treated as second-class citizens. From the early years of the communist regime to the present, their income and welfare have often lagged far behind those of the rest of the country. Nor have they been allowed to organize themselves politically to protect their interests.[62] During the reform era, urban labor has also been under assault in many ways. The reform of the SOEs has led to declining status and economic well-being of many urban workers—the so-called "masters of the socialist country."

---

60. On the attitude of the Chinese government toward foreign capital and its underlying rationale, see Gallagher 1999. On its pro-SOE policies, see Huang 2008.

61. These strategies are discussed in detail in Pearson 2000, Dickson 2003, and Tsai 2007.

62. Bernstein and Lü 2003.

Furthermore, workers lack representation and organization in the political process. In the 1980s, workers' representatives accounted for around 27 percent in the NPC. By the late 1990s, this had dropped to 11 percent.[63] Trade unions are supposed to speak for the interests of the workers, but in reality, they are not allowed to engage in collective bargaining on the workers' behalf. Instead, they help the state and corporations control the workers or, at best, mediate conflicts among the three parties.[64] These factors have contributed to wage stagnation and persistent underspending on social welfare programs.

The general public is also ill-equipped to protect its interest. Money-saving households and consumers stand to gain from reform of the financial system and public finance, but they face serious collective action problems.[65] The problem of collective action is made particularly acute in China by the CCP's extreme sensitivity to any form of organization outside its own control.[66]

Although most of the groups in favor of a new development model are politically left out of the mainstream, their interests have found some support within the Chinese government. One place where such support seems significant is the NPC. For instance, in 2007 the NPC promulgated the Labor Contract Law, which improved the protection of the rights of workers. In making this law, the NPC faced many obstacles coming from powerful groups in society and influential bureaucracies in the Chinese government. The lawmakers argued long and hard that the law should focus on protecting the rights of the workers rather than on offering equal protection of the interests of employees and employers. Within the framework given by the State Council, they fought over each clause to give the workers a better deal than they had before. The situation was quite similar in the making of the Social Security Law, which was promulgated in 2010.

---

63. See Li 2008, 258.

64. Chen 2003. On the plight of Chinese workers during the reform era, see Chan 2001.

65. As public choice theorists have long argued, in any society producers in import-competing industries tend to be highly motivated and well-organized to pressure the government for protectionist policies because of their small number and the potential of major losses to them posed by free trade. In contrast, consumers lack motivation and organization in pushing for free trade because the benefits are dispersed and relatively small for each actor. See Downs 1957. The same logic applies to Chinese consumers and savers.

66. On the CCP's attitude toward organized actions, especially protests, see Cai 2004.

Another base of support for a new development model is the People's Bank of China (PBOC). As David Steinberg points out in this volume, the PBOC represents the nontradable financial sector and is interested in controlling inflation. Therefore, it does not favor RMB undervaluation and has been a supporter of a more market-based exchange rate regime. More importantly, as noted by Yang Jiang in her chapter, under a reformist leader for the last ten years, China's central bank has been a bastion of reform-minded officials. The PBOC has taken some steps toward liberalizing the financial system, including allowing market forces to influence interest rates and exchange rates to some extent. Some observers argue that the PBOC's recent push for the internationalization of the RMB is "reform by Trojan horse," aimed at pushing the liberalization of China's financial system.[67] After all, in order for the RMB to be a credible international currency, China must expand capital account liberalization, float its currency, and let the market determine interest rates.[68]

Overall, the interest and power configuration in China have posed serious obstacles to a fundamental change of the development strategy. For example, as mentioned earlier in the paper, the Chinese government began to consider a plan to reform income distribution in 2004, and it was not until 2013 that the State Council even issued an opinion on the matter. It is not hard to imagine the strong political resistance and struggle that took place behind the scenes during those long years in between and will likely to go on in the years to come. Along with ideology and institutions, interest group politics has seriously limited the policy shift toward a domestic consumption–based growth model.

As noted early in the paper, the exchange rate weapon was used in the past to address global imbalances. Randall Henning argues that the US government used the dollar weapon to achieve two levels of effect. At one level, it tried to use depreciation of the dollar to make American exports more competitive, and thus reduce American trade deficits. At another level, the depreciation of the dollar or the threat of depreciation was intended to

---

67. See, e.g., Thornton 2012.
68. One might draw a parallel with the earlier efforts by reformists in the Chinese government to use foreign pressure regarding China's accession to the World Trade Organization to speed up domestic economic reforms (Kim 2002).

pressure other countries to adopt expansionist macroeconomic policies to compensate for its contractionary effect.[69]

The use of the exchange rate weapon by the United States with regard to China may have had some first-level effect, inasmuch as the appreciation of the RMB in recent years has reduced the competitiveness of Chinese labor-intensive exports. But it has not had any significant second-level effect. Although US government officials have often urged China to adopt expansionist macroeconomic policy, it has not been an integral part of the exchange rate negotiations. Perhaps American negotiators recognize that the second-level effect of the exchange weapon depends on generating domestic pressure on the targeted government to adopt expansionary policies, which in China's political system is not likely to happen.

But more importantly, China's external imbalance is rooted in the country's development model. Short-term macroeconomic adjustment cannot fundamentally solve this problem. While China's current account surplus has decreased in the last few years due to a combination of factors, thereby ameliorating the external imbalance, the internal imbalance has actually worsened, largely because of the massive investments made by the government's stimulus programs. The enlarged manufacturing capacity is turning out products that have to be sold in either the international or the domestic market. If they are not, there will be serious problems with unrecoverable investments.[70] If domestic consumption in China continues to be kept low, there will be tremendous pressure to export these products, rejuvenating large trade surpluses and again worsening the external imbalance.

Reform of the development model is crucial to rebalancing the Chinese economy domestically and internationally. What is the likely trajectory of reform in China in the future? As long as the political foundations of the current model remain in place—ideology, institutions, and interest configuration—it is reasonable to expect minor tinkering to continue without fundamental changes. Corporate and government accumulation of wealth will continue to suppress household consumption, which will likely spill over to external surpluses.

---

69. Henning 2006.

70. The IMF has noted this issue in its annual Article IV consultation report in 2013. Also see Ahuja et al. 2012.

However, a serious crisis in China could affect the direction of this trajectory. If the economy suddenly hits a major bump or some political or environmental calamity leads to an outburst of public discontent, those at the apex of the political system may be forced to recalculate the "encompassing interest" of the regime.[71] They may be persuaded to look beyond the ideological confines of statist nationalism, abandon some of the institutional pillars of state capitalism, and "sacrifice" the interest of some bureaucracies and corporations in exchange for the survival of the regime. The remaking of the development model will be part and parcel of broader political reforms in China.

---

71. The concept of "encompassing interest" originates in Olson 1982.

5

CHINA'S ENGAGEMENT WITH INTERNATIONAL MACROECONOMIC POLICY SURVEILLANCE

Andrew Walter

China's relationship with the process of international economic policy surveillance associated with the International Monetary Fund[1] evolved from relative passivity in its early phase toward growing tension by the mid-2000s. When the Chinese authorities blocked the annual Article IV consultation process with the IMF in 2007, it appeared that Beijing's relationship with the surveillance regime had reached the point of breakdown. Some prominent commentators, especially in the United States, accused China of holding down the value of its currency for mercantilist purposes and of an abrogation of its responsibilities as an IMF member.[2]

I thank the editors, two anonymous reviewers, and the workshop participants for very helpful comments on an earlier draft of this chapter. All remaining errors are the responsibility of the author.

1. Surveillance is the process by which the IMF oversees the international monetary system and monitors economic and financial policies of member countries.
2. Bergsten 2008, Subramanian 2010; Minxin Pei, "China: The Big Free Rider," *Newsweek,* January 21, 2010.

In a broader sense, the controversy could also be seen as a decisive test of the robustness of the post-1945 liberal international order—an order some claim is "hard to overturn and easy to join"[3]—in the face of a rising great power that might not accept its basic norms, rules, and procedures. It also seemed to contradict claims that China's relationship with global institutions and associated regimes and norms has been characterized by greater convergence over time.[4] If China was neither a rule-taker nor a rule-maker in this important area of global economic governance, might it be in the process of becoming a rule-breaker? And if the liberal economic order had neither constrained nor socialized China, did this lend support to realist arguments that extant international economic regimes would erode when faced with rapid shifts in the balance of power?[5]

I argue in this chapter that this interpretation is too simplistic and in important respects misleading. China has certainly been slow to respond to growing concerns about its currency policy and its willingness to accept responsibility for international adjustment. This reflects its now considerable power-as-autonomy in the global system and the leadership's determination not to jeopardize its own domestic political monopoly, which has relied heavily on the delivery of rapid economic growth. Since 2005, however, China has accepted modest real currency appreciation and has taken measures to boost domestic demand. China's leadership is also committed since 2008 to an enhanced international macroeconomic surveillance process under the auspices of the G20. It did so primarily out of self-interest: a desire above all to preserve its domestic political position; to avoid undermining the domestic coalition in the United States that has opposed trade sanctions against China since the early 1990s; and to prevent the "stigmatization" of China as a "currency manipulator" by the IMF. These are largely negative goals, which the leadership has increasingly pursued by what is referred to throughout this volume as the exercise of power-as-autonomy. China's positive objectives as regards the reform of global monetary governance currently lack coherence and persistent commitment (see also Yang Jiang in this volume), but in one respect it has sought to achieve more influence: to

---

3. Ikenberry 2008, 24.
4. Kent 2007, Johnston 2003, 2008.
5. Gilpin 2001.

modify the international surveillance regime to encourage adjustment and policy stabilization measures by others, above all the United States. This objective has met with uncertain success, and it has entailed that China itself submit to a modest level of increased international surveillance over its own policies.

This renewed willingness to accept international oversight, however, has not yet substantially shifted the balance of forces regarding Beijing's stated objective to rebalance its economy toward consumption-led growth. Here, China's autonomy in the global political economy remains substantial and the main obstacles to such rebalancing are domestic. The leadership's response to the global financial crisis was particularly revealing: the credit-fueled boost to domestic demand was aimed primarily at the further promotion of investment projects rather than of domestic consumption.[6] There were some new measures to boost domestic consumption, including increased public spending on health and education, but these were insufficient to prevent a further decline in the contribution of consumption to total demand. The opportunity provided by the crisis to take decisive steps to accelerate the transition toward a new consumption-led growth model simply was not taken.[7] The main beneficiaries of this strategy have been local authorities and businesses who benefit from large subsidies to investment and production; the main loser has been Chinese society at large. Whether the new leadership will succeed where the previous one failed remains to be seen.

In what follows, I first describe China's evolving relationship with the international macroeconomic policy surveillance regime associated with the IMF. I then address the strengths and shortcomings of some standard theories that might account for this relationship, and outline an alternative explanation that focuses attention on the asymmetries of power relations between domestic and international actors and provides a better account of China's changing relationship to this important international regime. The conclusion develops the broader implications of the argument.

---

6. Wen Jiabao, "How China Plans to Reinforce the Global Recovery," *Financial Times,* June 23, 2011, www.ft.com/intl/cms/s/0/e3fe038a-9dc9-11e0-b30c-00144feabdc0.html#axzz2lmUS4R2e.

7. Naughton 2011.

China and the Macroeconomic Surveillance Regime

"Global imbalances" became an important preoccupation of policymakers, journalists and academics concerned with problems of international economic governance in the early 2000s, and they came to play a central role in the debate about such governance since 2008.[8] From a longer perspective, concerns about international current account imbalances date back to at least the interwar period. They played an important role in the deliberations that led to the Bretton Woods agreement of 1944, in the final years of the Bretton Woods system, and after the 1970s in the context of intra-G7 debates over macroeconomic adjustment responsibilities.[9]

China's contribution to global imbalances and its relationship to the international economic surveillance regime, however, only recently became matters of controversy. China emerged as a significant current account surplus country in 2003–4 and its emergence in 2005 as the world's largest surplus country was sudden and unexpected, not least in Beijing. China's leadership was evidently also ill prepared for the growing tension this produced in relations with the major developed countries, especially the United States, and with the IMF-led process of policy surveillance.

Until the early 2000s, China's relationship with the Fund had been comparatively unproblematic. It joined the IMF and World Bank in 1980, after the diplomatic deal between Washington and Beijing that brought the PRC into a variety of Western-dominated international institutions.[10] At the time, China's government almost certainly saw few costs and considerable benefits from membership of the Bretton Woods institutions. Its early relations with both the Fund and the Bank were cordial. China was a significant consumer of technical advice and eventually became the largest client for World Bank loans. It developed a good working relationship with IMF staff over this period, who were generally supportive of Beijing's reforms.[11]

China borrowed only twice from the IMF, in 1981 and 1986, but conditionality on these occasions was neither intrusive nor inconsistent with the

---

8. For an overview of the macroeconomic surveillance regime, see Foot and Walter 2011.
9. See De Cecco 2012.
10. Jacobson and Oksenberg 1990.
11. Author interview with IMF staff in Beijing, November 2008.

leadership's own desire to control inflation in the context of rapid growth. In this early period, China's current account was approximately in balance and its small size meant that it was not deemed in Washington to pose significant systemic risks. The Fund's attention was also closely focused on Latin America during this period. All this allowed China's leadership considerable practical policy autonomy, and Fund surveillance through the Article IV process was unintrusive despite Beijing's extensive use of capital controls and its dual exchange rate regime, which was replaced with a unified peg in 1994.

China's low global economic status in the first decade of its reforms also meant that its macroeconomic policies attracted limited attention from other major governments. This began to change in the early 1990s. The United States, the most important member of the IMF and Asia's largest trading partner, was still far more concerned with the economic threat from Japan and other Asian emerging countries at this time. The US Treasury's new reporting obligations under the 1988 Trade and Competitiveness Act focused in the first few years on Japan, South Korea and Taiwan. The latter two were cited for "currency manipulation," which as section 304 of the 1988 Act specified (in language that approximated that in the IMF's Second Amendment of 1977) was "for purposes of preventing effective balance of payments adjustments or gaining unfair competitive advantage in international trade."[12] The Treasury's report noted for the first time in May 1991 that the US bilateral trade deficit with China had grown rapidly to become the third largest with emerging Asia.[13] For the following three years, the Treasury cited China as a currency manipulator. From the American perspective, the United States was acting as the self-enforcer of the IMF's own exchange rate surveillance rules, which since 1977 had proscribed currency manipulation but which proved too politically sensitive for the Fund to enforce.[14]

This policy produced few obvious results. In 1993, the newly elected President Clinton linked the renewal of China's Most Favored Nation status, first granted in 1980, to improvements in China's human rights, a salient issue in the years after Tiananmen Square. However, under pressure

---

12. See US Treasury 1990.
13. US Treasury 1991.
14. International Monetary Fund 1977.

from major business leaders who argued that denial of MFN status would hurt US exports whilst having little impact on human rights policy, Clinton backed down in 1994 and announced that in future MFN and non-trade issues would be delinked.[15] Later that year, the US Treasury took China off the currency manipulation list, citing the end of China's dual currency system.[16]

Subsequent US administrations have taken the line that the best way of encouraging political reform in China is to support its continued integration into the global economy. Notably, the United States supported China's entry into the World Trade Organization in 2001, further reducing the likelihood of trade sanctions. The growing dependence of many large US companies on Chinese assembly production and on imports from China has also reduced the appetite among large firms for a trade dispute with Beijing. Since 2008, the Obama administration's goal of doubling US exports may also have strengthened the hand of pro-trade forces in America.[17]

China's growing regional importance was underlined during the Asian financial crises of the late 1990s, when China maintained its fixed dollar peg despite large currency depreciations among other emerging Asian economies. Its economic growth also remained robust throughout the crisis, serving as an important engine of regional growth during a period in which the far larger Japanese economy continued to stagnate. For Beijing, the lesson of the Asian crises was that the growing volatility of capital flows and the detrimental impact of IMF policy conditionality in its lending programs necessitated national protection and autonomy via continued capital controls and much larger foreign exchange reserves.[18] It is almost certainly the case that no one at this time anticipated just how large China's foreign exchange reserves would grow over the following decade.

China's trade and current account surpluses rose suddenly and sharply from 2003, as did its bilateral trade surpluses with the United States (figure 5.1). It is also notable that until 2004, its bilateral surplus closely

---

    15. Noland 1996.

    16. US Treasury 1994.

    17. International Trade Administration, National Export Initiative Introduction, http://trade.gov/nei/nei-introduction-state-of-the-union-012710.asp.

    18. Zhou 2011.

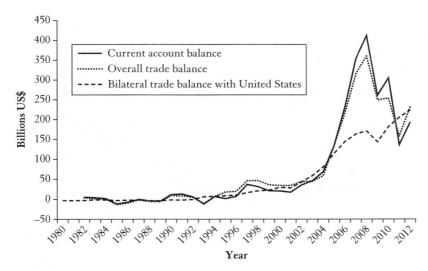

Figure 5.1. China's current account balance, overall trade balance, and bilateral trade balance with the United States, 1980–2012, US$ billions. IMF, Direction of Trade Statistics and International Financial Statistics Databases.

followed its overall trade and current account surpluses—from 2005, these noticeably diverged, although the bilateral surplus remained by far the largest element in the overall trade surplus. By 2006, China had overtaken Japan and Germany as the world's largest current account surplus country and rivaled the Middle East in importance (Figure 5.2).

This sudden emergence of China as a large surplus country prompted growing calls, especially from certain industry groups, unions, and Congress in the United States, for China to revalue the renminbi and to adopt a more flexible exchange rate policy more generally. Similar American demands had been directed at other major surplus countries since the 1960s, but in China's case these concerns were sharpened because China (uniquely) was also perceived as a potential strategic rival.[19] By mid-2005, the George W. Bush administration sought to defuse the growing domestic

---

19. The demand that China should "move to a market-based, flexible exchange rate regime" was also contained in the Bush administration's second-term security strategy review (National Security Council 2006).

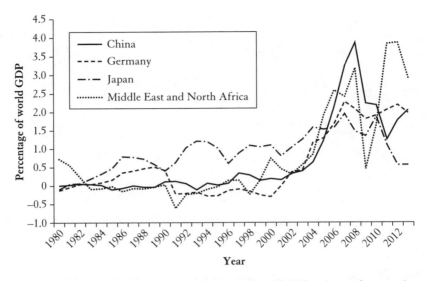

Figure 5.2. Current account balances as a percentage of world GDP, major surplus countries and regions, 1980–2013 (estimates from 2012). IMF, World Economic Outlook Database, April 2013.

political salience of China's surplus by arguing that it was actively encouraging the Chinese in bilateral and multilateral forums to shift their policy stance.[20] Concern over China's currency policy was also growing in Japan and Europe, although both took a far lower profile on the issue than did Washington.

Supported by this soft consensus among the G7 countries, the IMF in its bilateral surveillance discussions with the Chinese authorities adopted an increasingly critical stance toward Chinese currency policy. A series of increasingly robust policy discussions ensued. Like the US government, the IMF argued for a more flexible exchange rate policy and accelerated appreciation.[21] Prominent critics of China's stance, including Fred Bergsten and a number of his colleagues at the Petersen Institute for International Economic Policy in Washington, argued that Chinese policymakers evidently had mercantilist objectives and that the IMF and

20. Taylor 2007, 291–300.
21. International Monetary Fund 2005, 15–17, and 2006, 17–20.

the US administration needed to take robust action to end Beijing's currency manipulation.[22] For Bergsten, the Chinese case was a decisive test of the willingness of the United States and other major developed countries to defend and uphold the norms and rules of the postwar international economic order.

Over time, these critics became increasingly frustrated with what they perceived as fundamental weaknesses in the international surveillance regime and in the Bush administration's and the IMF's unwillingness to enforce the Articles of Agreement. Senators Charles Schumer (D-NY) and Lindsey Graham (R-SC) tabled the first bill in 2003 that would authorize unilateral trade sanctions against China if bilateral negotiations failed to achieve a substantial renminbi appreciation against the dollar. Dozens of bills focusing on China's commercial practices followed over the remaining years of the Bush administration, with a growing focus on renminbi undervaluation from 2005.[23] However, as Hufbauer and Brunel note, although Congress was not divided on the question of the need for renminbi appreciation, there was little consensus on the appropriate levers, especially as regards the automaticity of trade sanctions.[24]

The Bush administration's response, especially during the tenure of Treasury Secretary Hank Paulson, was to maintain the policies of previous administrations in insisting that persuasion rather than sanctions was the appropriate strategy and that Congress was making it harder rather than easier to achieve its objectives. This preference reflected a desire not to disrupt America's broader relationship with China and the influence of a range of voices in banking, high technology, and other sectors who favored engagement rather than confrontation with Beijing. Elsewhere in G7 countries, there was even less appetite for a more aggressive stance toward China's currency policy.[25]

---

22. Bergsten 2008.
23. Hufbauer and Brunel 2008, 219–21.
24. Hufbauer and Brunel 2008.
25. In a speech in Beijing in February 2005, Peter Mandelson, European commissioner for trade, argued for "the gradual liberalization of the exchange rate of the Yuan," but took care to emphasize that Europe also favored trade liberalization (Peter Mandelson, "The EU and China: Partnership and Responsibility in the Global Economy," University of International Business and Economics, Beijing, February 24, 2005), http://europa.eu/rapid/press-release_SPEECH-05-105_en.htm.

Faced with this uncertain degree of external threat of trade sanctions, China's leadership might simply have chosen to maintain its fixed currency peg even in the face of a rapidly growing external surplus. Instead, however, it decided in mid-2005 to shift to a policy of managed, very gradual renminbi appreciation against the dollar. Bush administration insiders argue that the combination of US persuasion, multilateral diplomacy, and IMF surveillance pressure was an important contributor to this shift.[26] But rising domestic inflation in 2005 provided another reason to move in this direction, one more aligned with the party leadership's core interest in maintaining social stability and its own domestic political monopoly.[27] In the absence of knowledge of the senior leadership's true motivations, it is very difficult to know how much external factors mattered in the final decision that was taken.

What seems clearer is that, although the new policy of nominal appreciation did contribute to a gradual rise in China's real effective exchange rate from 2005 (figure 5.3), it proved a failure in a variety of ways. The current account surplus continued to grow rapidly over 2005–8, external pressure for accelerated renminbi appreciation increased rather than dissipated, and market expectations of continued currency appreciation encouraged large speculative capital inflows that required China's central bank to intervene ever more vigorously in exchange markets and to accumulate massive dollar reserves. United States and IMF criticism of China's policies intensified and China's relationship with the Fund worsened substantially.[28] In an indication of Beijing's growing frustration with IMF surveillance and its perceived bias in favor of Washington, Beijing took the unusual step of voting against the adoption of the 2007 Decision on Bilateral Surveillance (seen as directly aimed at lowering the bar for declaring China in breach of its IMF commitments).

As it also became clear that the Fund was under growing American pressure to declare the renminbi "fundamentally misaligned," the Chinese leadership effectively blocked and withdrew from further bilateral surveillance discussions with the Fund over 2007–8.[29] This reflected a sharp

---

26. Taylor 2007, 291–300.
27. Shih 2008.
28. For a detailed discussion, see Blustein 2012.
29. Foot and Walter 2011, 113–16.

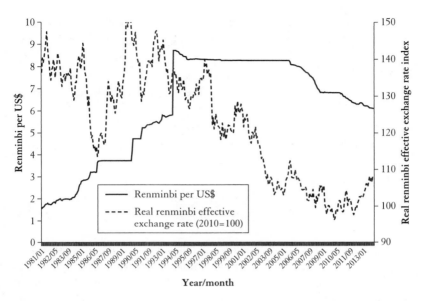

Figure 5.3. Chinese renminbi nominal exchange rate against the US dollar (left scale) and estimated real effective exchange rate index (right scale), 1981–2013. US Federal Reserve FRED database, and BIS real exchange rate database.

break with what had hitherto been a fairly cooperative and pragmatic working relationship with the Fund, and indeed a general policy of joining key multilateral institutions. One concern of the Chinese government was that a fundamental misalignment finding by the IMF would raise the likelihood of US trade sanctions, even if from a low level, and the more distant possibility of trade restrictions authorized by the World Trade Organization.[30] China's opposition to the 2007 decision failed to prevent its adoption, underlining its limited power-as-influence in a Western-dominated IMF. Fund staff continued to prepare an Article IV report on China for 2008 that would state "significant concerns that the exchange rate may be fundamentally misaligned and exchange rate policies could be a significant contributor to external instability," requiring ad hoc consultations with the Fund.[31]

---

30. Blustein 2012, 20.
31. Cited in Blustein 2012, 21.

However, the deepening of the financial crisis in September 2008 led to the abandonment of initiatives to declare China in potential breach of its IMF commitments. Indeed, Beijing ceased currency appreciation in mid-2008 as external demand began to fall sharply. In this very different environment, Beijing agreed to return to the Article IV surveillance process in 2009. The divergent paths of economic recovery between China and the advanced countries in 2009 did generate renewed criticism, but China only reverted to its previous policy of slow appreciation in June 2010. Since then, the nominal and real appreciation of the renminbi has been modest (figure 5.3), prompting continuing calls on China to engage in more rapid currency liberalization.[32] Overall, however, US discussion and criticism of Chinese exchange rate policy have been significantly lower than in the few years preceding the global financial crisis.

The IMF's stance has also shifted significantly. In the 2012 Article IV consultation, the emphasis was upon China's internal rather than external imbalances. The IMF argued that the renminbi was "moderately undervalued against a broad basket of currencies," a significant change from its 2011 assessment of "substantial undervaluation."[33] The Fund has recognized the significant decline in China's external surplus, a development that it failed to predict, but it argued that this decline had been achieved in part through increased investment, which only worsened the "internal imbalances" in the Chinese economy.[34] In the IMF view, the growing overdependence of growth on investment is unsustainable because it is increasingly inefficient and has been fed by a rapid expansion of bank lending, in particular to local governments for infrastructure investment.[35] Although some further currency appreciation would be desirable, the Fund's new emphasis is upon what it sees as crucial structural reforms: financial sector liberalization and development, a strengthened social safety net, state-owned enterprise (SOE) sector reforms, and public sector finance reforms (including at the local government level).

Similar reforms have also been proposed by the Chinese government itself, which has also accepted that the Chinese economy is characterized by unsustainable imbalances. Most famously, Premier Wen Jiabao stated

32. International Monetary Fund 2011b, 18–19.
33. International Monetary Fund 2012d.
34. International Monetary Fund 2012b, 3.
35. See International Monetary Fund 2012c, Ahuja et al. 2012.

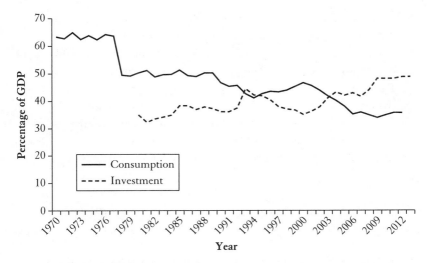

Figure 5.4. Chinese final household consumption expenditures and total investment, percent of GDP, 1970–2013. IMF, World Economic Outlook Database, and World Bank, Databank. Estimates from 2012.

after the National People's Congress of March 2007 that "China's economic growth is unsteady, unbalanced, uncoordinated, and unsustainable."[36] Without pressing ahead with domestic reforms, the IMF claimed, the Chinese authorities would not achieve their own expressed objective of rebalancing the economy toward consumption, an objective that has to date been met with failure (figure 5.4).

Despite this attempt by the IMF to frame its advice in less confrontational terms and in ways that were consistent with the leadership's own declared policy priorities, the Chinese authorities remained unhappy. They continued to oppose the view that the currency was undervalued, but they also expressed "some reservations about characterizing China's investment rate as being excessive."[37] They also continued to perceive "bias" in the surveillance process, including being overly "focused on policy gaps in emerging markets, while missing key policy features of advanced economies that had contributed to the last crisis . . ."[38] China has also stepped up arguments

36. Quoted in Lardy 2008, 5.
37. International Monetary Fund 2012c, 24.
38. International Monetary Fund 2012c, 20.

for a more fundamental reform of the IMF and the international monetary system,[39] and argued vigorously for more extensive IMF surveillance of the United States and for guarantees from Washington that it would pursue more responsible monetary and fiscal policies.[40]

Thus, although China's relationship with the process of international macroeconomic surveillance has improved considerably since the trough of 2007–8, significant tension and disagreement remain over the policy advice it receives from the Fund. Beijing also continues to criticize the procedural and distributive legitimacy of the surveillance process itself.

Explaining China's Stance on Macroeconomic Surveillance: Some Prominent Theories

At one end of the spectrum, some authors argue that China has become increasingly convergent with global norms and associated rules and institutions, driven by a mixture of self-interest, mimicking, and (perhaps over the longer term) normative socialization. At the other end, there are authors who argue that China's leadership is primarily driven by the statist objective of policy autonomy and increased global influence via export-led growth and financial independence—in short, a form of neomercantilism. Others put less emphasis on leadership preferences and instead argue that dominant societal interests have constrained the government's economic policy choices, preventing full convergence with the international surveillance regime. I briefly review each of these theories, assessing their strengths and shortcomings.

Normative Convergence?

The trend described above toward rising divergence between China and the international surveillance regime, followed by partial reconciliation since 2009, stands in tension with general claims about increasing Chinese

39. Zhou 2009.
40. "China Rules Out 'Nuclear Option' on T-bills," *Financial Times,* July 7, 2010, www.ft.com/intl/cms/s/0/5f038fc8-89a3-11df-9ea6-00144feab49a.html#axzz2lmUS4R2e.

convergence with global norms, rules, and institutions,[41] or about an international liberal order that is constraining even for rising great powers.[42] Of course, this case is only one among many and so is insufficient by itself to overturn general claims of this kind and the assumptions about the effectiveness of convergence mechanisms on which they focus. There has after all been a general tendency in Chinese policy toward a higher level of behavioral consistency with norms in a number of important areas of global politics and economics.[43] However, there are important exceptions to this generalization besides macroeconomic surveillance, including the global climate protection regime, where China has also found it very difficult to accept existing norms. These cases suggest that the combination of material self-interest, normative socialization, and the incentives for convergence provided by the norms and institutions of international society has been insufficient to ensure Chinese convergence in crucial instances.

Moreover, China's leadership has come to see the IMF and the international surveillance regime as lacking sufficient legitimacy to constitute international public goods that deserve respect and adherence. Beijing's growing frustration with the surveillance process was partly due to a perceived lack of recognition by the United States and the IMF as to how much it had done. But the dispute reflected a deeper discomfort with what Beijing perceived as an unfair asymmetry in the surveillance regime, with its emphasis on rules relating to currency policy and its relative weakness vis-à-vis what it saw as US macroeconomic policy irresponsibility. In China's view, the proscription of currency manipulation disadvantages relatively poor countries that choose to manage their exchange rates for purposes of economic development, a policy associated in China and in other parts of East Asia with rapid growth in trade and output.[44] By contrast, the surveillance regime placed little constraint on the policy choices of the major developed economies with floating exchange rates, above all the United States.

Even so, despite this perceived bias in the international surveillance regime, China's stance has not been one of outright opposition or persistent

---

41. Kent 2007, Johnston 2008.
42. Ikenberry 2008.
43. Foot and Walter 2011.
44. Commission on Growth and Development 2008, 49–50; Independent Evaluation Office of the IMF 2011, 20, 35.

defection. The withdrawal from the bilateral surveillance process signaled the limits of China's willingness to accept what it perceived as illegitimate and disruptive external criticism, but its subsequent return to this process and recent involvement in modest enhancement of the multilateral surveillance process also indicates a longer-standing preference to work within the system. At a minimum, China does appear to want increased influence over these norms and rules, in particular a more balanced surveillance process that increases pressure on the United States and other major developed countries to adjust their policies to promote external stability.[45] This and China's continued participation in the Fund and related surveillance activities implies a minimum Chinese acceptance of the basic principle of the IMF's right to undertake macroeconomic surveillance of its members. China also supported, along with a number of other countries, the G20 decision after the crisis to intensify surveillance of the most systemically important economies, with the IMF playing a key advisory and analytical role. If this modification of the international surveillance process renders it more effective and legitimate in the eyes of China's leadership, it is possible that over time it will become a more committed participant. At present, China's participation in this regime might best be seen as tentative, pragmatic, and contingent on its continued reform.

Leadership Preferences

As noted above, some prominent commentators have interpreted China's stance on international surveillance since the early 2000s as reflecting a state-led mercantilist strategy in which the objective of rapid national economic development is a means of consolidating political power at home and obtaining greater power—in terms of both autonomy and influence—abroad.[46] In this view, China's emergence as a major economic and political power represents a sharp challenge to the extant liberal economic order, requiring a decisive response. The urgency of meeting this challenge has often been seen as greatly increased by the global financial crisis.

---

45. "Transcript: Wen Jiabao," *Financial Times,* February 2, 2009, www.ft.com/intl/cms/s/0/795d2bca-f0fe-11dd-8790-0000779fd2ac.html#axzz2lmUS4R2e; International Monetary Fund 2008.
46. Bergsten 2008, Subramanian 2010.

In a popular diagnosis, global payments imbalances—and China's large and growing contribution to them—threaten the stability of the US dollar-based international monetary system, of global finance, and of the world economy more generally.[47]

It is difficult to dispute that the Chinese leadership has prioritized rapid economic development as a means of retaining power at home and maintaining considerable autonomy vis-à-vis a variety of external actors and pressures. How much the leadership wishes to enhance its power over regional and global outcomes is hotly disputed within China and abroad, but is not easy to discern given the secretive nature of China's policymaking process. As noted above, Chinese officials have indicated that they support the objective of removing the perceived bias in the international surveillance regime and increasing the pressure on developed countries to accept greater responsibility for adjustment. Despite recent developments in the G20-sponsored surveillance process, it is unlikely that China (and others) have achieved their goal of subjecting US economic policies in particular to substantially greater international constraint. China's ability to (re)shape international rules thus remains low at present.

The weaknesses in the mercantilism thesis are several. First, China's export promotion strategy has entailed a rapidly rising level of export dependence on foreign markets, particularly the United States and the European Union, on imported components from factories elsewhere in Asia, and on multinational firms, which played a crucial role in the development of manufacturing in China, particularly in the very trade-intensive consumer electronics sector that boomed from the 1990s. The leadership has therefore accepted reduced autonomy as one of the prices of rapid economic development—a sharp break from the Maoist strategy of self-reliance. Standard objections to this argument are that it exaggerates the real extent of China's dependence on foreign firms and markets because the level of value added in the foreign-owned firm export sector is low, and that China's economic rise means that other states are also increasingly dependent on China, canceling out this apparent decline in autonomy. However, both objections understate the extent of change in China's relations with the outside world, both real and perceived. If Beijing really thought

---

47. Brender and Pisani 2010, Obstfeld and Rogoff 2009.

the foreign-owned firm export sector in China to be of marginal value, it is difficult to understand why it has put so much effort into attracting such foreign direct investment in the past, or why it has been so unwilling to risk jeopardizing China's competitiveness as a manufacturing base for domestic and global firms by accepting "unreasonable" Western demands for rapid and sharp currency appreciation. Many Chinese analysts have also drawn lessons from the negative experience of Japan since the early 1990s, including the idea that overly rapid currency appreciation might undermine growth and manufacturing competitiveness.[48] It is therefore much more likely that the leadership attributes significant economic and political importance to this part of the Chinese economy and to its perceived growth and employment benefits. IMF economists estimate that net exports and fixed investment linked to the traded sector accounted for nearly two-thirds of China's total output growth over 2001–8, compared to 40 percent in the 1990s.[49]

As for the argument that mutual interdependence cancels out China's rising dependence on external markets and foreign direct investment, it has long been recognized that mutual interdependence makes it more difficult for countries to maintain policy autonomy and to exert external leverage, except in situations of asymmetric interdependence.[50] Rising interdependence with the United States in particular has aspects of considerable asymmetry that do not always work in Beijing's favor. Most notably, China's exports to the United States still far exceed US exports to China. This asymmetry is tempered by the fact that many US imports from China come from production and sales networks linked to US multinational firms, who as noted earlier do not favor aggressive policies toward China and who may benefit from renminbi undervaluation. This, and perhaps the unprecedented extent of the US government's indebtedness to China, reduces America's incentive to engage in the kind of "aggressive unilateralism" that characterized policies toward Japan in the 1980s.[51]

But as Beijing is well aware, Japan was an ally and China is not, and it cannot be sure that America might not choose to tighten the screws at some

---

48. Yu 2006.
49. Guo and N'Diaye 2009.
50. Keohane and Nye 1977.
51. Bhagwati and Patrick 1991; Yu 2006, 28.

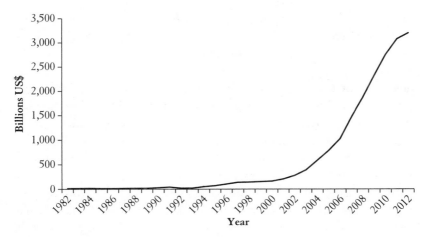

Figure 5.5. Chinese foreign exchange reserves, US$ billions, 1980–2012. World Bank.

point. This possibility fits another popular narrative in China in which the United States systematically tries to prevent the emergence of viable challengers to its predominance. This narrative goes back some time, including to Mao's concerns that US efforts to prevent nuclear proliferation were designed to entrench superpower monopoly over nuclear weaponry.[52] It was reinforced by events such as the Asian financial crisis of the late 1990s, in which America was seen as taking advantage of the leverage the crisis afforded it over allies such as South Korea.

This has led China to attempt to preserve autonomy through means such as foreign reserve accumulation and capital controls, as discussed by Eric Helleiner and Jonathan Kirshner in the introduction, but reserve accumulation (figure 5.5) has only served further to erode China's policy autonomy in another respect. Large reserve holdings have substantially increased China's dependence on macroeconomic, financial, and regulatory policy decisions in the United States and the eurozone, as the period since 2007 has demonstrated. This new dependence comes in the form of the credit and market (i.e., price) risk involved in holding a large proportion of the Chinese state's own savings in foreign currency debt instruments. Most

---

52. Li 2003, 58–60.

analysts have focused on China's so-called "dollar trap," but a dual "euro-dollar trap" emerged with the European sovereign debt crisis, raising the vexing question of whether China should contribute even more financial resources to rescue the relatively prosperous eurozone. Given its considerable exposure to euro government bonds and its dependence on European investment and imports, Beijing continued unilateral bond purchases. It initially resisted European requests to make direct contributions to Europe's bailout fund, pledging instead to lend money indirectly via the IMF.

It is doubtful that in doing so China has gained substantial power-as-influence over European or American policies. That is, even after the global financial crisis, China still seems unable to convert its creditor status into foreign policy leverage.[53] A recent example occurred when the German chancellor indicated on a visit to Beijing in August 2012 that she would not support a European Commission enquiry into China's solar power sector subsidies, but the commission launched an investigation anyway.[54] China has also been unable to link some major specific demands, such as IMF governance and quota reform, to its bilateral lending to the IMF.[55]

There may be some more diffuse benefits for China flowing from the West's need for financial assistance since 2007. China's $43 billion bilateral loan pledge to the IMF in 2012 strengthens the case for governance and quota reform at the Fund (though this is still unachieved), whilst providing China with assurance that European borrowers will continue to be subject to close monitoring and policy conditionality. In the longer term, the crisis may also have helped to reduce the asymmetries of the international surveillance process to China's advantage. As noted above, the G20 has collectively accepted the need for enhanced monitoring of all systemically important countries, including the United States and China. In July 2012, the IMF executive board also agreed to broaden the scope of international surveillance of internal policies, consistent with China's long-held view that it had hitherto been excessively focused on exchange rate policies.[56]

---

53. Drezner 2009.
54. Kathrin Hille and Joshua Chaffin, "Merkel Faces EU Clash over China," *Financial Times,* August 30, 2012, www.ft.com/intl/cms/s/0/c74f6a1c-f273-11e1-ac41-00144feabdc0.html#axzz2lmUS4R2e.
55. International Monetary Fund 2012e.
56. International Monetary Fund 2012a.

These are modest but significant shifts in the nature of the surveillance regime in a direction that China favors, as long as the consequences for China itself are not overly constraining (discussed below).

A third problem with the mercantilism thesis is that it underestimates the increasing differences of opinion within China on key policy questions and their consequences. In recent years the leadership has explicitly recognized the costs of the existing economic model, pledging to rebalance the economy toward domestic consumption, which has steadily fallen to the exceptionally low level of about a third of GDP today. The goal of rebalancing and reshaping the Chinese growth model has been conceptualized under the slogan of "Scientific Developmentalism," and received prominent emphasis in the Twelfth Five Year Plan.[57] As Wen Jiabao stated in his speech to the National People's Congress in March 2011, "Expanding domestic demand is a long-term strategic principle and basic standpoint of China's economic development as well as a fundamental means and an internal requirement for promoting balanced economic development."[58] Much more than external trade dependence is at stake. A low exchange rate has been associated with exceptionally high levels of investment in capital-intensive manufacturing, very low employment growth, rising dependence on commodity imports, and rapidly increasing pollution and greenhouse gas emissions. The central bank has also openly voiced its concerns over the erosion of monetary control and the financial instability that a highly controlled exchange rate entails. There has also been open disagreement over the appropriate path of China's exchange rate policy.[59]

Since the crisis, net exports have diminished in importance but growth has been maintained through even higher levels of investment, retarding the hoped-for shift toward consumption-led growth. Concern that this investment and debt bubble could prefigure a "hard landing" has been rising in various quarters, including in the State Council's own influential think

57. Naughton 2011, 3.

58. Wen Jiabao, "Report on the Work of the Government (2011)" speech delivered at the Fourth Session of the Eleventh National People's Congress, March 5, 2011, http://english.gov.cn/official/2011-03/15/content_1825268.htm.

59. "China Officials Wrestle Publicly over Currency," *New York Times,* March 25, 2010; Freeman and Yuan 2011; Yu Yongding, "China Can Break Free of the Dollar Trap," *Financial Times,* August 4, 2011, www.ft.com /intl/cms/s/0/2189faa2-bec6-11e0-a36b-00144feabdc0.html#axzz2lmUS4R2e.

tank, the Development Research Center.[60] There are also signs that China's new leadership team, led by Xi Jinping and Li Keqiang, share these concerns and view the Hu-Wen years as a lost opportunity for reform.[61] Rather than describing China's leadership as "mercantilist," it seems more accurate to describe important parts of this leadership as having recognized the problems with China's economic trajectory but as so far unable to take decisive measures to divert it toward a more sustainable path.

Interest Group Pressures

The shortcomings of the mercantilism thesis could be interpreted as good news for a society-centered account of China's difficulties with the international macroeconomic surveillance framework. From this perspective, Chinese policy can be seen as the product of a weak and divided central leadership that recognizes the need for change but which has been increasingly constrained by divergent societal preferences—a far cry from a strong, mercantilist state.[62] It is clear that key policymaking institutions such as the Commerce Ministry, the National Development and Reform Commission, and the State Council have periodically promoted the interests of the export lobby.[63]

However, the often close relationship between Chinese domestic firms and the party-state apparatus indicates that the Chinese political economy does not fit comfortably into the standard interest politics model. In the Chinese system, local party bosses have acquired a powerful political and often personal interest in the continuation of the export boom and associated inward foreign investment, and in infrastructure spending. The Chinese firms in the export sector are often closely connected with the party-state, including SOEs and the state-owned banks that lend to them. More generally, all firms in China still operate within the policy and political boundaries established by the party-state.[64] To a much greater extent

---

60. World Bank and Development Research Center of the State Council, the People's Republic of China 2012, 9, 31, 57.

61. Naughton 2013.

62. For accounts that emphasize the role of at least some parts of China's export sector, see Eichengreen 2005, He 2011.

63. Naughton 2008a, 2008b.

64. Breslin 2012.

than in developed democratic countries, this is also true of foreign firms operating in China, including those utilizing abundant Chinese labor in the manufacturing export sector.

In short, it is very difficult to draw a clear line between the respective interests of the state, the party, and the societal interest groups that have brought pressure on officials to block reform. The party is at the center of the system and prioritizes its own survival. On the question of exchange rate policy, the decision since 2005 has been to opt for a cautious, gradualist path that has not entirely satisfied either exporting interests, proponents of monetary and financial stability, or foreign critics demanding greater currency flexibility. As regards internal rebalancing, however, outcomes have been disappointing, suggesting that core interests in the CCP have been able to resist reform.

Power Asymmetries in International and Domestic Politics

Why has China's leadership so far failed to achieve its internal rebalancing objectives? The key obstacle is domestic. The main potential beneficiaries of a consumption-led growth strategy, the general Chinese public, have been unable credibly to threaten to sanction China's leadership for a failure to achieve internal rebalancing.

As Yang Jiang notes in this volume, there are a variety of mechanisms that have allowed the leadership to minimize the domestic costs of this reform failure that extend beyond the standard collective action problems facing consumers and citizens. First, growth itself and the employment opportunities it provides have helped to maintain social stability. Second, political repression, the maintenance of an effective monopoly on the means of violence, media censorship, and the repression of organized labor have all helped to contain the potential for social unrest in a system in which the gains from growth have been increasingly unequally distributed.[65] Third,

---

65. As one recent example of the role of censorship relating to failures to live up to promises to society at large, the Chinese authorities blocked access to the *New York Times* when it reported that Premier Wen Jiabao's family had amassed wealth in excess of US$2.7 billion (Wen has been closely associated with anticorruption policies). "Billions in Hidden Riches for Family of Chinese Leader," *New York Times,* October 25, 2012.

besides corruption, some of the largest transfers of wealth from consumers to the corporate and government sectors are relatively hidden, particularly those due to negative real interest rates on savings accounts and factor price subsidies.

The most powerful domestic opposition to internal rebalancing reforms is arguably located within the party itself. Minxin Pei estimates that over five million party members enjoy executive positions in SOEs and would stand to lose from reforms promoting internal rebalancing.[66] From this perspective, China's leadership has consistently delivered private goods to a relatively narrow party-state-business elite that increasingly benefited from the status quo during the Hu-Wen years, at the expense of society at large. This elite includes what Susan Shirk termed the "selectorate" (the party elite that selects leaders),[67] the families and friends of party leaders with increasingly extensive business interests,[68] key bureaucrats in economic ministries, SOEs, and other state-connected banks and firms, and parts of the army.[69]

Quite how trapped the party leadership is by this antireform coalition is uncertain. The Hu-Wen leadership continued to advocate internal rebalancing and it also permitted pro-reform voices to advocate an acceleration of measures to promote the shift toward consumption-led growth. This is one of the key recommendations of the "China 2030" report of the World Bank and Development Research Center of the State Council, for example. The report argued among other things for the fundamental reform of the SOE sector, which has benefited considerably from access to subsidized factor inputs and is a core component of the investment-oriented growth model. These arguments apparently met with strenuous resistance from the SOE sector and their bureaucratic supporters, including the State Asset Supervision and Administration Commission, the state holding company

66. Minxin Pei, "China's Politics of the Economically Possible," www.project-syndicate.org/commentary/china-s-politics-of-the-economically-possible, March 16, 2012. See also Pei 2011.

67. Shirk 1993, 10. For an extension of the selectorate argument to authoritarian and democratic politics see Bueno de Mesquita et al. 2003.

68. "Billions in Hidden Riches for Family of Chinese Leader"; "Xi Jinping Millionaire Relations Reveal Fortunes of Elite," Bloomberg, June 25, 2012, http://www.bloomberg.com/news/2012-06-29/xi-jinping-millionaire-relations-reveal-fortunes-of-elite.html; "As China Official Rose, His Family's Wealth Grew," *New York Times,* April 23, 2012.

69. On the relationship between the party-state and business, see Breslin 2012.

responsible for managing state-controlled assets.[70] It also argued for the dismantling of the system of financial repression, estimated to transfer 4–7 percent of GDP from consumers to the corporate and government sectors annually, which would unravel a system that has operated primarily in the interests of SOEs and connected firms.[71] By limiting both the savings options and the real returns on savings for Chinese consumers, this system has allowed banks to recapitalize and to write off past bad loans. It also provides very low-cost capital to large firms and local authorities. Similar arguments could be made about the general repression of organized labor in the Chinese political economy, as well as various other means by which the state has provided implicit and explicit price subsidies to business.[72]

Nevertheless, the leadership allowed the Development Research Center to make public the case for extensive reform. There are also signs that it has accepted the need for a reinvigoration of reform and the setting of more specific targets for internal rebalancing. In February 2013, the State Council approved targets to boost minimum wages to at least 40 percent of average salaries, to loosen interest rate controls, to boost spending on education and public housing, and to increase SOE dividend payments by 5 percent of revenues by 2015.[73] The new Xi-Li leadership has also signaled that it will seek to revive Deng Xiaoping's reformist zeal and to persuade opponents of reform.[74] Whether this will be sufficient is uncertain, but it acknowledges the failure of past reform and recent statements raise the stakes for all concerned.

The process of international policy surveillance has been supportive of these reform proposals, but it can do little to alter the basic parameters of Chinese domestic politics. There is a greater potential for intrusiveness in the G20's Mutual Assessment Process, with its more extensive focus on and analysis of the external effects of economic policy decisions by major countries ("economic spillovers") compared to the G8.[75] By November 2011, the

---

70. "New Push for Reform in China," *Wall Street Journal,* February 23, 2012.
71. Lardy 2008, Pettis 2012.
72. See Lee 2012.
73. "China Approves Income Plan as Wealth Divide Poses Risks," Bloomberg, February 5, 2013, http://www.bloomberg.com/news/2013-02-05/china-approves-income-plan-as-wealth-divide-poses-risks.html.
74. Naughton 2013, 5.
75. See Group of 20 2011.

IMF had produced reports on seven countries identified under these criteria: China, France, Germany, India, Japan, the United Kingdom, and the United States. The report on China argued that "rebalancing the [Chinese] economy . . . requires wide-ranging reforms, including strengthening social insurance, appreciating the exchange rate, and raising domestic interest rates. Such steps would improve welfare, both in China and the rest of the world. That is why the Chinese authorities have made these measures the crux of the nation's new Five-Year Plan."[76]

This does little more than repeat what the leadership itself has already said. Furthermore, on the question of internal rebalancing, the IMF is toothless as regards a major creditor country such as China. United States or European sanctions for a failure to achieve a decisive shift toward consumption-led growth are even less likely than they were for currency manipulation in the mid-2000s. Nor are IMF attempts at persuasion helped by the tendency in China and much of the rest of Asia still to see it as a biased tool of Western influence.[77] In short, where it really matters for the leadership, the international surveillance process remains a bystander in the politics of domestic rebalancing.

The 2011 IMF spillover report argued that "the roots of China's imbalances lie deep in the economy's structure."[78] More accurately, they lie deep in China's political structure and in the way in which it has interacted with other powerful actors and forces in the global political economy. How else to explain the increasingly sharp divergence between leadership objectives and policy results? As regards the former, Wen Jiabao appeared to signal the leadership's sensitivity to mass societal interests in his speech to the People's Congress in March 2011:

> We are keenly aware that we still have a serious problem in that our development is not yet well balanced, coordinated or sustainable . . . . Moreover, we have not yet fundamentally solved a number of issues that the masses

76. International Monetary Fund 2011c, 2.

77. "Wen Warns against Renminbi Pressure," *Financial Times,* October 6, 2010, www.ft.com/intl/cms/s/0/f92d794e-d16d-11df-96d1-00144feabdc0.html#axzz2lmUS4R2e; "Time for RMB Appreciation?" *People's Daily Online,* June 9, 2010, http://english.people.com.cn/90001/90778/90859/7018757.html.

78. International Monetary Fund 2011c, 2.

feel strongly about, namely the lack of high-quality educational and medical resources, and their uneven distribution; increasing upward pressure on prices, and exorbitant housing price increases in some cities; increasing social problems resulting from illegal land expropriations and housing demolitions; significant problems concerning food safety; and rampant corruption in some areas. We must therefore have a strong sense of responsibility toward the country and the people and work tirelessly and painstakingly to solve these problems more quickly to the satisfaction of the people.[79]

The Chinese leadership's rebalancing objectives have been at the top of its stated policy agenda for nearly a decade. There is also a growing consensus among the key international institutions and some Chinese analysts about the package of measures needed to shift the economy from investment to consumption-led growth.[80] And yet the results have been disappointing. This should be puzzling for those who laud the Chinese government's technocratic expertise and political power to get things done.[81]

Rather than a powerful technocratic state with rising global influence, we have seen that China is simultaneously "weak and strong": weakest regarding domestic actors opposing reform, increasingly strong regarding most external actors, and strongest regarding the broad mass of domestic society who would benefit most from internal rebalancing. Furthermore, to understand the failure of internal rebalancing compared to external rebalancing, it is necessary to understand the Chinese leadership's economic policy incentives within the political system in which it operates—not simply with that system's authoritarianism, but with its increasingly divided nature and its complex interaction with the external world. Internal rebalancing that would favor the mass of Chinese citizens has not been as high a priority as external rebalancing for the United States and other countries, despite their broad interest in the success of China's reform project.

This analysis also has important implications for the concerns of this volume. First, in terms of its power in international monetary relations, China has enjoyed varying degrees of policy autonomy. As its integration

---

79. Wen 2011.

80. International Monetary Fund 2011a, 2, 19; World Bank and Development Research Center 2012.

81. E.g. Wilsdon and Keeley 2007.

with the global economy rose, it found it increasingly difficult to claim that it should enjoy full autonomy on exchange rate policy. Chinese policy autonomy has been much higher in other areas relevant to internal re-balancing. China's power over outcomes in the global political economy remains limited, though as we have seen the global financial crisis since 2007 both reduced external pressure on exchange rate policy and facilitated a modest realignment of the international macroeconomic surveillance process in ways favored by China. Fundamental reforms that would give China much more influence over this process and over international monetary arrangements generally have not been achieved, however. The crisis may have reduced Western dominance but it has not yet delivered significant international monetary rule-making power to new actors such as China.

Second, the mercantilism thesis is misleading. Although China's attitude toward international surveillance is critical and thus cannot be described as a rule-taking stance, neither has it been a rule-breaker. It chafes constantly against the dominant positions of the dollar, of the US financial system, and of the United States itself in the processes of international monetary governance. We have seen that it aspires in important areas to reform of the system, but its power-as-influence in this regard is still limited. Instead, it has sought change from within, particularly since 2008. It has accepted the broad principle of international macroeconomic surveillance but it has objected to what it perceives as a fundamental bias in the rules and procedures of surveillance, especially the formerly heavy focus on exchange rate policies and the lack of attention to the destabilizing macroeconomic policy choices of the United States and, increasingly, parts of Europe. Nevertheless, China exhibits a clear preference for international surveillance to constrain others more than itself, a considerable policy tension. One prerequisite of exerting power-as-influence would be for China to articulate not only what it does not like about global monetary governance, but what kind of future order it prefers. It is difficult to find evidence of a coherent vision in this regard, as Yang Jiang discusses in her chapter.

Third, China's stance has been broadly consistent with those of many other emerging and developing countries. The view that the international surveillance process has been biased against the interests of these countries and insufficiently constraining for the major developed countries is widely shared.[82] China has not been isolated in its calls for the reform of international surveillance and more generally for the reform of international monetary governance. Since 2008, this has helped to facilitate the reorientation of international surveillance toward greater symmetry and a renewed focus on internal policies in the major countries. But it also implies considerable challenges ahead. As we have seen, the political difficulty this agenda presents for China itself is considerable and its success will be contingent on the uncertain ability of China's new leaders to achieve domestic reforms that eluded their predecessors. The challenges regarding the surveillance of other major countries, above all the United States, are also formidable and failures in this regard will on past evidence weaken the perceived legitimacy of the revised framework in China and elsewhere.

Fourth, as the scope of international surveillance has expanded in recent years, including into a range of domestic policy domains seen as relevant to international monetary and financial stability and to the perennial problem of adjustment, the range of relevant actors in China has also expanded. It has long been the case that the ultimate decisionmaking body on important policy matters has been the Politburo Standing Committee. The People's Bank of China, the Finance Ministry, the Commerce Ministry, the China Investment Corporation, the State Asset Supervision and Administration Commission, and a range of other bodies have implementation responsibilities and some input into the policy process, but their preferences have often diverged. The party has also been divided, with powerful local bosses able to pursue policies that conflict with the objectives of the central government. The senior leadership has been unable decisively to cut through this policy conflict, producing an increasing gap between Chinese policy rhetoric and reality, as well as growing uncertainty about China's real intentions in economic policy. China's readiness for international monetary leadership, and its ability to achieve further influence on a range of international issues, will also remain in considerable doubt as long as these domestic challenges remain unresolved. In this respect, it is hardly alone given the challenges and domestic policy conflicts that have grown in the United States and Europe in recent years. This suggests hard times ahead for global monetary governance.

---

82. See reports by the Independent Evaluation Office of the IMF, including 2013, esp. 29–32, and 2007, 25–27.

6

The Limits of China's Monetary Diplomacy

Yang Jiang

There is now a widespread expectation that China will become a global monetary power. Such expectations arise not only from China's economic weight, but also from its active monetary diplomacy. The latter is defined here as the use of monetary measures to pursue foreign policy objectives, or the use of diplomacy—intergovernmental talks and arrangements—to pursue monetary objectives. Chinese official rhetoric emphasizes China's international contribution as a "responsible great power," resonating with Robert Zoellick's expectation for China to be a "responsible stakeholder."[1] Pursuing the status of a global monetary power with a global currency seems clearly on Beijing's agenda. However, to what extent is China

---

1. "Zhongguo rushi 10 nian: Biaoxian zhuoyuefeifan, wei fuzeren daguo jianxinyu" [10 Years since China's entry into the WTO: Extraordinary performance, establishing credit as a responsible great power], *China Daily,* October 20, 2011. Robert Zoellick, "Statement on Conclusion of the Second US-China Senior Dialogue," Washington, DC, December 8, 2005, http://2001-2009. state.gov/r/pa/prs/ps/2005/57822.htm.

actually preparing itself for the role of a global monetary power through monetary diplomacy?

Gregory Chin and Jonathan Kirshner are optimistic in their chapters in this volume about the possibility of RMB internationalization and China's rising role in international monetary relations. Here I provide a more pessimistic view. The priority of the party-state is to maintain control and stability, and the domestic politics of China's financial policy are dominated by conservatives who are against reform and liberalization for this reason. Because RMB internationalization requires reform of the interest rate and exchange rate regimes, which would in turn hurt core interest groups in China, no meaningful liberalization of China's monetary policy can be carried out without the leadership's fierce intervention. The leadership, however, may not do so because the regime's priority is to avoid instability, and financial liberalization risks undermining the state's control of finance which has been at the core of China's export-oriented, investment-driven growth model.

Evidence of China's reservations about liberalization can be found in the country's monetary diplomacy. China prefers bilateral to multilateral monetary arrangements that are often shallow in content—not requiring significant domestic reforms—and aimed more at practical and political gains than at preparing itself for the role of a global monetary power that possesses a global currency and participates in multilateral monetary governance. Because China's bilateral arrangements require little domestic adjustment or monetary policy coordination between the partners, and their conditionalities bear little resemblance to those of existing global institutions, China's monetary bilateralism is more of a stumbling block than a building brick for global monetary cooperation.

Three considerations are driving forces behind China's preference for bilateralism in monetary diplomacy. First, bilateral monetary diplomacy follows China's traditional preference for bilateralism to achieve foreign policy goals. Beijing can strengthen relationships with targeted countries as a benefactor, rather than being lost behind a multilateral framework (such as the IMF and EU rescue mechanisms). Bilateral monetary diplomacy also helps China build an image of a "responsible great power." It starts a domino effect among nonpartners to demand the same treatment from China, as was the case with bilateral swap arrangements (BSAs), offshore renminbi centers, and holding of RMB reserves, putting China in the position of being the one in demand. That way, China can negotiate other political gains, such as support on human rights and "One China" issues. China also uses bilateral or bloc diplomacy to ally with other countries (e.g. through groupings of the BRICS, East Asia, and developing countries) to create a stronger voice at global institutions to challenge the existing dominant powers and to defend its own monetary policies.

Second, bilateralism offers China flexibility in policy choices. China's bilateral arrangements do not require it to reform domestic financial institutions, nor to follow the neoliberal template prescribed by global monetary institutions. China can control the degree and pace of RMB internationalization and capital account liberalization. It can also avoid requirements to coordinate its exchange rate with other countries, as a regional currency union would necessitate. In addition, it can minimize international surveillance of its financial institutions and policy. China's confidence in multilateral monetary institutions is also not high. The IMF is regarded as an institution of global governance that is failing to regulate the global financial and monetary order. European monetary cooperation is also perceived to be suffering from a spectrum of institutional, economic, and political ills. With bilateral arrangements, China can decide on the scope and depth of cooperation— who can benefit from the scheme and the amount of transactions allowed.

Third, China's bilateral monetary arrangements meet its short-term, pragmatic needs. China does not have a clear aim or a domestic consensus regarding the goal of making the RMB an international currency. Selective RMB internationalization facilitates trade and investment and reduces exchange rate risks between China and its major trade partners, although the usage of RMB in trade has so far been limited by other policy constraints. Bilateral monetary diplomacy also creates issue linkages for China to get recognition of its market economy status and shop for natural resources, infrastructure projects, and investment opportunities. In particular, it benefits state-owned enterprises (SOEs) regarding their overseas investment, construction projects, importing of natural resources, and financing opportunities. The government—or the Ministry of Finance and sovereign wealth funds—can also raise capital through overseas RMB bond markets.

The above policy preferences are determined by domestic politics. Although Chinese financial policymakers recognize that RMB convertibility is inevitable in the long term, recent steps of RMB "internationalization" at best represent a partial success of some liberal actors in China. Any further reforms that would affect the vested interests of state commercial banks, SOEs, and their regulators are very difficult to carry out in today's China because of their strong political power within the party-state. The priority of the state remains keeping control over the national economy and ensuring domestic stability and national security, for the purpose of regime survival. That priority reflects its lack of confidence in both domestic and international financial institutions, the stronger power of conservatives than liberals in domestic politics, as well as its preference for symbolic gestures and pragmatic measures in diplomatic strategy rather than for idealistic commitments to reform. China's future contribution to multilateral monetary cooperation and its global monetary power are dependent upon continued reform, which in turn depends on whether liberals can accommodate, or if not, overpower vested interests.

The Importance of Domestic Politics

The fundamental reason for China to adopt bilateralism as the main approach to monetary diplomacy lies in domestic politics: it is a compromise between reform-minded liberals and conservatives. Although both groups argue from the premise of maintaining national stability and sustaining the Party's rule, they differ drastically over the pace and content of financial reform. Their debates and power struggles are intense because the state's control over financial and monetary policy has been a cornerstone of China's model of political economy. Artificially low interest rates effectively transfer the Chinese population's savings to subsidize state banks and SOEs, while a managed exchange rate encourages export of labor-intensive goods. Any change of financial and monetary policy would have wide repercussions for the Chinese political economy. Liberals push for reform as they regard the current model as unsustainable and hazardous for China's future; some of them also suffer economic losses from the current system. Conservatives resist reform because they do not want to lose control over certain policies and the rents generated from them.

The liberals are represented by the People's Bank of China (PBOC), private banks and some small and medium enterprises, some local governments, and lately the China Securities Regulatory Commission under Guo Shuqing. The conservatives are represented by the Ministry of Finance (MOF), the National Development Reform Commission, state commercial banks, and SOEs, which would like to retain their control over policy and national economy. The conservatives and liberals try to influence, and have representatives within, the summit of China's decisionmaking apparatus—the Communist Party's Central Committee, its Politburo and the Politburo's Standing Committee. Many government officials and managers of SOEs are appointed by the Party's Organization Department and are at the same time Party cadres; some of them are members of the Central Committee. The above-mentioned government units and top managers of big SOEs are therefore part of the party-state, and their conflicts are at the same time battles within the Party, or examples of what the Party likes to refer to as "intra-Party democracy." Such a conservative-liberal division exists within the Party's core as well. For instance, four of the nine-member Standing Committee under the Hu-Wen leadership and four of the seven-member Standing Committee under the Xi-Li leadership are widely considered to be conservatives. The power game within the Politburo and its Standing Committee, however, is far more complicated and secretive than their policy preferences and is therefore beyond the scope of this paper.

Since China entered the WTO at the end of 2001, it has become increasingly difficult to carry out further reforms, especially those that would affect vested interests including state commercial banks, SOEs, and government units that are supposed to regulate them. As Zhou Xiaochuan said in a speech in 2010, many reforms before and in consequence of China's WTO accession were carried out in a top-down fashion, whereas now bottom-up reform has become crucial because it is difficult to find a unified model of financial reform from the top.[2] For liberals, bilateral monetary arrangements may help bring Chinese practices to international standards, while for conservatives they expand China's political influence in the world vis-à-vis the West and Japan, offering an opportunity to change the rules of the game.

Liberals hope that currency swaps, offshore RMB centers, and trade and investment settlement in RMB will have a "spillover effect" and pave the

2. Zhou Xiaochuan, "Zhou Xiaochuan tan zhengti gaige lun: Zishang'exia he zixiaeshang xiangjiehe" [Zhou Xiaochuan talks about holistic reform: Integrate top-down and bottom-up], speech at the Annual Forum of Chinese Economists, December 1, 2010, http://www.rmlt.com.cn/News/201012/201012010948579619.html.

way for RMB internationalization as well as capital account and exchange rate regime liberalization. "Experiment" is the word currently used in Chinese official language to describe the nature of such policies, denoting their tentative and retractable nature. Experimenting at a local level has been a typical way to get bandwagons of national reform rolling in China, including the household contract responsibility system that started national agricultural reform in the late 1970s, and Special Economic Zones that started market reform and opening in the early 1980s. Liberals hope that the expansion of an external market and increased international exposure will create an unstoppable momentum that will lock in domestic reform. As Zhou Xiaochuan put it, sometimes "the government intentionally encourages the enthusiasm for reform from enterprises and local governments in order to let them propel reform."[3] He notes that local enthusiasm for obtaining permission for financial experiment is prevalent. Zhou also emphasized their purpose of "experimenting mistakes" (*shicuo*)—finding out which measures are mistaken and which not—in order to justify "bottom-up reform" and forestall the whole package of reform being scrapped due to partial failures. However, the dominant view regarding experiments is still that they may have uncontrollable negative spillover effects, and therefore they should only be carried out with extreme caution and in a top-down fashion.[4]

Private businesses are in general supportive of the liberals' call for financial reform because they have enormous difficulty in getting financing from state commercial banks, which prefer to lend to SOEs. The state commercial banks and SOEs, however, are so closely tied with the party-state that private businesses are pessimistic about interest rate reform in the near future, since it concerns the core interests of state banks and SOEs.[5]

---

3. "Zhou Xiaochuan: Zixiaershang shi gaige shi woguo jinrong gaige zhongyao zucheng bufen" [Zhou Xiaochuan: Bottom-up reform is an important part of nation's financial reform], November 11, 2012, http://news.xinhuanet.com/fortune/2012-11/17/c_113711667.htm.

4. "Zhou Xiaochuan: Woguo jinrong gaige zhong zishangexia de zuchengbufen" [Zhou Xiaochuan: The bottom-up parts of China's financial reform], speech at the 2012 International Financial Forum, December 3, 2012, http://www.pbc.gov.cn/publish/goutongjiaoliu/524/2012/20121203092006577585996/20121203092006577585996_.html.

5. "Lilv guanzhi de beiju" [Tragedy of interest rate control], November 2, 2012, http://opinion.hexun.com/2012-11-02/147521411.html; "Chen Gong: Liugei zhongguo jingji gaige de shijian zhisheng shinian" [Chen Gong: China only has ten years left for economic reform], January 17, 2012. http://finance.ifeng.com/news/people/20120117/5466699.shtml.

One who speaks out about such close ties within China's financial structure and the difficulty of financial reform is Li Jiange, president of China International Capital Corporation. According to Li, "the government has strengthened supervision and intervention in recent years to an incomprehensible and intolerable degree," and it was "very inappropriate" that some financial supervisory agencies sent officials to sit on the boards of directors of companies under their supervision.[6] On another occasion, Li openly criticized Xie Xuren, the minister of finance, for his "false argument" that government revenue was not related to the people's income. Li decoded the oft-used official term of "stably progressing reform" as no progress, and added that the timing of reform should never be left to "those with no sense of historical responsibility and mission."[7]

For conservatives, recent initiatives of China's monetary diplomacy, including bilateral currency arrangements, serve the pragmatic needs of the chiefs of the public economy—in financing and importing commodities and in SOEs' overseas businesses—without depriving them of control over their policy areas. For instance, rather than leading financial reform, the president of the Bank of China Xiao Gang promotes the international business of the BOC and supports RMB internationalization for the purpose of enabling Chinese enterprises to "go global."[8] He is also the only person from the four state commercial banks to become one of the 205 members of the Eighteenth Central Committee of the Party, the core of political power. It should be noted that the BOC and the China Construction Bank were recapitalized in 2003 by the PBC, while the Ministry of Finance assumed control of recapitalizing the Industrial and Commercial Bank of China and the Agricultural Bank of China in 2005 and 2007. It seems, however, that BOC does not share the enthusiasm of the central bank for financial reform. The representatives of major state banks had heated debates with the central bank governor Zhou Xiaochuan in a closed-door meeting in June 2012, resisting reforms that would break their monopoly. Xiao Gang reportedly

---

6. "Li Jiange: xiayibu gaige rengyao jianchi shichanghua fangxiang" [Li Jiange: Next-step reform should continue marketization], November 17, 2012, http://economy.caixin.com/2012-11-17/100461892.html.

7. "Li Jiange: Xie Xuren qiangciduoli" [Li Jiange: Xie Xuren's false argument], March 13, 2012, http://business.sohu.com/20120313/n337591174.shtml.

8. "2012 nian tuidong jinrong gaige bada renwu" [Eight people in 2012 who push for financial reform], *Zhengquan Ribao* [Securities Daily], January 4, 2013.

expressed strong opposition to proposed interest rate reforms and pounded the table many times in strong emotion.[9] When China changed leadership in 2013, Xiao Gang replaced reformist Guo Shuqing to become the new president of the China Securities Regulatory Commission, making the latter's term surprisingly short. The chief economist of the BOC, Cao Yuanzheng, said that China's current monetary policy was appropriate and there was no need to change its major components.[10] The state banks do not wish to give up their grip on the domestic financial system, even after Wen Jiabao commented in April 2012 that it was too easy for state banks to earn profits. In fact, neither state commercial banks, nor their major clients (SOEs), nor their regulators want to give up their profits or the dominant position in the national economy. As Lardy as well as Walter and Howie stress, financial repression based on the state's control over banks and the financial system has been a cornerstone of China's development model.[11]

Conservatives have gained power in domestic policymaking vis-à-vis liberals since China's WTO accession. Recent steps of RMB internationalization and experiments with local financial reform appear to be successes of the liberals. Conservatives, however, have snatched the decisionmaking authority over crucial issues and expanded their power base in domestic politics. Decisionmaking power in China on foreign reserve and exchange rate policy used to belong to the central bank only, but now the MOF also has a say in monetary policies.[12] At the G20 finance ministers' and central bank governors' meeting in Moscow in February 2013, Finance Minister Xie Xuren stated that China would adopt an expansive fiscal policy in 2013 despite wide domestic calls for reform including financial reform as well as constraining investment and inflation[13].

---

9. "Zhongguo zhengfu youyi pochu daxing guoqi longduan diwei dan guoqi lingyou tumou" [Chinese government intended to break monopoly of big SOEs but SOEs have another plan], Reuters, October 18, 2012, http://cn.reuters.com/article/wtNews/idCNCNE89H05L2012 1018?sp=true.

10. "Cao Yuanzheng: Quannian jingji jiangzeng 8% meibiyao chutai tebie ciji cuoshi" [Cao Yuanzheng: Annual growth will reach 8%, no need for special stimulus], June 9, 2012, http://news.hexun.com/2012-06-09/142290033.html.

11. Lardy 2012, Walter and Howie 2011.

12. Author's interviews in Beijing, 2007.

13. "Xie Xuren: Jianshao lianghua kuansong huobi zhengce fumian waiyi xiaoying" [Xie Xuren: Reduce negative externalities of quantitative easing], February 18, 2013, http://finance.ifeng.com/stock/roll/20130218/7671382.shtml.

Even among liberals, there are different voices. In the central bank, there are some who push back against RMB internationalization. The Ministry of Commerce, which usually supports economic liberalization, is concerned over the pace of RMB appreciation as it has a power base among exporters.[14] Liberals lost ground to conservatives particularly thanks to the global financial crisis. At the onset of the crisis, the Chinese leadership made a swift decision to stimulate the economy with massive investment. Much of the stimulus has gone to SOEs and publicly funded projects, exacerbating the problem of "advance of the state and retreat of the private" (*guojin mintui*). The National Development Reform Commission worked to make sure that projects under the four-trillion-yuan stimulus program would have enough funding. Although such investment has created huge problems of inflation and debt, and some banks did not feel confident about repayment of their loans, the central bank had to be flexible about the principle of controlling inflation so as to give special support to the projects.[15] Walter and Howie observe that "2009 marked the end of banking reform as advanced since 1998," and that the "massive stimulus package reliant on bank loans may have washed away for good the fruits of the previous 10 years of reform."[16]

At the end of 2011, public anger turned against China's banking sector following a speech by the president of China Minsheng Banking Corporation, China's first real private bank, in which he said that the profits of Chinese banks were so high that it was sometimes too embarrassing for banks to publish them.[17] Calls for financial reform, in particular interest rate reform, came from many scholarly and public discussions. The PBC also tried to set up a deposit insurance scheme to pave the way for interest rate reform. In April 2012, however, Zhou Xiaochuan said that the deposit rate would not be changed, indicating that meaningful interest reform was not possible in the short term. Apart from the fear of arbitrage by hot money,

---

14. Thornton 2012.

15. "Yanghang da huobi zhengce ji jinrong gaige" [Central Bank answers questions about monetary policy and financial reform], press conference during the two congresses, March 12, 2012, http://topic.eastmoney.com/hbzc2012/.

16. Walter and Howie 2011, 76, 81.

17. "Li Ruoyu: jinrong gaige jinru shenshuiqu, yinhang yali da" [Li Ruoyu: Financial reform enters deep water, huge pressure on banks], July 4, 2012, *Shanghai Securities Daily,* http://bank.hexun.com/2012-07-14/143564523.html.

Zhou cited the reason that the banks (read: the state commercial banks) under hard budget constraint did not want to increase the deposit rate.[18] When the media pursued the question with Zhou of whether China's reserve requirement and interest rate would be adjusted, Zhou replied, "you know I can't answer this question."[19] His response reflects the fact not only that those two policies are decided by the State Council, but also that it is a politically sensitive issue over which the central bank does not have much control. Interest rate reform and RMB convertibility have been discussed for twenty-nine years in the PBOC, according to a former staff member, but are still not realized.[20]

Overall, to the Chinese government, financial security is an important part of national security, encompassing the ability to defend against domestic and foreign attacks and international financial crises, and to maintain financial sovereignty. It is defined mostly in terms of stability rather than flexibility, particularly the stability of the exchange rate and the financial market.[21] The Chinese government set up overall guidelines for financial opening: "adequate for national conditions, gradual progress, safe and controllable, compete and cooperate, win-win mutual benefit," (*yiwo weizhu, xunxujianjin, anquan kekong, jingzheng hezuo, huli gongying*), which was written in the Twelfth Five Year Plan. Therefore, keeping control is a precondition to any reform. James Liu, vice president of the Shanghai Stock Exchange, concedes that Beijing remains wary of capital markets that act like "an unbridled horse."[22]

The greater strength of conservatives vis-à-vis liberals in domestic financial politics as well as the government's priority of maintaining control have determined that China's monetary arrangements are often symbolic only, intended for political gain, or shallow and short term—oriented, for pragmatic commercial gain. An overview of Chinese monetary diplomacy will underline this point so far as bilateral arrangements are concerned.

---

18. "Su Peike: shichanghua gaige xupo cunkuan lilv guanzhi" [Su Peike: Marketization reform requires breaking interest rate control]," *Meiri Jingji Xinwen* [Economic News Daily], April 27, 2012, http://opinion.hexun.com/2012-04-27/140850491.html.

19. "Yanghang hangzhang Zhou Xiaochuan de gongguodeshi" [Achievements and mistakes of central bank governor Zhou Xiaochuan], February 7, 2013, http://opinion.hexun.com/2013-02-07/151028172.html.

20. "Tragedy of interest rate control."

21. People's Bank of China 2009, Yeung 2008.

22. "Long March to Renminbi Convertibility," *Financial Times*, August 25, 2010.

Bilateralism in Chinese Monetary Diplomacy

The features just described have been characteristic of Chinese monetary diplomacy, in which bilateralism has been a central strategy. This can be seen in the crisis rescue provided by China for the eurozone, in its RMB aid and currency swap arrangements, in its role in multilateral monetary cooperation, and in its approach to the internationalization of the RMB.

Eurozone Crisis Rescue

When the stability of the eurozone was threatened in early 2011, European countries looked to China to provide financial support. While Japan purchased 100 billion yen (US$1.2 billion) of bonds through the European Financial Stability Facility, China preferred to deal with individual countries, using bilateral talks to obtain commercial and political benefits. It sent out shopping tours—each typically led by a high-level official with a group of business representatives—across Europe.[23] Some European countries reportedly requested China to provide financial assistance to deal with the debt crisis, including Greece, Sweden, and Germany. There is no transparency about how much European sovereign debt China actually bought; market estimates put it at 25 percent of China's currency reserves,[24] including German, French, Greek, Hungarian, and Spanish debt. China utilized that opacity to cut bilateral deals with individual European countries. Greece, Hungary, Portugal, and Spain, among others, kept quiet about matters such as human rights and pledged political support for China on various issues within the EU.[25] Spain and Portugal came to favor lifting the arms embargo against China after the latter publicly committed to their economic recovery.[26]

---

23. Xi Jinping visited Belgium, Germany, Romania, Bulgaria, and Hungary in October 2009. In June 2011 Wen Jiabao visited Hungary, the UK, and Germany. In October 2011, Jia Qinglin visited Greece, the Netherlands and Germany. In April 2012 Wen visited Iceland, Germany, Sweden, and Poland, member of the Standing Committee of the Politburo Li Changchun visited the UK, and Li Keqiang visited Russia. In June 2012, Hu Jintao visited Denmark.

24. Parello-Plesner 2012.

25. European Council on Foreign Relations 2012.

26. Parello-Plesner 2012.

China showed a particular interest in buying commercial projects and shares in companies. A sale of European assets was what China favored for its companies, as Minister of Commerce Chen Deming commented in regard to the euro crisis. China has done quite well in this respect. The amount of Chinese investment in Europe surged, with Europe becoming China's fastest growing foreign direct investment destination in 2011.[27] During the crisis, Chinese companies bought the largest Hungarian chemicals manufacturer and a Portuguese state-owned energy company, and won Greek and British infrastructure contracts. Poland is proposing assets that China could invest in even after the latter pulled out of a major highway project. Thanks to China's shopping sprees, Germany, the UK, Italy, Bulgaria and Spain promised to support acceptance of China's market economy status within the EU.[28]

China eventually bought bonds of the European Financial Stability Facility after French President Nicolas Sarkozy made an emergency call to Hu Jintao in October 2011. At the same time, China made three major demands on the EU: recognition of China's market economy status, lifting of the arms embargo, and support of China's demand for more voting power at the IMF.[29] China's policy toward the European rescue reflects its priority of risk aversion, as well as dexterous usage of bilateral monetary diplomacy to win commercial deals and political support. As a result of the crisis, there is little scope left in the EU for a coordinated approach

---

27. Parello-Plesner 2012, 42.

28. "Deguo yuantui oumeng chengren zhongguo shichangjingji diwei" [Germany willing to push EU to recognize China's market economy status], October 6, 2010, http://www.bbc.co.uk/zhongwen/simp/china/2010/10/101006_germany_china.shtml; "Yingguo zhichi zhongguo jinzao huo shichangjingji diwei" [UK supports China in obtaining market economy status early], September 28, 2011, http://www.chinese.rfi.fr/中国/20110928英国支持中国尽早获市场经济地位. "Yidaliwaizhang: Zhichi geiyu zhongguo shichangjingji diwei" [Italian foreign minister: Support given to China's market economy status], July 19, 2011, http://world.people.com.cn/GB/15194122.html; "Baojialiya zhuhuadashi tan zhongbao jianjiao 60 zhounian ji zhongbao guanxi" [Bulgarian ambassador to China talks about sixty years of bilateral diplomatic relations], September 24, 2009, http://www.people.com.cn/GB/32306/143124/147550/10112136.html; "Xibanya jiangcushi oumeng jinzao chengren zhongguo shichangjingji diwei" [Spain will urge EU to recognize China's market economy status as soon as possible], May 26, 2009, http://www.china.com.cn/news/txt/2009-05/26/content_17833896.htm.

29. "China Extends Help to Tackle Euro Crisis," *Financial Times,* December 21, 2010. Also see ECFR (2012). "Wang Qishan: xiwang oumeng jinkuai chengren zhongguo shichangjingji diwei" [Wang Qishan: Hope for EU to recognize China's market economy status as soon as possible]," December 21, 2010, http://news.sina.com.cn/c/2010-12-21/112721680357.shtml.

toward China. As the European Council on Foreign Relations put it in 2012, "the European Commission mostly fights alone while member states sweet-talk China."[30]

RMB Aid and "Currency Swap Diplomacy"

China has increased the usage of RMB for aid, not so much for RMB internationalization but for politico-strategic purposes and energy needs. China has pledged RMB aid to Egypt and Yemen for restoring order and reconstruction.[31] Beijing was worried that the "Arab Spring" would spread to China and that the new governments would hurt local Chinese businesses because of their good relations with the outgoing regimes. China has also pledged RMB 150 million aid to Afghanistan, and supported the latter's observer status at the Shanghai Cooperation Organization (SCO). Apart from its energy and resources, Afghanistan is a key neighboring country for China in its crackdown on separatist Uighur groups. In May 2012, the People's Liberation Army signed a contract with its Cambodian counterpart to provide the latter with 120 million yuan in aid, as part of a diplomatic offensive of the PLA among ASEAN countries to win support in the territorial dispute with the Philippines over Scarborough Shoal, and in other disputes in the South China Sea.[32]

BSAs are so far the most actively used form of Chinese monetary diplomacy. They are, however, shallow, flexible, and largely symbolic. Between 2008 and October 2013, China has signed BSAs with twenty-three jurisdictions worth approximately RMB 2.5 trillion (see table 6.1). They typically have a maturity of three years and can be extended.

It can be seen from table 6.1 that many of China's swap partners are also China's current or potential free trade agreement partners. That is because China chooses currency swap and FTA partners for similar reasons: it

30. European Council on Foreign Relations 2012, 28.

31. In April 2012, China pledged 90 million yuan aid to Egypt in support of the latter's economic projects. In May 2012, at a meeting of the Friends of Yemen (held by Yemen, Saudi Arabia, and the UK), China pledged aid of 100 million yuan.

32. "Zhongguo jiang chuzi 1.2 yi yuan renminbi yuanzhu jianpuzhai junshi xuyao" [China will fund 120 million yuan RMB to aid Cambodia's military needs], May 30, 2012, http://news.dayoo.com/world/201205/30/53871_24098012.htm.

TABLE 6.1. China's bilateral swap arrangements

Sign Date	Central Bank	Value (billions of yuan)	FTA Partner
October 9, 2013	European Central Bank	350	No
October 2, 2013	Indonesia (renewal)	100	Yes, in ASEAN
September 30, 2013	Iceland (renewal)	3.5	Yes
September 12, 2013	Albania	2	No
September 9, 2013	Hungary	10	No
June 22, 2013	UK	200	No
March 26, 2013	Brazil	190	Proposed
March 7, 2013	Singapore (expansion)	300	Yes
June 26, 2012	Ukraine	15	No
March 22, 2012	Australia	200	Under negotiation
March 20, 2012	Mongolia (expansion)	10	Under study
February 21, 2012	Turkey	10	No
February 8, 2012	Malaysia (expansion)	180	Yes, in ASEAN
January 18, 2012	UAE	35	Under negotiation, in Gulf Cooperation Council
December 23, 2011	Pakistan	10	Yes
December 22, 2011	Thailand	70	Yes, in ASEAN
November 22, 2011	Hong Kong (expansion)	400	Yes
October 26, 2011	South Korea (expansion)	360	Under negotiation
June 13, 2011	Kazakhstan	7	Proposed, in SCO
May 6, 2011	Mongolia	5	Under study
April 19, 2011	Uzbekistan	0.7	Proposed, in SCO
April 19, 2011	New Zealand	25	Yes
July 24, 2010	Singapore	150	Yes
June 9, 2010	Iceland	3.5	Yes
March 29, 2009	Argentina	70	No
March 23, 2009	Indonesia	100	Yes, in ASEAN
March 11, 2009	Belarus	20	No
February 8, 2009	Malaysia	80	Yes, in ASEAN
January 20, 2009	Hong Kong	200	Yes
December 12, 2008	South Korea	180	Under negotiation

prioritizes neighboring, energy-rich, and strategically important countries. These include countries in ASEAN + 3, the SCO, and BRICS. ASEAN + 3 is an important target of China's "good neighbor" diplomacy, for both security and economic reasons, and it is Beijing's preferred configuration of regional groupings compared with ASEAN + 6 or the Asia-Pacific countries.

The swap between China and Brazil of about $30 billion signed in March 2013 was the first of proposed swaps among BRICS, the details of which are expected in 2013. Although observers regard BRICS swaps as a challenge to the dominant role of the US dollar and the G7 in the global monetary order and as a means of RMB internationalization, the Sino-Brazilian agreement is first and foremost aimed at avoiding exchange rate volatility of the US dollar, as China seeks to buy Brazilian energy and raw materials, and to abate Brazilian protectionism against its cheap products. China has been Brazil's biggest trading partner since 2009, with bilateral trade volume exceeding $75.5 billion in 2012.[33] Upon signing the swap, the two countries also agreed to elevate their relationship to a "global strategic partnership."[34]

China also uses BSAs to strengthen its strategic relationships with other SCO members (including Kazakhstan and Uzbekistan), observers (Afghanistan, Pakistan and Mongolia), and dialogue partners (Belarus and Turkey), because SCO is another organization that China promotes to balance off Western influence in global politics and constrain the activity of Xinjiang Uighur separatists labeled by Beijing as terrorists. Accordingly, Xinjiang Uighur province became the first in China in 2009 to experiment with RMB settlement for cross-border trade and investment with other SCO countries.[35] The strategic significance of the SCO and some other countries—Latin American countries, Australia, and Gulf countries—to China also lies in their energy and natural resources. When China and Kazakhstan agreed to a $1 billion currency swap, they announced the upgrading of bilateral relations to a strategic partnership and the decision of Kazakhstan to supply nuclear fuel pellets to China from 2013.[36]

The use of the above BSAs is pragmatic and short term–oriented: to avoid exchange rate risk with countries with which China trades

---

33. "China, Brazil Sign $30 Billion Swap Accord to Bolster BRICS," Bloomberg, March 26, 2013, http://www.bloomberg.com/news/2013-03-26/china-brazil-sign-currency-swap-agreement-for-30-billion.html.

34. "Brazil and China Agree Currency Swap," *Financial Times,* June 22, 2012; "Qianshu ju'e huobi huhuan xieyi, zhongguo basi raokai meiyuan gao maoyi" [Huge currency swap signed, China and Brazil trade without dollar], March 28, 2013, http://news.xinhuanet.com/world/2013-03/28/c_124514601.htm.

35. Zhou, "Bottom-up parts of China's financial reform."

36. "Beijing Agrees Currency Deal with Kazakhs," *Financial Times,* June 13, 2011.

extensively, particularly with countries rich in energy and raw materials, and to a lesser extent to facilitate border trade and trade with bilateral FTA partners. Currency swaps may help Chinese companies pay for commodities, enable partner countries to import Chinese products, or assist companies in both countries to get RMB financing in resource-related activities. They do not serve to bring Chinese institutions to the standards of a market economy.

China has also signed currency swaps with small countries that are not significant trade partners but are strategically important. After Iceland's sovereign debt crisis erupted in 2008, China was in talks with Iceland about ways it could assist recovery, in contrast to the perceived bullying by UK and other European countries over the country's debts.[37] China signed a currency swap with Iceland in June 2010. The country's significance for China lay in its subarctic position, in a region with energy reserves and important shipping routes. Iceland was also a member of the Arctic Council that might support China's permanent observer status. China's aggressive diplomatic efforts in the Nordic countries bore fruit—it eventually gained this status in May 2013 despite Canada's caution.[38] In late 2011, China also signed a currency swap with Pakistan. That country has also enjoyed special friendship with China because of its strategic position adjoining both China and India, and China has prioritized Pakistan in aid and bilateral trade arrangements. The Chinese central bank has also suggested a currency swap with Chile, seen as a doorway to Latin American markets, resources, and infrastructure projects.[39]

China's swaps for preventing short-term crises are largely symbolic. China has learned from its experience with the Chiang Mai Initiative (CMI) that currency swaps are a low-cost arrangement that can generate political and commercial benefits. They are controllable and flexible, because the conditionality for activation, interest rate, and maturity can all be bilaterally negotiated. Only 20 percent of the available drawing under the CMI was not attached to IMF conditionalities (it increased from 10 percent in 2005). China in fact preferred a rigorous activation process—100 percent

---

37. "Iceland Secures China Currency Swap Deal," ibid., June 9, 2010.
38. "Six Nations Win Seats on Arctic Council," *Wall Street Journal,* May 15, 2013.
39. "China, Chile to Establish Strategic Partnership, Boost Trade," http://news.xinhuanet.com/english/china/2012-06/27/c_123334167.htm.

linkage of the CMI funds to IMF conditionality.[40] China has changed from insisting on strict conditionality to a more lenient attitude in its recent BSAs, as it now has more foreign reserves, and swaps are seldom activated. For smaller economies such as Belarus and Iceland, however, the BSAs feel like a lifeline, in particular when IMF or EU conditionality restricts their ability to obtain loans.

There was no plan for setting up a central decisionmaking mechanism or compulsory information sharing under CMI; countries had the choice to opt out of the arrangement when a crisis happened. Likewise, China supports multilateral pooling of CMI swaps (CMIM) but has been more wary of independent surveillance at CMIM. Currency swaps do not require exchange rate coordination or domestic reform. Swaps with the sole aim of preventing short-term liquidity crisis do not contribute much to the internationalization of the RMB either, as they are in the form of temporary loans. The consideration of a foreign exchange reserve pooling and currency swaps among BRICS may look like signs of China's enhanced activity in multilateral monetary cooperation. If they take a similar form to that of the CMIM, however, they will still be largely shallow and symbolic.

China's Role in Multilateral Monetary Institutions

China's diplomacy at multilateral monetary institutions is largely symbolic. This can be seen from its reluctance to contribute funds to them, its resistance to the surrender of sovereignty, and its use of bilateral or bloc diplomacy to challenge them and to protect its own economic model.

First, China is reluctant to contribute resources to multilateral monetary institutions, unless such contributions carry minimal risk compared with alternative options and bring clear benefits. It also uses bilateral or bloc diplomacy at the IMF to justify its resistance to making higher contributions and its demands for greater voting power. At the onset of the global financial crisis, China stated that it had fulfilled its quota in the IMF and that if other countries wanted it to contribute more, they should allow its voting power in the Fund to increase.[41] At the G20 meeting in Washington

---

40. Amyx 2008, Grimes 2006.
41. "Interview with Her Excellency Fu Ying, Chinese Ambassador to UK," *The Andrew Marr Show,* March 29, 2009, http://news.bbc.co.uk/2/hi/programmes/andrew_marr_show/7970581.stm.

in November 2008, neither China nor the Gulf states intended to step forward with funding. Japan's subsequent announcement that it would extend $100 billion to the IMF in February 2009, however, prompted new pledges from China as well the United States and the EU.[42] At the G20 summit in London in April 2009, China pledged $50 billion as part of a $500 billion increase in IMF resources.

China subsequently tried to ally with Japan to jointly seek a greater voting share in the Fund by reducing that of overrepresented countries (in particular some European countries), thereby constituting themselves representatives of an "Eastern bloc." In a rare display of unity, in February 2012, China and Japan jointly stated that the eurozone would need to lift the €500 billion cap on its bailout funds if it hoped to persuade the non-European G20 countries to increase their funding of the IMF.[43] In late March 2012, under pressure from the IMF, the OECD, and the G20, EU finance ministers approved an increase in total lending capacity of the bloc to €700 billion. On April 7, the Chinese and Japanese finance ministers restated their willingness to cooperate on the issue of IMF contributions. On April 17, however, Japan unilaterally increased its contribution to the IMF by $60 billion, a diplomatic coup against China, stating that Japan hoped to encourage other nations to follow suit. In Chinese official media, Japan's move was seen as aimed at consolidating its voice at IMF and containing China.[44]

China also attempted to use the BRIC grouping as a handy sounding board to voice its preferences at the IMF. In 2009, the BRIC countries refused to contribute funds directly to the IMF for fear that such lending would go through the New Arrangements to Borrow facility which has no effect on their relative quota. Instead, the BRIC countries and South Korea agreed to inject money into the IMF through a new SDR bond system,

---

Also see Shusong Ba (at the State Council Development Research Center), "Quanqiu jingji tiaozheng zhong de zhongguo tiaozhan he jiyu" [China's challenges and opportunities in global economic reshuffle], February 18, 2009, http://www.cei.gov.cn/LoadPage.aspx?Page=ShowDoc& CategoryAlias=zonghe/jjfx&ProductAlias=50lt&PAlias=50lt&BlockAlias=50sjjj&filename=/ doc/50sjjj/200902202296.xml.

42. Grimes 2009.

43. "China and Japan Unite on IMF Resources," *Financial Times,* February 19, 2012.

44. "Riben shuaixian chuzi EMF qianzhi zhongguo" [Japan offers contribution to EMF first, containing China], *Cankao Xiaoxi* [Reference News], April 22, 2012.

which involved a temporary purchase of SDR-denominated securities. These IMF bonds were tradable and limited to a one-year maturity—a key condition demanded by the emerging market economies for safety.

After Japan's unilateral increase of its IMF contribution in April 2012, China announced its decision at the G20 meeting in Mexico in June 2012 to increase its contribution to the IMF by $43 billion. China made the pledge as part of a group action of the BRICS (now including South Africa), which stated that their new contributions were based on the assumption that key powers at the IMF would move forward on governance reform that would give the emerging economies greater power. As for the specific amount, China explained that it was based on its quota at the IMF (10 percent of $430 billion total pledged by the G20 at their previous summit on April 21), and its capacity as a developing country, implying that a larger contribution from China should correspond to a larger quota and that it was understandable if China contributed less than Japan or other developed countries. Upon the announcement, Chinese president Hu Jintao also urged the IMF to implement quota reform, referring to the IMF decision in December 2010 to shift more than 6 percent of quota shares to dynamic emerging market and developing countries, within which China was expected to get its quota increased from 4 to 6.39 percent. Hu's reminder reflected domestic opinion, which regarded IMF's decision to increase the quota of EMDCs in 2010 as a diplomatic success, but the hitherto unimplemented increase of China's quota as disappointing.[45]

The symbolic value China pursues through multilateral monetary diplomacy is the image of a responsible great power. Chinese leaders have on many occasions reiterated the position that their country won't be absent from the international effort to boost IMF resources, based on international consensus.[46] At the same time, China is careful not to be burdened by the "China's responsibility" discourse with "unduly high or even unrealistic

45. "Woguo zengzi IMF beihou: Zhongfang gongxian da huayuquan xiao" [Behind the nation's increase of IMF funds: China contributes much but has little voice]. *China Daily,* June 23, 2012.

46. "Emerging Markets Pledge IMF Funds," *Washington Street Journal,* June 19, 2012; "China Will Boost IMF Resources," *China Daily (USA),* July 18, 2012, http://usa.chinadaily.com.cn/china/2012-06/18/content_15509206.htm.

expectations."[47] He Jianxiong, IMF Executive Director for China, stated that "China should focus on putting its own house in order."[48] Moreover, Beijing does not want to aggravate domestic anger over its usage of the people's savings, as the government's stimulus programs have already been criticized for corruption and waste, as well as for "advance of the public and retreat of the private."[49] Both He and Zhu emphasized that China's decision to increase its IMF contribution was based on the safety and profitability of IMF credit.

Second, in both global and regional monetary institutions, Beijing is not willing to surrender sovereignty over economic policy, thus making its participation in monetary multilateralism largely symbolic. As is widely known, China criticizes IMF's conditionality for loans and refuses to accept a flexible exchange rate as one of the ultimate goals of the national reform project. Even though China supported the multilateralization of the bilateral swaps under CMI, it resists giving CMIM supranational power. As Andrew Walter points out in this volume, China's relationship with the international surveillance regime has also deteriorated. Beijing is not comfortable with releasing detailed information about its domestic financial system, not to mention with subjecting national policy to international surveillance. Consistent with the analysis of domestic politics here, Walter underlines that this discomfort comes mainly from a narrow set of domestic interests—the party-state-business elite.

China also rejects the possibility of exchange rate coordination in Asia, although many Chinese academics believe that participating in a regional currency is the best way to promote RMB internationalization. The Chinese government has dismissed the significance of a Japan-proposed Asian Currency Unit, not only because of competition with Japan for regional leadership and disagreement over its composition,[50] but also because the ACU cannot satisfy simultaneously three important objectives of China's

---

47. "Bufuzeren de zhongguo jingji zeren lun" [Irresponsible "China economic responsibility" talk], *China Daily,* July 30, 2010, http://www.chinadaily.com.cn/zgrbjx/2010-07/30/content_11069733.htm.

48. "Emerging Markets Pledge IMF Funds," *Wall Street Journal,* June 19, 2012.

49. "Guojin mintui jiang ehua shouru fenpei" [Advance of the Public and Retreat of the Private Will Exacerbate Income Distribution], *Financial Times* (Chinese), January 7, 2010, http://www.ftchinese.com/story/001030661.

50. Jiang 2010.

current economic strategy: maintaining export competitiveness and stabilizing import cost, restoring external and internal balance, and reducing excessive exchange rate fluctuations.[51] The ACU idea was not even a point for discussion at the 2009 ASEAN + 3 finance ministers' meeting.

Third, China uses bilateral and bloc diplomacy to challenge existing powers and neoliberal ideology in global monetary governance. Without offering feasible alternatives, China is only making symbolic gestures and really seeking to protect its own economic model. As mentioned earlier, China positions itself as a representative of developing countries and calls for reform of the global monetary system. China prides itself on the rise of the G20 against the G7 in global economic governance and in the decision of IMF to give larger quotas to EMDCs. China also calls for strengthening regulation of developed economies. In so doing, China tries to divert attention from its policies to those of developed countries.

A key issue in global monetary governance is the international reserve currency. PBOC Governor Zhou Xiaochuan's provocative call in 2009 for reform of the international monetary system and his suggestion for a global reserve currency caught the world by surprise.[52] Thanks to Zhou's essay, there was renewed interest in the use of the SDR as a reserve currency in academic and policy circles, including the IMF and its Executive Board. Thinly veiled as an expression of personal opinion, the article expressed the wish of the Chinese central bank to have more say in global monetary governance, an objective that China has followed for decades, both at the creation of the Bretton Woods institutions and since China resumed membership in them in 1980 (see Eric Helleiner and Bessma Momani's chapter). China has also pressed for the RMB to be one of the currencies included in the IMF's SDR basket. Li Daokui, member of the Monetary Policy Committee of the central bank, has argued that the SDR without the RMB would be "ridiculous" and "lack legitimacy," and that the inclusion of the RMB in the IMF basket should not be linked with the currency's convertibility.[53]

---

51. Zhang and He 2007.

52. Zhou 2009.

53. "PBOC Adviser Says SDR System Without Yuan Is 'Ridiculous,'" Bloomberg, March 31, 2011, http://www.bloomberg.com/news/2011-03-31/pboc-adviser-says-sdr-system-without-yuan-is-ridiculous-1-.html.

Zhou Xiaochuan and the central bank do not represent the whole spectrum of Chinese opinion, but only the more liberal side that advocates reform and liberalization. Many Chinese policy elites, including Nie Qingping from the China Securities Regulatory Commission, do not think inclusion of the RMB in a supranational reserve currency is feasible in the foreseeable future.[54] The reason they cite is the inconvertibility of the RMB. If the RMB became an international reserve currency, China would lose control over its monetary policies, a scenario that the beneficiaries of the existing system do not want to see. The Chinese government denied in July 2009 that Zhou Xiaochuan's proposal represented the official standpoint and said that China expected the US dollar to maintain its role for "many years to come"[55] In September 2011, even Zhou Xiaochuan made a statement that China was in no hurry to have the RMB added to the SDR basket.[56] China's call for international monetary reform is best seen as largely symbolic. Li Jianjun, an analyst with the Bank of China, said: "The crux of issuing a super-sovereign currency is determining who gets the final say. Both issuance and allocation involve a lot of political give-and-take. Without seeing great benefits, countries will have little incentive to take the onus."[57]

Internationalization of the RMB

Many Chinese academics and policymakers regard the ownership of an international currency as a symbol of great power status. Zhang Yuyan, director of the World Economy and Politics Institute at the Chinese Academy of Social Sciences, thinks that internationalization of the RMB is a necessary support for the rise of China, and notes that hegemonic powers

---

54. "Nie Qingping: Chaozhuquan huobi hennan zhaodao huobimao" [Difficult for the supranational currency to find an anchor], *First Finance News,* April 1, 2009, http://bond.hexun.com/2009-04-01/116251849.html. Also see Bowles and Wang 2008.

55. Mark Deen and Simon Kennedy, "Russia, India Question Dollar Reliance before Summit (Update 2)," Bloomberg, July 6, 2009, http://www.bloomberg.com/apps/news?pid=20601087&sid=aaPXSTHmf02I.

56. "China's Zhou Says No Hurry to Include Yuan in SDR: Xinhua," MNI Deutsche Börse Group, September 8, 2011, https://mninews.deutsche-boerse.com/content/chinas-zhou-says-no-hurry-include-yuan-sdr-xinhua.

57. "With or Without Yuan Added in SDR, Global Monetary System Should Reform," November 3, 2011, http://news.xinhuanet.com/english2010/indepth/2011-11/03/c_131228404.htm.

in recent history—Britain and the United States—have had internationally dominant currencies.[58] However, in contrast to the market-led process of dollar internationalization, it is believed among the Chinese policy elite that RMB internationalization has been and should be led by the state in a gradualist fashion. Starting in June 2009, the Chinese government has come up with a series of policies to expand the usage of the RMB, through trade and investment, bilateral local currency settlement agreements, offshore RMB centers, and RMB aid. These appear to be steps toward internationalization of the RMB and liberalization of the Chinese financial and monetary regime. However, the PBOC's experiments with RMB internationalization have been allowed because they suit vested interests and the state's strategic considerations. RMB internationalization continues to be constrained by other key policies insisted on by conservatives as well as by the state's priority of maintaining control.

China has signed bilateral local currency settlement agreements with fourteen economies.[59] The list of economies clearly shows three purposes, which may coexist in some agreements. First, the agreements facilitate border trade: either by bringing RMB usage into formal channels where the RMB had been an informally accepted currency, as with Laos, Mongolia, Myanmar, Nepal, North Korea, Taiwan, and Vietnam; or by creating channels to promote RMB usage where the currency had not been much used, as with Kazakhstan, Kirgizstan, and Russia,.[60] Second, they support payment for energy and raw materials, as with Brazil, Kazakhstan, Kirgizstan, Russia, and South Africa. Third, they carry political symbolic value, for instance within the BRICS; so, too, would the proposed agreements among SCO members. However, as will be discussed later, the usage of the RMB is still limited by other conflicting policies, and the US dollar remains important. For instance, Russia demands US dollars for commodities trade.

In June 2012, China and Japan started direct currency trading on the foreign exchange market, making it possible to settle bilateral trade

58. "Zhang Yuyan: Renminbi guojihua shi zhongguo jueqi de biyao zhicheng" [Zhang Yuyan: RMB internationalization is a necessary support for the rise of China]," May 31, 2011, http://www.cnr.cn/gundong/201105/t20110531_508052770.shtml.

59. These include Belarus, Brazil, India, Kazakhstan, Kirgizstan, Laos, Mongolia, Myanmar, Nepal, North Korea, Russia, South Africa, Taiwan, and Vietnam.

60. Lv and Wang 2012.

without the US dollar, and since 2009, China has been diverting part of its US dollar reserves to Japanese debt, and has accelerated its Japanese debt purchases since the euro crisis erupted in 2010. Some Chinese analysts acclaim yuan-yen convertibility as a significant step in China's exchange rate reform and RMB internationalization.[61] Its impact on the RMB, however, is limited. According to Tan Yaling of the China Forex Investment Research Institute, because of the declining status of the Japanese yen in international economy, as well as the importance of the US dollar to the value of the Japanese yen in the foreign exchange market, commercial banks would change yen into US dollars outside of their trading hours to avoid exchange rate risks. It is also difficult for Chinese investors to access the Japanese market.[62] Moreover, because of the limited degree of openness of the Chinese financial market, Japan would have very little impact on China's bond market.

The major trigger for the initiatives vis-à-vis Japan was political. The summit between Chinese Premier Wen Jiabao and Japanese Prime Minister Yoshihiko Noda in December 2011 served as a stimulant to bilateral cooperation, against the background of improved diplomatic relations. The two countries had been compelled by the momentum of East Asian financial cooperation to assume co-leadership, demonstrated by their agreement to contribute equal amounts of funding to the multilateral pool of CMI in May 2009. However, when the territorial dispute between the two countries over the Diaoyu/Senkaku Islands escalated in 2012, financial tensions between the two countries also grew. China's official newspaper *China Daily* published an article by Song Jinbai at a think tank affiliated with MOFCOM calling for sanctions against Japan, saying that "with Japan's national debt at stake, the proverbial straw that can save the Japanese economy seems to be in the hands of China. And China can use it to find ways to impose sanctions on Japan in the most effective manner."[63]

---

61. "Renminbi dui riyuan zhijie jiaoyi 6 yue qihang, huigai zaimai yibu" [RMB convertible with Japanese yen, exchange rate reform a further step from June], *First Finance News,* May 30, 2011, http://finance.sina.com.cn/china/jrxw/20120530/014612175687.shtml.

62. "Zhuanjia cheng zhongri huobi zhidui jin qianjin yixiaobu, geng youli riben" [Expert says yuan-yen convertibility is only a small step, more beneficial for Japan], May 29, 2012, http://finance.sina.com.cn/roll/20120529/145812172107.shtml.

63. "Consider Sanctions on Japan," *China Daily,* September 17, 2012, http://www.chinadaily apac.com/article/consider-sanctions-japan.

A representative of the Tokyo Stock Exchange in Beijing also said that its business in China was almost halted due to cancellation of meetings by Chinese government officials and difficulties in communicating with Chinese companies.[64]

Regardless of the risk in handing a "proverbial straw" to Beijing, other countries (including Australia) have been seeking similar convertibility arrangements with China. Moreover, some central banks (including those of Austria, Indonesia, and Pakistan) and the World Bank have been allowed access to China's onshore RMB-denominated interbank bond market through bilateral agreements with the Chinese central bank since it launched its pilot program in August 2010. The PBOC hopes that these examples would start a domino effect, attracting other foreign institutions to apply for access to China's interbank bond market as well, although these arrangements are mostly symbolic.[65] A political domino effect has also started, as countries compete to become offshore centers for the RMB.

In addition to bilateral convertibility arrangements, the Chinese central bank would like to use offshore centers to internationalize the RMB and propel opening of the onshore RMB market. These experiments are allowed as long as they suit vested interests—of SOEs, state commercial banks, and their regulators—and remain controllable. Hong Kong is also used as a platform for financing for mainland institutions and corporations. By the end of August 2012, MOF has issued bonds of 51 billion yuan, together with a number of big SOEs, policy banks (the Exim Bank or the Development Bank), and state commercial banks.[66]

The bilateral approach to considering candidates for offshore RMB centers also suits some of China's political aims. A political domino effect has been initiated by China's preferential treatment for Hong Kong as the first offshore RMB center, with other major cities—Singapore, London, Tokyo, Taipei, Sydney, and Paris—now seeking the same status. Beijing hopes the link with Taipei will promote political integration between the

64. "Diaoyudao zhengduan zhi zhongrihan ziyoumaoyiqu hengshengbianshu" [Diaoyu Islands dispute impedes China-Japan–South Korea FTA], *21st Century Business Herald,* September 19, 2012, http://stock.cjzg.cn/caijing/1348012320812281.html.

65. Thornton 2012.

66. "Xianggang zhuyao renminbi zhaiquan faxing qingkuang yilan" [Major RMB bonds issued in Hong Kong], October 31, 2013, http://cn.reuters.com/article/currenciesNews/idCNL3S0II0ME20131031?sp=true.

mainland and Taiwan. London won support from the Bank of China to become an offshore RMB center thanks to much diplomatic work. As mentioned previously, however, BOC does not wish for domestic financial reform. Offshore centers are regarded by BOC as financing houses for Chinese companies to "go global." But China won political clout with its deal with Britain: the UK promised to support China's market economy status at the EU and also resolved to recognize China's full sovereignty over Tibet.

The inconvertibility of the RMB and China's largely closed capital account greatly limit the development of offshore RMB centers. In other parts of the world, inconvertibility makes the RMB unattractive in major international markets. According to a survey in 2012, 42 percent of American companies and 23 percent of European companies are unwilling to use RMB for settling trade. Even among Chinese domestic companies, more than 40 percent are unwilling to use the RMB, because of inconvertibility and inconvenient transaction procedures. In particular, the US dollar is still the de facto pricing currency for global commodities.[67] Therefore, even if offshore RMB centers were established in London or New York, they would be largely symbolic.

Despite the above intergovernmental arrangements since 2004 and a series of policies since June 2009,[68] the attraction of the RMB in international trade is limited by other policy constraints. According to studies by the Development Research Center of the State Council, the usage of the RMB in international trade and investment has been largely limited to border trade. The US dollar remains the main currency for China's trade, and the acceptance of RMB investment is even lower.[69] The reasons include RMB inconvertibility, the strictly controlled capital account, and the lack

67. "Cong kuajingjiesuan dao kuajingdaikuan, renminbi guojihua zhengyizhong qianxing" [From cross-border settlement to loans, RMB internationalization continues to be debated]," *21st Century Business Herald,* July 7, 2012, http://www.21cbh.com/HTML/2012-7-7/4NMzY5XzQ2OTY4NQ.html.

68. In June 2009, China launched a pilot scheme for cross-border trade settlement in RMB in a few mainland cities and Hong Kong, and subsequently expanded it to the whole of China and any trading partner. In January 2011, the central bank launched a pilot scheme for the settlement of foreign direct investment in RMB, followed by further easing of RMB FDI regulations. In June 2012 Qianhai Financial Special Zone was set up to open up a channel for RMB to flow between Hong Kong and mainland.

69. Development Research Center of the State Council 2011, 45.

of bilateral currency settlement agreements between China and most of its trade partners.

Moreover, China's politico-strategic environment constrains the RMB's potential to become a dominant regional currency. Some countries in the region try to protect the status of traditional economic powers and their currencies, namely the US dollar and the Japanese yen.[70] Obviously, recent maritime territorial conflicts have not helped in dispersing the fear of China in its neighborhood, despite Beijing's charm offensive through FTAs, aid, and investment since the 1997–98 Asian financial crisis.

Finally, there appear to be co-ordination problems amongst Chinese government agencies. The Ministry of Finance and the National Bureau of Taxation came up with regulations that disqualify many companies from export tax deduction if they use RMB. The State Administration of Foreign Exchange and China Customs put a cap on the amount of RMB cash that can be brought across the border. Besides, there is a cap on the net inflow and outflow in trade settlement through commercial banks, which means that these banks have to have both import and export business in similar amounts.[71] Chairman of the China Banking Regulatory Commission Liu Mingkang emphasizes that maintaining control and exercising caution remain priority in the experiment of RMB free convertibility.[72]

In conclusion, recent activity in China's monetary diplomacy does not foreshadow faster domestic reform or financial liberalization in the foreseeable future. The arrangements that China has made through monetary diplomacy are often symbolic for political gains, or shallow and short term—oriented for pragmatic commercial gains. They are at best a compromise between domestic liberal and conservative actors. Their trajectory depends on not only the position of the next-generation leadership but also to what extent such measures suit vested interests. Such interests, which try to preserve financial repression, state bank dominance, and SOEs' monopolies,

---

70. Development Research Center of the State Council 2011, 45–48.
71. "Zhongxin yinhang fuhangzhang Cao Tong: Liujie renminbi guojihua zhidu jianshe" [Vice President of Citibank Cao Tong: Six interpretations of institutional building of RMB internationalization], January 8, 2010, http://forex.stockstar.com/JL2010010800002012_3.shtml.
72. "Liu Mingkang: Qianhai renminbi zibenzhang kaifang shiyan xu shenshen [Liu Mingkang: Qianhai RMB capital account opening should be cautious]," http://finance.sina.com.cn/stock/hkstock/hkstocknews/20120703/154412467257.shtml.

have become so entrenched in China's political power structure that they have become virtually untouchable. Unless the new political leadership of Xi Jinping and Li Keqiang can overcome resistance from the entrenched interests, any meaningful financial reform is not likely in the near future.

China's initiatives also do not indicate that it is preparing to assume the role of a global monetary power, nor greater interest in multilateral monetary co-operation. China is reluctant to contribute to multilateral resource pools, unless they provide clear-cut benefits. Its bilateral arrangements require little monetary policy co-ordination between the partners that might lead to global co-operation, and their conditionalities bear little resemblance to those of existing global institutions. Furthermore, China's bilateralism may encourage other countries to follow suit, as is already seen in the bilateral swaps between Japan and India and local currency settlements between Iran and India, and Iran and Russia.[73]

---

73. "Iran, Russia Replace Dollar with Rial, Ruble in Trade, Fars Says," Bloomberg, January 7, 2012, http://www.bloomberg.com/news/2012-01-07/iran-russia-replace-dollar-with-rial-ruble-in-trade-fars-says.html. "India, Iran to Settle Some Oil Trade in Rupees—Source," Reuters, January 20, 2012, http://www.reuters.com/article/2012/01/20/india-iran-idUSL3E8CK3C120120120.

7

CHINA'S RISING MONETARY POWER

Gregory Chin

The study of power in China's international monetary relations is at a rudimentary stage. Direct forms of power are better understood. "Direct power" can be defined as the ability of one state to get another state to do what it would not otherwise do, either by persuasion or coercion. Scholars have focused on China's ability to influence US policy behavior, or lack thereof. Sester and Drezner, for example, each examine whether China has been able to convert its large holdings of US debt into influence over US policymaking. They each run different tests; and reach different conclusions. Sester suggests there is growing Chinese influence, while Drezner is more skeptical.[1] More recently, Cohen has explored whether the currency

I thank Benjamin Cohen, Andrew Walter, the participants at the Cornell workshop, and the two anonymous reviewers for their comments, and especially Eric Helleiner and Jonathan Kirshner for their editorial guidance and suggestions. I thank the Social Sciences and Humanities Council of Canada for supporting the research for this chapter.

1. Sester 2008a, Drezner 2009.

swap agreements that the People's Bank of China has signed with other central banks are latent tools of Chinese direct monetary power, a future tool of monetary statecraft to counter Western state power.[2]

A second face of direct power is the ability of one state to avoid direct pressure from another state to do what the former would not otherwise do. Cohen has shown that China has gained this increased "power-as-autonomy" in the sense of avoiding external pressure on its exchange rate. Beijing's vastly increased foreign currency reserves position it to postpone externally requested policy adjustments when it wishes. As Cohen puts it, "power to delay is clearly enhanced"[3] However, Cohen also finds that China's increased capacity to deflect exogenous pressure is a somewhat passive mode of monetary power, and does not automatically translate into greater influence, or a more active, purposive exercise of international power.

The aforementioned studies of direct Chinese power make important contributions, but direct power is only part of the power calculus. Its study leaves unexamined the broader, indirect, structural ways in which China is beginning to exercise monetary power internationally. Structural power also has two faces.[4] The first face is a constraining effect. To paraphrase Strange, it is the power to shape or determine the broader context within which other states and market actors have to operate; in short, the power to shape frameworks that condition how things are done and the context within which states and people relate to each other, to delimit the range of options.[5] The second face is the possessor's capacity to expand the range of choices open to others, by giving them opportunities they would not otherwise have had, by opening or extending their options.[6]

The main conceptual argument in this chapter is that China is exercising the second face of structural power in the international monetary realm by expanding the range of reserve currency options that states and market actors have in the international monetary system. It is doing so by promoting reserve diversification within the international monetary system. China is reshaping the monetary frameworks, and the international

---

2. Cohen 2012.
3. Cohen 2008, 461.
4. I thank Benjamin J. Cohen for highlighting this conceptual point.
5. Strange 1988, 24–25.
6. Strange 1988, 31.

currency markets, within which states, market actors, and people relate to each other. China's actions aim to induce institutional adaptation by opening up and broadening the range of international currency options in the name of fostering an international monetary system that is "fair, orderly and stable." At the same time, Beijing's international currency interventions may have the medium-term effect of indirectly constraining the "exorbitant privilege" of the United States—the first face of structural power. In brief, China, by promoting reserve diversification, may, over the medium term, have a disciplining effect on US economic policy, imposing higher debt-servicing costs on the United States if it chooses to continue to pursue a loose monetary and fiscal policy. The statements by leading Chinese monetary and financial elites reproduced in this chapter highlight such system-level thinking, and indicate that it is a core element of the strategic culture and medium-term objective that is guiding China's global monetary interventions.

The analysis here highlights three main empirical findings. First, that China is promoting international monetary and reserve diversification through a number of channels, that include the collective efforts of the BRICS nations to expand the role of the Special Drawing Right (SDR), (a multilateral asset issued by the IMF), and support its development into a multilateral reserve option; the enactment of formal agreements and currency cooperation measures between China and the BRICS countries, to increase the use of their national currencies to settle trade and investment within the grouping, and to develop international financial markets for the BRICS currencies; and concerted steps to increase cross-border use of China's national currency, the renminbi, as an international currency for settling trade and investment, as a store of value, and ultimately, as one of the world's major reserve options.[7]

Second, the negative effects of growing volatility in the value of the US dollar on China's foreign exchange holdings became a growing concern for the country's senior government leaders from 2007 onward. These currency concerns converged with the 2007–9 global financial crisis (GFC),

---

7. Two other components of China's current international monetary interventions that are not covered in this chapter, due to limits of length, are China's support for ensuring the survival of the euro, and its currency internationalization efforts at the regional level, especially within the Asian region.

especially the dollar liquidity freeze, which affected China's trade relations. Amid this critical juncture, and the emergence of the G20 Leaders process, China's leaders responded with more activist monetary diplomacy.

Third, the Chinese strategic thinking on international monetary reform that is examined in this chapter traces back more than a decade, and its origins are rooted in Asian criticism of US and IMF handling of the 1997–98 Asian financial crisis. The call from China's central bank to reform the international monetary system, which gained widespread notoriety at the height of the GFC, was actually based on growing Chinese disillusionment with US management of the world's de facto reserve currency. Since 1999, senior Chinese central bank and financial officials have flagged their concern for the major reserve-issuing countries to act more responsibly at a succession of IMF and World Bank gatherings, and they have highlighted the importance of the IMF putting more emphasis on surveillance of the advanced economies, developing a multilateral reserve option, and moving toward a multi–reserve currency system. These warnings went unheeded. We begin with the relevant history.

The Origins

In March 2009, as the international community looked anxiously for global leadership to put a floor under the free fall of Anglo-American finance and bring order back to the world economy, China's central bank published a landmark essay by its governor, Zhou Xiaochuan, titled "Reform the International Monetary System." This was received by international observers as bolt from the blue. It read like a Chinese treatise on global monetary change that outlined succinctly the technical and governing rationale for moving toward a more diverse reserve system. Due to its timing, and to China's weight in international financial and currency markets, the essay drew widespread global attention. But as we will see, the Chinese critique of the existing international monetary system had been building for more than a decade.

Governor Zhou focused on the problem of relying on "credit-based national currencies as major international reserve currencies," and argued that the "current crisis and its spillover in the world" had confronted the global community with the "still unanswered question" of "what kind of international reserve currency do we need to secure global financial stability and facilitate world economic growth?"[8] Observers took notice of the People's Bank of China (PBOC) governor's understanding of the "Triffin Dilemma": of the irresolvable conflict of interest involved in the government of a reserve-issuing country placing priority on domestic policy goals while also trying to meet international currency needs that are shared with other countries. In brief, the issuing countries of reserve currencies cannot maintain the value of reserve currencies while also providing stable liquidity for the world.

The solution, according to Zhou, is to establish a reserve currency that is "disconnected from individual nations and is able to remain stable in the long run, thus removing the inherent deficiencies caused by using credit-based national currencies." The governor suggested that the reserve asset should satisfy three conditions: first, "theoretically, an international reserve currency should . . . be anchored to a stable benchmark and issued according to a clear set of rules . . . to ensure orderly supply"; second, "its supply should be flexible enough to allow timely adjustment according to the changing demand"; and third, "such adjustments should be disconnected from economic conditions and sovereign interests of any single country." Perhaps most important, he suggested that the SDR, as a "super-sovereign" reserve currency, could be the "light in the tunnel" for the reform of the international monetary system. Zhou reexamined why the SDR had been created initially by the IMF in 1969 (namely, to mitigate the anticipated risks of relying on sovereign reserve currencies at a time when the dollar-gold system was experiencing serious stress), and he suggested that a super-sovereign reserve currency "eliminates the inherent risks of credit-based sovereign currency," and "makes it possible to manage global liquidity" via global multilateralism. As monetary diplomacy, Zhou's essay showed a deft touch as it did not explicitly mention the dollar.[9]

The origins of the strategic thinking in Zhou's essay actually stretched back more than a decade to the late 1990s. At almost every biannual IMF and World Bank gathering from 1998 to 2007, stemming back to the aftermath of the 1997–98 Asian financial crisis, Chinese central bank and finance representatives warned about the adverse effects of the existing

8. Zhou 2009, 1.
9. Zhou 2009, 1–2.

international monetary system in terms of exchange rate volatility and currency instability; called on the IMF to exercise stricter surveillance over the major reserve-issuing countries; warned of the "irrationality" of overrelying on any single nation's currency; and proposed moving toward a multipolar reserve system. Since the crisis, Chinese disillusionment with US handling of the dollar-centered international monetary system has only increased.

As resentment intensified in Asia toward the negative effects of the IMF's bailout packages, in April 2000 PBOC Deputy Governor Xiao Gang told the International Monetary and Financial Committee (IMFC)[10] gathering: "We think the major industrial economies have systemic significance, therefore, the Fund should put more effort into monitoring these members under its bilateral and multilateral surveillance exercise, particularly, by analyzing the possible impact or spillover effect of their policies on both regional and global economies."[11] Governor Dai Xianglong followed with similar warnings at the April 2002 IMFC meeting, as the negative effects of the IMF's medicine became more evident.[12]

As early as 2002, Chinese monetary elites highlighted the supposed "irrationality" of the existing international monetary system, stated their preference for "multipolarity," and first raised the SDR as a reserve asset option. At the spring meeting of the IMF and the World Bank, Governor Dai drew attention to the fact that

> The irrationality inherent in the international monetary system has contributed to the uneven allocation of global resources and large fluctuations among major currencies ...
>
> We support "multi-polarization" of the world economy. This will help promote harmonized and balanced development of the global economy and the establishment of a new international political and economic order that is

---

10. The IMFC reports to the IMF Board of Governors on the management of the international monetary and financial system, and advises on the IMF's work program. The committee, with twenty-four members, monitors developments in global liquidity and the transfer of resources to developing countries, considers proposals by the Executive Board to amend the Articles of Agreement, and assesses unfolding events that may disrupt the global monetary and financial system. It usually meets twice a year, at the autumn Bank-Fund annual and spring meetings. See International Monetary Fund 2013b.

11. Xiao 2000.

12. Dai 2002b.

fair and rational. In this regard, it is obviously beneficial to expand the use of SDRs as an international reserve currency. Conditions should be created to encourage such an effort. Being the center of the international financial system, the IMF should attach greater importance to the reform of the international monetary system, paying more attention to the unbalanced development of the world economy in finding possible solutions.[13]

At successive Fund and Bank meetings from 2002 to 2004, Chinese officials repeated the message about the "irrationality" of the system, and called for the creation of a "new, rational and fair international economic order," a "new international monetary system."[14] This criticism built on the Chinese Communist Party's official foreign policy line, outlined in General Secretary Jiang Zemin's speech at the Sixteenth National Party Congress in November 2002, which referred to "multipolarization and economic globalization" as growing trends that have brought "opportunities and favorable conditions for world peace and development."[15] He warned that "the old international political and economic order, which is unfair and irrational, has yet to be changed fundamentally. . . . We stand for establishing a new international political and economic order that is fair and rational. We oppose all forms of hegemonism and power politics. China will never seek hegemony and never pursue expansionism."[16]

The Chinese criticism was ratcheted upward at the April 2003 IMFC gathering, when then PBOC Assistant Governor Li Ruogu explicitly singled out US macro and monetary mismanagement for criticism:

> At present, the depreciation of the dollar has put pressure on the economic recovery of the euro area. If exchange rate volatility and international capital flows were to affect each other, there will be an even greater impact on the emerging market economies whose financial sectors are still not robust.
>
>   . . . The United States should pay more attention to its existing macroeconomic weaknesses and enhance policy coordination with other countries to prevent the negative impact of sharp exchange rate volatility on the vulnerable world economy.[17]

---

13. Dai 2002a.
14. Dai 2002b; Li 2003; Zhou 2004a.
15. Jiang 2002, 56.
16. Jiang 2002, 56.
17. Li 2003.

At the IMFC meeting in April 2004, Zhou also singled out US misman-agement, and offered a warning about the US economy: "First of all, the wealth effect on which this recovery relies may be difficult to sustain. Second, the expansion of the US fiscal deficit is detrimental to private sector investment and capital market stability. Third, the U.S. current account deficit continues to grow, inevitably resulting in an adjustment of the U.S. dollar exchange rate, and may perturb the global economy."[18] Again at the joint discussions of the IMF and the World Bank on October 3, 2004, Zhou returned to the links between US macro mismanagement and the destabilization of global finance: "The economic structural problems of the major developed countries are having a potentially negative impact on global economic development, exchange rates, and even financial market stability."[19] And Li Ruogu followed on the theme of US destabilization of financial markets at the April 2005 IMFC meeting: "Since last September, U.S. dollar exchange rates have been declining. Not only does this place great pressure on the export growth of some economies, but it also threatens the stability of U.S. domestic financial markets. If the U.S. fiscal and current account deficits continue to expand, the U.S. dollar will depreciate further, which may in turn lead to upheavals in financial markets and the real economy."[20]

China's central bank authorities focused on redirecting the Fund's surveillance onto the major industrial nations and economies that have greater debt vulnerability. They pushed the Fund to encourage these major reserve-issuing countries to better coordinate their economic policies, and to maintain exchange rate stability in the major currencies.[21] The senior Chinese representatives reiterated this message at every IMF and World Bank biannual gathering from 2005 to 2008. The rationale they provided was that these economies and their financial markets have a great effect on global or regional development. This was also the period when the US Treasury, the US Congress, and the IMF began pressuring China on exchange rate "misalignment."[22]

---

18. Zhou 2004a.
19. Zhou 2004b, 1.
20. Li 2005, 1.
21. Zhou 2006a.
22. Blustein 2012, 12–23.

In April 2006 in Washington, PBOC Governor Zhou Xiaochuan offered the following comments on the SDR, presaging the main themes he would reinforce in the March 2009 essay:

> There is a fundamental need for the Fund to enhance the effectiveness of its surveillance since global trade, settlements, and reserve assets are heavily reliant on a single currency. On the one hand, the Fund should give priority to establishing a surveillance and check-balance mechanism of the major reserve currency countries while on the other hand giving thought to reforming the international monetary system. To this end, the continuous enhancement of the role of the SDR in the international monetary system remains an important issue.[23]

Zhou returned to the same themes at the IMF and World Bank gathering in Singapore in September 2006.[24] The successive Chinese warnings, and calls for systemic change, however, went unheeded, and were largely ignored by central bank and finance representatives of the G7 governments. Much did change, however, with the free fall of Anglo-American finance in 2008.

Coordinated Pressure

In the decade before the GFC, China's monetary statecraft and diplomacy were largely the preserve of senior technocrats from the central bank, and to a lesser extent, the finance ministry.[25] However, as the world economy descended into crisis with the collapse of Lehman Brothers in September 2008, and when US President George W. Bush gathered the leaders of the world's largest economies at the first G20 Leaders summit on November 15, 2008 China's leaders elevated financial and monetary policy, and monetary diplomacy to top priority. As the crisis worsened and spread, the governments of other countries, including those of the leading economies,

---

23. Zhou 2006a.
24. Zhou 2006b.
25. For the role of central bank and finance officials in China's international monetary relations see Jacobson and Oksenberg 1990; Lardy 1999; Pearson 1999.

looked to Beijing to play a key part in helping to stabilize the world economy. China's party and government leaders gave their support to China's central bank to lower its interest rate on bank lending on October 8, 2008, and again on October 31, 2008, as part of a series of measures by central banks in the leading economies to try to contain the negative effects of the crisis. At the G20 finance ministers' and central bank governors' meeting in São Paulo on November 8, Zhou reassured the assembled participants that China would help stabilize international financial markets by maintaining its economic growth and by expanding domestic demand; that China's central bank was monitoring the situation of the financial markets very closely, and was ready to make further adjustments to its policies and interest rate if needed; and that the PBOC would cooperate with the IMF to stabilize financial markets.[26] On the second day in São Paulo, Chinese officials informed their counterparts that Beijing had just announced a RMB 4 trillion (about US$570 billion) stimulus package that would be spent over two years to offset the adverse effects of the GFC by boosting domestic growth.[27]

The GFC generated three important changes in China's monetary diplomacy: a shift in the primary actors; a massive increase in financial contributions; and coordinated action with the group of rising states known as the BRICS. In terms of actors, Communist Party General Secretary and State President Hu Jintao, primus inter pares among the Party's collective leadership, became the lead spokesperson on China's global monetary thinking, when he called on the G20 Leaders at their first summit to give priority to restoring financial stability, "improving the international currency system and steadily promoting the diversity of the international monetary system."[28] During this period, Chinese Premier Wen Jiabao became the key messenger of the government's growing concerns over Washington's management of the dollar, which had a direct bearing on China's reserve holdings.[29] Prior to the London G20 summit on April 2, 2009, Wen

---

26. Jiang Yuxia, "China to Stabilize Global Financial Markets by Maintaining Growth," November 9, 2008, http://news.xinhuanet.com/english/2008-11/09/content_10330101.htm.

27. The stimulus package provided financing for low-income housing, rural infrastructure, water, electricity, transportation, the environment, technological innovation, and rebuilding from several natural disasters.

28. Hu 2008.

29. On the inherent vulnerability of China's foreign exchange holdings see Wang 2007.

stated to the US media: "We have lent a huge amount of money to the U.S . . . . to be honest, I am definitely a little worried."[30]

The publication of Zhou Xiaochuan's essay in the days before the London G20 grabbed the attention of the Western media, and Vice Premier Wang Qishan's vision of a new monetary order where "developing countries have more voice," published in the London *Times,* set the tone of the Chinese leadership going into the G20 summit.[31] However, it was Hu Jintao who played the key role actually at the meeting, calling on the G20 Leaders to instruct the IMF to "reinforce and improve supervision over the macroeconomic policies of related parties, especially the major economies issuing reserve currencies. Particular focus should be put on the regulation of currency issuance policies."[32] Hu echoed the earlier message of the PBOC: "We should improve the international monetary system and the reserve currency issuing regulatory mechanism, maintain the relative stability of the exchange rates of major reserve currencies and promote a diverse and reasonable international currency system."[33] In the midst of a crisis at the heart of the global financial system, the message was difficult to ignore, and was delivered as a rallying cry on behalf of the major emerging economies and the G77.

The second new dimension of China's monetary diplomacy is that Beijing is marshaling large amounts of financial resources, especially by its historical standards, to back up its global interventions with tangible contributions. Its speeches and the proposals on international monetary reform are backed up with money. For example, China was among the first countries at the London G20 summit to agree to contribute to refilling the coffers of the IMF. The Chinese leadership emphasized that it hoped that China's $50 billion contribution would help stabilize the world economy as a whole, and provide support especially to the most vulnerable developing countries to buffer them against the fallout from the GFC, a crisis not of their making.[34] The third way in which China broke new ground with its

30. Michael Wines, Keith Bradsher, and Mark Landler, "China's Leader Says He is 'Worried' Over US Treasuries," *New York Times,* March 13, 2009, http://www.nytimes.com/2009/03/14/world/asia/14china.html?_r=0.

31. Wang Qishan, "G20 Must Look Beyond the Needs of the Top 20," *The Times*, March 29, 2009 http://www.thetimes.co.uk/tto/law/columnists/article2048640.ece.

32. Hu 2009.

33. Hu 2009.

34. "Analysis: At G20, China Finds Way to Raise Stature in World Finance," April 4, 2009, http://news.xinhuanet.com/english/2009-04/04/content_11129289.htm.

monetary diplomacy post-GFC was its close coordination with other rising states, namely Brazil, Russia, India, and South Africa (as well as other governments in East Asia)[35] to promote international monetary reforms. Chinese officials worked with their counterparts in Brazil and Russia to insist that their contributions of US$10 billion each would be directed, together with China's $50 billion, to purchase the new issuance of SDR-denominated funds from the IMF.

Political Obstacles to the Special Drawing Right

After making their well-publicized contributions to the IMF via the SDR in June 2009, China and the rising states continued their advocacy for reserve diversification onto the next global leaders summit, the gathering of the G8 + G5 in L'Aquila, Italy, on July 9, 2009.[36] According to a European G8 source, in the leadup to the L'Aquila meeting Beijing requested that proposals for a global reserve currency to be put on the agenda.[37] Another source reported that at preparatory talks for the meeting, Beijing had proposed that on the second day of the summit a joint statement on reform of the international monetary system be issued on behalf of the G8 + G5 and Egypt.[38] Prior to the start of summit, Deputy Foreign Minister He Yafei, the Chinese sherpa for the G8 + G5 and the G20, suggested to the Western media that it would be "normal" if the discussion at the summit expanded to include currency issues.[39]

China's advocacy was countered by representatives of the G7 governments, in particular those of Japan, Canada, and Britain. The traditional powers tried to block the upstart from adding the reserve currency issue to the agenda of what was traditionally their club meeting. Japanese representatives dismissed the questioning of the global reserve system as a side

---

35. Chin 2010.

36. The "Group of Five" emerging countries, which met on the sidelines of the G7/8 summit at the invitation of the G8, included Brazil, India, China, South Africa, and Mexico.

37. "Dollar Status Unlikely to be in G8 Communique: G8 Source," Reuters, July 3, 2009, http://www.reuters.com/article/2009/07/03/us-g8-summit-currency-idUSL325178220090703.

38. Ibid.

39. Noko Yishikawa, "Major Nations Should Back Dollar as Key Currency: Japan", Reuters, July 3, 2009, http://www.reuters.com/article/2009/07/03/us-g8-summit-japan-sb-idUSTRE5621 DR20090703.

issue that could be discussed at the "side meetings" of the G5 emerging economies.[40] Canadian Finance Minister James Flaherty defended the dollar as the reserve currency, saying that it had been a stabilizing force during the ongoing financial crisis.[41] British Prime Minister Gordon Brown questioned the appropriateness of raising the reserve currency question, and suggested that attention should be focused instead on containing the global economic crisis and restoring stability.

Despite the stonewalling from the G7, China, with strong backing from Brazilian President Luiz Inácio Lula da Silva, forged ahead in trying to advance the idea of an expanded role for the SDR. At the morning meeting of the G8 + G5 on July 9, 2009, Chinese State Councillor Dai Bingguo delivered China's official statement on behalf of President Hu Jintao,[42] which included the recommendation that "We should have a better system for reserve currency issuance and regulation, so that we can maintain relative stability of major reserve currencies' exchange rates and promote a diversified and rational international reserve currency system."[43] This message was delivered despite the displeasure of the US and the efforts of the G7 allies to prevent the issue from being discussed.

For China and the BRICS, however, the SDR issue was turning into an uphill battle, despite the fact that the IMF managing director was on side. The American hosts for the next G20 gathering in Pittsburgh (September 29, 2009) once again deflected the calls from the BRICS to place international monetary reform on the agenda. The hosts of the subsequent G20 gathering in Toronto (June 2010) gave no additional backing to discussing the enhancement of the role of the SDR, and kept the discussion to the items that were included in the regular IMF review process.[44] These two summits turned out to be a washout for the BRICS international

40. Ibid.

41. Karim Bardeesy, "Calls Grow to Supplant Dollar as Global Currency," *The Globe and Mail,* July 5, 2009, http://www.theglobeandmail.com/report-on-business/economy/calls-grow-to-supplant-dollar-as-global-currency/article4278221/.

42. Hu Jintao returned to China the night before the G8 + G5 meeting to deal with domestic unrest in the country's far western region.

43. Simon Rabinovitch and Matt Falloon, "China Demands Currency Reform at G8 Summit, Britain Skeptical," Reuters, July 9, 2009, http://www.reuters.com/article/2009/07/09/us-china-economy-currencies-idUSTRE56840F20090709.

44. Brazilian President Lula da Silva chose not to attend the Toronto G20 meeting.

monetary reform agenda.[45] The G7 governments effectively railroaded the calls from the rising powers to focus on international monetary reforms by placing emphasis instead in Pittsburgh and Toronto (and again at the Seoul G20 summit in November 2010) on developing a "Mutual Assessment Process" that was supposed to aid the correction of global imbalances of trade and finance, the principal concern of the deficit countries.

Despite the lack of receptivity from the G7 to further expanding the multilateral reserve asset option (beyond their agreement to support a new SDR allocation in April 2009)[46], Zhou Xiaochuan was undaunted, and at the October 2010 meeting of the IMF and World Bank he again stated his position:

> We hope that the IMF and the World Bank could sum up the experiences and lessons of this global crisis, be modernized with creative thinking and innovation, and rebuild the global economic and financial architecture accommodating new developments and features. The IMF shall adjust its focus of surveillance, paying more attention to the macroeconomic policies of major reserve currency–issuing economies, the financial sector, and the cross-border capital flows. Moreover, it shall refine the international monetary system, keeping the exchange rates of the major reserve currencies relatively stable, while diversifying and rationalizing the system.[47]

The next day (October 9), in China's statement to the IMFC, Zhou singled out the role of the dollar, and the need to move beyond over-reliance on "a" national currency as the world's reserve currency:

> Forty-one years ago, in response to a serious U.S. dollar crisis, the Fund established the Special Drawing Right (SDR) to help maintain international

---

45. The Chinese leadership used Hu Jintao's speeches to stress that the international community needed to strengthen the capacity of the IMF and strengthen supervision of the macroeconomic policies of all economies, especially the major reserve currency-issuing economies. Hu Jintao's speech is summarized in "The Fourth Summit of the Group of Twenty is Held in Toronto, President Hu Jintao Attends the Summit and Delivers an Important Speech," Ministry of Foreign Affairs of the People's Republic of China, June 27, 2010, http://www.fmprc.gov.cn/eng/topics/hjtfwjnd4thG20/t712730.htm.

46. The new SDR allocation in April 2009 was the first since the early 1980s. I thank Eric Helleiner for highlighting this nuance.

47. Zhou 2010a.

monetary stability. However, as developed countries successively moved toward floating exchange rate regimes, the role of the SDR has been overlooked. The current global financial crisis and economic recession, the most severe since the Second World War, has alerted us to the necessity to accelerate the reform of the international monetary system. Conditions should be created to strengthen the role of the SDR. The Fund is about to conduct its review of the SDR. We hope that positive progress will be achieved in a broad range of fields, including improvements in the basket of currencies and strengthening of the SDR's role.[48]

Despite the PBOC's ongoing advocacy on behalf of the SDR at IMF and World Bank meetings for more than a decade, and the fact that the G7 did agree to the first new allocation of SDRs since the early 1980s in April 2009 at the London G20 summit, Beijing found that its efforts to push together with the BRICS nations for further use of the SDR were running into obstacles. The traditional powers remained set on a system anchored on the dollar and the euro as the main options, and with the British pound and the Japanese yen included in the rankings of world's most-traded currencies. The political limits to pursuing international monetary reform and expanded use of the SDR via "global committee" were becoming increasingly apparent to the Chinese.

The limits on China's actual willingness to promote the SDR were also tested during the year of the French presidency of the G20 (January–December 2012). The French had long been critics of America's "exorbitant privilege." French President Sarkozy, and Christine Lagarde as finance minister, continued the tradition of questioning the dollar order at press briefings. In the year prior to taking over the G20 presidency, Nicolas Sarkozy built on the unique diplomatic relationship that his predecessor had forged with China to court the Chinese on working jointly to promote the reform of the international monetary system. Sarkozy believed that gaining unprecedented Chinese support for his agenda would enable him to make some dramatic breakthroughs as global leader. Sarkozy set his sights ambitiously on reining in the US "exorbitant privilege," developing mechanisms for limiting volatility in commodity prices, but also on striking a new consensus on exchange rate management. With the latter, the intentions of the French president ran up against Beijing's interests.

---

48. Zhou 2010b.

Early on, the Chinese leadership reciprocated. In early November 2010, the Chinese president flew to Nice to meet with Sarkozy, prior to then flying back to Asia to attend the Seoul G20 Summit. In statements to the media, Sarkozy said that the "French side is willing to enhance coordination and cooperation with China on international affairs," especially to "cooperate with China closely within the G20 framework and to enhance communication and coordination on . . . efforts to push forward reform of the international monetary system."[49] Upon assuming the G20 presidency in January 2011, Nicolas Sarkozy declared that reform of the international monetary system would be the top priority for the Cannes G20 summit in November.

However, the offer from Sarkozy did not come in the form of a suggestion to co-host an event or a set of meetings, but rather of a request to host and take the lead in a seminar on reforming the international monetary system, early in the French G20 presidency. The French tried to persuade the Chinese that by doing so, they could set the tone and the course for year-long discussions on how to build a more stable and robust international monetary system that would reach a new consensus on currency and exchange rate reforms, trade imbalances, and expanded the use of the SDR. Sarkozy furthermore tried to press Beijing to join the G7 finance grouping, but the Chinese leadership did not reciprocate. Not surprisingly, they maintained the strategic position of "engage, but do not join the G7/8."[50] Chinese policy insiders referred to the G7/8 as the "forum of the rich countries."[51] China's leaders chose to avoid the limelight, and the central bank did not take the lead on the event with the French. In the end, the preparations were devolved to the Track Two level, with a Chinese think tank (the China Center for International and Economic Exchanges) given the task of hosting the meeting, which was held in Nanjing instead of Beijing. Sarkozy attended the event, which took place on March 13, 2011, but his counterpart, Chinese President Hu Jintao, did not attend, nor did Prime Minister Wen Jiabao. The Chinese leadership was represented by

---

49. Both Sarkozy's and Hu Jintao's remarks are summarized in "Hu Jintao Holds Talks with His French Counterpart Sarkozy," Ministry of Foreign Affairs of the People's Republic of China, November 5, 2010, http://www.fmprc.gov.cn/eng/topics/hujintaofangwenfaguoheputa oya/t767230.htm.

50. For the details of China's "engage, but do not join" approach to the G7/8 see Chin 2008.

51. Yu 2005, 194.

Vice Premier Wang Qishan, the lead official on the financial and monetary portfolios.

Skeptics could argue that Beijing balked when it was actually faced with the opportunity to play a bigger role (see Yang Jiang's chapter in this volume for a more extensive treatment of the limits of Chinese monetary diplomacy). They question the seriousness or real desire on the part of the Chinese leadership to advance a program of international systemic change.[52] Such interpretations ignore or misread how the Chinese authorities perceived Sarkozy's intentions at a deeper level. Not without reason, Chinese officials saw the French president's offer for them to host the G20 preparatory meeting as laden with another agenda: the G7 finance agenda of the United States, Britain, and Canada, to push for a more dramatic revaluation of the Chinese currency, and continue to nudge China toward a more flexible exchange rate regime. In field interviews, the author was told that PBOC officials sensed at the initial G20 finance ministers' and central bank governors' meeting under the French G20 presidency in Paris, on February 18–19, 2011, that the Americans and their G7 allies—with the support of the French G20 presidency—would use the March meeting in China to press Beijing on "exchange rate flexibility."[53] The strategy was to put China in the glare of the host's seat, which would make it difficult to deflect the pressure from the United States and the G7 on exchange rate policy. The incentive for China to take on such a role was further reduced when the Obama administration made it increasingly obvious, in the lead up the Nanjing meeting, that it would block the inclusion of the RMB in the SDR basket, threatening a veto at the IMF. Treasury Secretary Geithner stated that the United States would only support the inclusion of the RMB in the SDR basket if China agreed to fulfill three conditions: making the RMB fully convertible, the PBOC fully independent, and the capital account fully open.[54] The Americans knew that the Chinese side would not accept these conditions.

52. I thank one of the anonymous reviewers for emphasizing this point.

53. Author's discussions with researchers of the Chinese Academy of Social Sciences, Beijing, July 2011, September 2012.

54. Jamil Anderlini, "G20 Struggles to Ease Monetary Reform Tensions," *Financial Times,* March 31, 2011, http://www.ft.com/intl/cms/s/0/cb9ee2d8-5b6a-11e0-b965-00144feab49a.html#axzz2h6kxsmCh.

The Chinese response to the French offer could be seen as a lost opportunity to advance the cause of the SDR. This may have been so. Much depends on one's reading of the political feasibility of any effort to advance an alternative reserve currency option by "global committee." A nuanced read would be that the Chinese reaction is an example of China's "transactional diplomacy," where Chinese officials carefully weigh national costs and benefits against those of contributing to the so-called "global public good," and where issues of trust in the Chinese worldview and on the Western side continue to inhibit collective action on "common goals."[55] As it turned out, the meeting in Nanjing was described by those who took part as one of the least constructive G20 gatherings since the crisis. The *Financial Times* reported that the delegates found it difficult to agree on the right way to measure global imbalances, which prevented them from discussing measures that might lead to the imbalances' resolution, while Sarkozy's efforts to instigate a discussion on expanding the SDR basket to include the RMB were met with little enthusiasm.[56] For Beijing, its experience up to that time as a member of the G20 would not have inspired optimism. In Zhou Xiaochuan's 2009 essay, there were hints that Chinese monetary strategists were well aware of the political obstacles to any effort to advance a multilateral reserve option, or any nondollar reserve option: "The reestablishment of a new and widely accepted reserve currency with a stable valuation benchmark may take a long time. The creation of an international currency unit, based on the Keynesian proposal, is a bold initiative that requires extraordinary political vision and courage."[57]

Around the time of the Nanjing G20 gathering, Vice Premier Wang Qishan expressed the view (one that is held widely among the Chinese financial and monetary elite) that global monetary reform is a "long and complex process" that can only be explored and implemented gradually.[58] Li Ruogu similarly warned that despite the "irrationalities" of the current dollar-centered international monetary system, "it would be difficult to find and implement a feasible replacement plan in the short term, so we will still have to travel a relatively long road for reform of the international

---

55. Shambaugh 2013, 127, 154.
56. Anderlini, "G20 Struggles to Ease Monetary Reform Tensions."
57. Zhou 2009, 2.
58. Anderlini, "G20 Struggles to Ease Monetary Reform Tensions."

monetary system."[59] Equally telling about the Chinese strategic perspective is the fact that public opinion shapers such as Huang Xiaopeng, the editor of the *Securities Times* newspaper, injects a dose of realpolitik into the discussion, stating that it is unlikely that the United States will want to see a dilution of its monetary power, and that it will likely resist attempts to strengthen the role of SDRs.[60] Given such caution, and considering the pushback or deliberate evasion that China officials and their BRICS partners encountered when they tried to advocate on behalf of the SDR, there is little wonder the Chinese did not leap at the French offer.

Chinese representatives did, however, continue to push for expanding the role of the SDR and other reforms to the international monetary system at the IMF and World Bank meetings, as well as through the new multilateral dialogue with the BRICS. At the third BRICS summit (April 14, 2011) in Sanya, Hainan Island, which was hosted by China, the BRICS governments issued the following strongly worded assessment: "Recognizing that the international financial crisis has exposed the inadequacies and deficiencies of the existing international monetary and financial system, we support the reform and improvement of the existing international monetary system, with a broad-based international reserve currency system providing stability and certainty."[61] The Sanya Declaration further stated: "We support the reform and improvement of the international monetary system, with a broad-based international reserve system providing stability and certainty. We welcome the current discussion about the role of the SDR in the existing international monetary system including the composition of SDR's basket of currencies."[62] Two days later, at the IMFC meeting in Washington, Yi Gang, PBOC deputy governor, reinforced the Chinese message: "The common view is the current IMS [international monetary system] has drawbacks and needs reform. . . . It is encouraging that the Fund has made numerous studies . . . especially on the currency basket of

59. Simon Rabinovitch, "China Officials Call for Displacing Dollar, in Time," Reuters, July 6, 2009, http://www.reuters.com/article/2009/07/06/us-china-economy-currencies-sb-idUSTRE5650 WO20090706.

60. Huang Xiaopeng, "In Reforming the International Monetary and Financial System, China Should Be Pragmatic" (in Chinese), *Zhongquan shibao* [Securities Times], October 31, 2009, http://ifb.cass.cn/show_news.asp?id=20074).

61. BRICS Leaders 2011.

62. Ibid.

the SDR and the extension of the role of the SDR, and has offered a number of constructive recommendations."[63]

Alternative Multilateralism

In addition to their SDR interventions, the Chinese and other BRICS governments also began to pursue a second stream of intra-BRICS monetary statecraft, starting in 2009, to increase, through collective action, the international use of their national currencies, by using their own currencies for trade and investment among themselves. Brazil appears to have been the initial champion. During the height of the GFC, President Lula da Silva highlighted the instability of the dollar as the reserve currency, and declared boldly that the BRICs should work together to "change the political and trade geography of the world."[64] In May 2009, one month after the London G20 summit, the Brazilian president flew to Beijing to initiate discussions on how the central banks of China and Brazil could work together, so that a portion of their bilateral trade to be conducted in Brazilian reals and Chinese RMB.[65]

The joint communiqué from the first gathering of the BRICs leaders on June 16, 2009, in Yekaterinburg, Russia, did not mention either the SDR or using the currencies of the BRICS countries. In advance of the meeting, however, the Russian leadership stated that the world needed more reserve currencies, including expanded use of the SDR, and the Kremlin revealed that the BRICS leaders would discuss investing their reserves in each other's currencies, settling bilateral trade in domestic currencies and establishing currency swap agreements.[66] Reuters reported that the dollar fell 0.9 percent against a basket of currencies on world markets after these comments.[67] The Brazilian president also said: "We recognize the

63. Yi 2011.

64. Todd Benson and Raymond Colitt, "Brazil Lends IMF Money Ahead of BRIC Summit," Reuters, June 11, 2009, http://in.reuters.com/article/2009/06/10/idINIndia-40228820090610.

65. Ibid.

66. Gleb Bryanski and Guy Faulconbridge, "BRIC Demand More Clout, Steers Clear of Dollar Talk," Reuters, June 16, 2009, http://www.reuters.com/article/2009/06/16/us-bric-sb-id USTRE55F1HY20090616.

67. Naomi Tajitsu, "FOREX-Dollar Stung by Russian Comments, Euro Upon ZEW," Reuters, June 16, 2009, http://in.reuters.com/article/2009/06/16/markets-forex-idINLG43302920090616; Wanfeng Zhou, "Dollar Slides after Russia Comments, BRIC Summit," Reuters, June 16, 2009. http://www.reuters.com/article/2009/06/16/us-markets-forex-idUSTRE5530NQ20090616.

importance of the dollar, and we recognize the importance of the United States. But we also understand that, at this time of change in which no one really knows what is going to happen, it makes sense to start discussing things that five years ago seemed almost prohibited."[68] Chinese president Hu Jintao urged the BRIC countries to "promote diversification of the international monetary system."[69] The final communiqué did state: "We also believe that there is a strong need for a stable, predictable and more diversified international monetary system."[70] After the meeting, Russian President Dmitry Medvedev remarked: "As far as the supranational currency is concerned, all the parties stressed quite an obvious thing—the existing reserve currency baskets and the major reserve currency—the dollar—did not live up to the hopes."[71] The Russian president also suggested that the national currencies of the BRICS be used for their trade.

After Brazil helped to kick-start the currency co-operation, and the Russians provided their support at the initial BRICs gathering, the Chinese played an increasingly important role, especially from 2010 onward. They had already supported Lula's suggestion to explore currency co-operation among the G5 at the next gathering of the rising states, the G8 + G5 meeting in L'Aquila, less than a month after the first BRICS meeting. Lula led the discussion among the G5 countries on using their national currencies to promote trade within the grouping, during the preparatory discussions for the meeting with the G8 the next day.[72] Whereas the Indians reportedly showed little enthusiasm, the Chinese supported the Brazilian effort.[73] As the host of the next BRIC Leaders summit, in Brasilia on April 16, 2010, Lula pressed on, undeterred. The Brazilian

---

68. Benson and Colitt, "Brazil Lends IMF Money Ahead of BRIC Summit."

69. Chris Buckley, "Much-Trumpeted BRIC Summit Ends Quietly," Reuters, June 17, 2009, http://www.reuters.com/article/2009/06/17/us-bric-summit-idUSTRE55G20B20090617.

70. BRIC Leaders 2009.

71. "Medvedev Calls for Use of National Currencies in Trade," Russian Television, June 17, 2009, http://rt.com/news/medvedev-calls-for-use-of-national-currencies-in-trade/.

72. Group of Five 2009.

73. After the G5 meeting, Indian Foreign Secretary Shivshankar Menon acknowledged that the G5 had suggested the use of their own currencies to settle trade among themselves, but predicted that the issue was unlikely to see much progress as financial markets, which are wary to risks to US asset values, are highly sensitive to the debate. Phil Stewart and Matt Falloon, "G8 Welcomes Developing States, Eyes Climate and Trade," Reuters, July 8, 2010, http://mobile.reuters.com/article/topNews/idUSTRE5662VJ20090708?i=27.

president scored two achievements of particular note: first, the national development banks of the BRICS countries (and the State Export-Import Bank of India) signed a pact to facilitate mutual economic co-operation and trade, including co-financing of projects in infrastructure, energy, industry, high technology, and exports; and second, the leaders of the BRICS nations pledged in their joint communiqué to explore the potential for supporting regional monetary arrangements and local currency trade settlement arrangements.[74]

These initial discussions between the rising powers on international currency collaboration provided the base for more detailed intra-BRICS currency agreements by 2011, and especially from 2012 onward. At the Sanya summit of BRICS leaders in April 2011, the heads of the BRICS national development banks and the State Export-Import Bank of India forged ahead to sign an agreement on settlement of trade and investment using their own currencies, and a day later, signed a framework agreement on financial cooperation, before the leaders of the BRICS nations.[75] The China Development Bank lent its clout and resources to the cause. Chen Yuan, former central bank deputy governor and chairman of the CDB, provided normative support for pursuing reserve diversification together with the BRICS: "It is in the interest of all to practice lending and settlement in local [their own national] currencies," and he urged the BRICS nations to increase multicurrency trade settlement and lending in a "practical and efficient way."[76] Chen also registered China's commitment to the cause when he noted that although no specific details were listed in the framework agreement, it could nonetheless be expected that the CDB would provide RMB lending to the other four BRICS members of around RMB10 billion (US$1.53 billion) by the end of the year. It was a rather bold statement given that previous to 2011, the CDB had not lent in RMB to the other members of the group.[77]

---

74. BRIC Leaders 2010.

75. Wang Xiaotian, "BRICS Target Global Economic Reform," *China Daily,* April 15, 2011, http://www.chinadaily.com.cn/cndy/2011-04/15/content_12329794.htm.

76. The statements by Chen Yuan are quoted in Wang Xiaotian, Li Xiaokun, and Ma Liyao, "Banks Close to Agreement on Local Currency Settlement," *China Daily,* April 14, 2011, http://www.chinadaily.com.cn/china/brics2011/2011-04/14/content_12323493.htm.

77. Wang, "BRICS Target Global Economic Reform."

The intra-BRICS discussions of the bank chiefs at Sanya were especially important because they opened the way for more intensive examination among the BRICS governments of how the BRICS could act collectively to open up credit and financial markets in their currencies, as well as of possibilities for collaboration on bond issues in those currencies, and of establishing new markets for assets denominated in BRICS currencies.[78] The discussions at Sanya provided the foundation for the Indians to drive ahead at the next gathering of the BRICS Leaders on March 29, 2012 in New Delhi, when the heads of the national development banks signed two agreements that entailed more detailed commitments. Under the first agreement, credits were to be extended among the BRICS countries and denominated in their national currencies. According to the official statement, the agreement was "intended to reduce the demand for fully convertible currencies for transactions among the BRICS nations, and thereby help reduce the transaction costs of intra-BRICS trade."[79] The second agreement aimed to ease the confirmation of letters of credit upon receipt of a request from the BRICS country exporter, or the exporter's bank, or the indemnifying party, or the importer's bank. This agreement aimed to "help reduce trade transaction costs, besides promoting intra-BRICS trade."[80] Chinese officials and their BRICS partners envisage that these gradual steps will, cumulatively, strengthen co-operation among the BRICS development banks and promote intra-BRICS trade, and that as a result the international use of the currencies of the BRICS countries will increase, reliance on third-party currencies can be reduced, and foreign exchange and balance of payments pressures on the BRICS nations can also be minimized.

This element of monetary statecraft and diplomacy could gradually become more important over time to China and the other rising states, and appears to be a more direct means for them to work collectively to push for reserve diversification than the SDR route. As mentioned above, the SDR has run into growing disinterest, or conscious neglect, within

78. See the statements by Luciano Coutinho, president of BNDES, and Vladimir Dmitriev, chairman of Vnesheconombank, in Wang et al., "Banks Close to Agreement on Local Currency Settlement."

79. BRICS Development Bank 2012.

80. BRICS Development Bank 2012.

the G20 process. It needs to be acknowledged that these initiatives are only the beginning of experiments to move in this direction. Among the currencies of the BRICS nations, only China's ranks in the top ten most-traded currencies.[81] Nonetheless, data from the Bank for International Settlements (mid-2013) show that the Mexican peso, the Russian ruble, the Turkish lira, the South African rand, and the Brazilian real also accounted for a larger slice of global currency flows than before; which suggests that there is potential for emerging-market currencies to move up the rankings.[82] The litmus test for reserve diversification is whether the currencies of China and the BRICS can eventually displace some of the mid- and lower-range members of the current top ten, such as the Australian dollar, the Swiss franc, and the Canadian dollar.

The Pragmatic Option

After two years of advocacy together with the other rising states, it was becoming increasingly evident to Beijing that clear and present obstacles stood in the way of expanding the role for the SDR as a multilateral reserve option. One of the key policy entrepreneurs of "Greater China," Joseph Yam, the former chief executive of the Hong Kong Monetary Authority, has highlighted the geopolitical pushback that can be expected against any serious effort to promote a nondollar alternative reserve option. Yam writes that "there is little doubt" that the international monetary system "needs fixing. The difficult question, as always, is how."[83] Yam suggests that the political reality is that countries whose currencies currently play a reserve role are "unlikely to agree to any proposals to activate the SDR." Such a move would mean asking the major reserve-issuing countries to voluntarily give up a degree of their seigniorage, subject themselves to tighter fiscal and monetary discipline, erode some of the international competitiveness of their financial institutions, reduce international demand for assets denominated in their national currencies, and increase the cost of borrowing in their currencies. He argues that, given the political

---

81. Bank for International Settlements 2013.
82. Bank for International Settlements 2013.
83. Yam 2010, 6.

realities, "pragmatism dictates" that the best way to diversify the international monetary system is to encourage the more widespread use of a wider range of alternative reserve assets, and not focus only on the SDR. Yam emphasizes: "where encouragement is needed most is therefore in the use of the renminbi."[84]

Cross-border use of the RMB is, in fact, increasing rapidly, in a process that combines the interaction of states and market actors (see the chapter by Jonathan Kirshner in this volume). State intervention has been crucial in establishing the enabling policies, regulations, and institutional support for this. Since December 2008, China has signed currency swap agreements with twenty-three countries and regions, including trading giants Japan and South Korea, emerging economies such as Brazil and Turkey, and resource-rich Australia (totaling RMB 2.48 trillion, according to PBOC data cited by *China Daily* in mid-October 2013).[85]

Malaysia, Chile, Nigeria, Kenya, and other countries have now included the RMB as one of the foreign currencies in their reserve baskets. With respect to market actors, senior Chinese officials, such as Chen Yuan, suggest that "more and more trade and investment partners, in various countries, are willing to accept the RMB as a settlement currency."[86] The latest data from the Bank for International Settlements support this view, as well as the contention that RMB internationalization appears to be the path of least resistance, and the most direct route for China to promote reserve diversification.

According to BIS data, in early September 2013 the RMB climbed into the ranks of the most-traded international currencies when it surpassed the Swedish krona and the New Zealand dollar, rising to ninth most-actively traded currency globally.[87] Referencing survey data from April 2013, the BIS reported that trading in the Chinese currency had more than tripled over the past three years, to the equivalent of $120 billion a day in early 2013 (by comparison, US dollar trading averaged $4.65 trillion a

---

84. Yam 2010, 6.
85. Li Xiang and Zhang Chunyan, "Currency Swap Signed with the EU a 'landmark,'" October 11, 2013, http://www.chinadaily.com.cn/china/2013-10/11/content_17022147.htm.
86. The statements by Chen Yuan are quoted in Wang Yi, "Chen Yuan: Insist on International Reserve Currency Diversification," *Caijing,* November 10, 2011.
87. Bank for International Settlements 2013.

day in 2013), constituting a share of 2.2 percent of global foreign exchange volumes. Previously, in February 2013, the Society for Worldwide Interbank Financial Telecommunication (SWIFT) had reported that the RMB had surpassed the Russian ruble and the Danish krone, rising to thirteenth place on the list of payment currencies, a dramatic gain from twentieth place in January 2012 when the RMB had been used for 0.25 percent of global payments.[88] The proponents of RMB cross-border use would highlight that the increase in the RMB's use for global payments to 0.63 percent, though still relatively small, was an increase of 24 percent on the previous month and a year-on-year increase of 171 percent, measured by transaction value.[89] We should be mindful, however, not to overstate the recent trends. There is a long way to go before the dollar loses its singular dominance. As of early 2013, 62 percent of the world's currency reserves were still denominated in dollars ($3.7 trillion of the $6 trillion in allocated foreign exchange holdings of the world's central banks), according to IMF statistics.[90] The proponents of the dollar's continued dominance would suggest that the dollar has maintained its status as the general safe haven in times of recent trouble, including the GFC. The RMB skeptics would rightfully emphasize the small volume of the RMB's 0.63 percent of global payments in January 2013, that the leading world payments currency, the euro, accounted for 40.17 percent of transactions, and that the dollar accounted for 33.48 percent (which, according to SWIFT data, was an increase from 29.73 percent in January 2012).[91]

The growth in the international use of the RMB reflects the emerging reality that foreign and Chinese market actors can achieve benefits from using the RMB, such as payments flexibility and gains in their bottom lines. For corporations that trade with China, using RMB can lower their foreign exchange costs and risks. Some Chinese companies also offer price discounts for using RMB to settle payments and Chinese exporters tend to raise prices on foreign currency transactions as a cushion against potential foreign exchange fluctuations. One estimate is that overseas importers can

---

88. Michael Barris, "Yuan Rises to 13th as Payment Currency," *China Daily,* February 28, 2013, http://europe.chinadaily.com.cn/business/2013-02/28/content_16264385.htm.

89. For the data see ibid.

90. International Monetary Fund 2013a.

91. The data are in Barris, "Yuan Rises to 13th as Payment Currency."

save 2–3 percent on their invoices by paying in RMB.[92] These factors have contributed to a sixfold increase in RMB trade settlement in the past three years, with financial institutions in Asia, as well as in the UK, France, and Germany, increasingly adopting the RMB to support trade settlement for their corporate customers. While these gains are impressive, a senior business manager for SWIFT cautioned that the RMB is still a "very young currency" and "it takes many, many years to establish a currency" in the international marketplace.[93]

The scenario that is currently envisaged by the Chinese leadership is the RMB joining the top ranks of the world's two or three most-traded currencies, and becoming one of the major reserve currencies. Interestingly, while the use of the euro for global payments dropped to 40.7 percent by January 2013, from a previous high of 44.04 percent in January 2012, use of the RMB for global payments increased 171 percent during the same period.[94] Some observers predict that the plans of the US Federal Reserve to reduce its monetary stimulus could also hasten more widespread use of the RMB.[95] Perhaps most interesting and relevant, a survey by global payment services firm Western Union Business Solutions shows that RMB payments by American companies were up almost 90 percent during the first half of 2013 from the same period in 2012. The survey further showed that RMB transactions now represent 12 percent of US payments to China, up from 8.5 percent in the first half of 2012.[96]

In the wake of the 2008–9 GFC, China and its BRICS partners have pursued international monetary reform, and specifically reserve diversification, by trying to promote the international use of a multilateral asset, the SDR, as well as that of their own currencies. The analysis suggests that China and the BRICS have contributed to the modest increase in the role

92. Nathan Lai, "Why RMB Globalization Is Still a Ways Off," *Asian Banking and Finance,* September 18, 2013, http://asianbankingandfinance.net/custody-clearing/commentary/why-rmb-globalization-still-long-way-off.

93. James Wills, a senior business manager for SWIFT, quoted in Barris, "Yuan Rises to 13th as Payment Currency."

94. The data are from Barris, "Yuan Rises to 13th as Payment Currency."

95. Nicole Hong, Clare Connaghan, and Tom Orlik, "Milestone for Yuan Marks Rise of China," *Wall Street Journal,* September 5, 2013, http://online.wsj.com/article/SB10001424127887323623304579056704113253902.html.

96. Ibid.

of the SDR, when they helped to realize the new SDR allocation after the London G20 summit, but they have also become more aware of some of the political obstacles that stand in the way of further developing the SDR into a credible multilateral reserve option. Arguably more significant, over the medium term, is the fact that China and its BRICS partners have also forged a second stream of currency co-operation that focuses on increasing the international use of their own currencies to settle their trade and investment with each other, and on opening up, expanding, and reshaping global currency markets by developing money markets for their currencies. These initiatives are still more a pledge than a reality at this stage. Moreover, the current economic downturn in Brazil, India, and South Africa will likely affect the international demand for their currencies. Nonetheless, China and the BRICS are taking steps forward with each successive BRICS summit, putting more concrete detail, specific commitments, and action for follow-up into each set of formal agreements.

Most important, China has been taking concerted steps to increase cross-border use of the RMB. As of September 2013, the RMB only occupies the ninth place in the rankings of the world's most-traded international currencies. Furthermore, as a number of commentators have emphasized (including Jonathan Kirshner in this volume), some significant domestic constraints and obstacles must be overcome for the RMB to ascend to the top of the global payments and most-traded currency rankings. Nonetheless, the overall trend suggests that there is real demand for the RMB as an international currency, from state and market actors and across various regions of the world. The combination of structural trends and the policy and regulatory innovations introduced by the Chinese government and its currency partners, suggest that the currency of the world's second largest economy is set to play a greater role in the international monetary system.

It is still early days for each of the international currency initiatives that China is supporting or driving, including the internationalization of the RMB. If China is successful in advancing greater international use of the RMB and the RMB takes on the attributes of a reserve currency, and if the BRICS achieve even modest and incremental success in promoting increasing international use of their currencies (which would include the RMB), then the net effect, over the medium term, would be an expansion of the range of reserve currency options for states and market actors, and the reshaping and opening up of global currency markets, in which the national currencies of China and the BRICS nations play a more prominent role in the international monetary system. In so doing, China will have effectively exercised one dimension of structural power in its international monetary relations—expanding the range of options for itself and others.

Perhaps less obvious, by increasing the international use of the RMB and turning it into one of the major reserve currencies, China will have helped effect another major international monetary outcome: reducing or constraining the policy space of the United States. In such a scenario, through structural discipline China may, indirectly, prompt the United States to do something that it has been unwilling to take on during the last two decades: exercise greater fiscal discipline and tighten its monetary and financial policy. This is, arguably, the deeper meaning behind Chen Yuan's rather diplomatic words that, by proceeding in a manner that is "steady and orderly," the internationalization of the RMB will "exert correspond-ing influence in promoting the establishment of a scientific, reasoned, stable, and orderly international currency system."[97] Li Ruogu was more explicit in discussing how currency diversification, including RMB inter-nationalization, would have a constraining effect on US economic policy space. Speaking to a largely domestic audience at the Lujiazui Financial Forum in Shanghai, in April 2012, the forceful president of China Exim Bank, said: "If the US is not willing to discuss this problem [US financial debt and management of the dollar as a reserve currency], China has an old saying that 'the situation forces people to become strong,' and when the time comes, the United States will have to agree whether it likes it or not, because use of the US dollar would have decreased. As other currencies are used more, then this problem is solved."[98] At this point, these state-ments are more wishful thinking than a reality. However, the statements do hint at broader ambitions, and more fundamental adjustments to the international monetary system. The fact that the Chinese critique of the dollar-centered reserve system dates back more than a decade, and that its origins can be traced back to 1999, shows that these ambitions have deep strategic roots.

97. Quoted in Wang, "Chen Yuan."

98. Li Ruogu's statement is quoted in "Dai Xianglong: RMB Internationalization Depends on the Market Not Allies" (in Chinese), *Nandu City Newspaper,* April 4, 2012, http://sina.com.cn.

8

REGIONAL HEGEMONY AND AN EMERGING RMB ZONE

Jonathan Kirshner

Unless something goes terribly wrong with China's economy (a possibility not to be casually dismissed, even if it is not the most likely outcome), China will look to increase the international use of the RMB and eventually seek to establish its currency as the international money of East Asia. Over the coming years and decades the RMB will grow into this role at a rate determined by the shape of China's financial sector, the aggregate performance of its economy, and the pace and style of its financial liberalization. But these factors will influence the contours of the RMB's emergence; its growing role and influence are a virtual certainty. In this chapter I argue that two core motivations will guide this policy of facilitating and

I thank Eric Helleiner, Gregory Chin, Benjamin Cohen, Sarah Eaton, two anonymous referees, and the participants at the workshop on The Politics of China's Role in the International Monetary System for comments on earlier drafts of this chapter, as well as Wendy Leutert for research assistance (and all translations), and the Princeton Institute for International and Regional Studies, where I was the World Politics Visiting Fellow in 2012–13. This chapter draws on material in Kirshner 2014.

encouraging the emergence of the RMB as a regional currency: China's search for enhanced economic autonomy, and its quest for increased political influence. These are the two reasons that great powers have routinely sought to expand the international use of their currencies throughout modern history. And in the case of contemporary China, each of these motivations is particularly acute. Although the (often implicit) desire to enhance international influence has typically been the primary motive for states seeking to encourage the international use of their currencies, in the case of contemporary China the aspiration for greater autonomy in the wake of the global financial crisis has accelerated this impulse.[1] The crisis, especially understood in the context of the Asian financial crisis just ten years earlier, has undermined the legitimacy of the United States–championed, dollar-centric, unregulated financial order. After the crisis, China prefers to establish some distance from the dollar, and to explore distinct approaches to economic governance that offer some alternative to radically unmediated global finance. With regard to political influence, as an emerging great power (with aspirations to regional hegemony) in a crowded geopolitical neighborhood where states tend to pursue internationally oriented growth strategies and are wary of naked power plays, China will find that encouraging the regional use of the yuan in an effort to enhance its political influence an especially attractive strategy.

In this chapter, I first review how and why encouraging international use of home currency has been so instinctively appealing for powerful states throughout modern history. I then explain why China's ambitions for a more influential RMB, which had been cautiously emerging, have been accelerated by the global financial crisis. Key themes here include what I call "buyer's remorse," a greater desire for macroeconomic insulation, and the acceleration of the underlying trends that have been contributing to the emergence of the yuan as an international currency. An additional and crucial factor in motivating a greater role for the RMB is then considered—the delegitimization of the American model of capitalism, which had been in ascendance since the end of the Cold War, and was increasingly seen as the only game in town at the turn of the twenty-first century. I then review some of the official measures designed to promote

---

1. Beijing has always craved autonomy, even more than influence; in this instance, increasing the international role of the RMB will serve both objectives.

the increased international use of the RMB (and some of the potential limitations to that process). A brief conclusion considers some of the international political implications of the emerging global monetary order.

The framework laid out in the introduction to this volume is engaged in this chapter in the following way: my argument is that China is interested in promoting RMB internationalization and challenging the international dominance of the dollar, motivated to enhance both its "power-as-influence" (over other states, especially in East Asia) and "power-as-autonomy." To be clear, I do not argue that the yuan will displace the dollar as the preeminent global currency. Rather, I expect it to encroach on the influence of the (still formidable) US dollar and eventually emerge as the dominant currency in East Asia. As such, I see China as a rising power that is no longer a "rule-taker," accepting the status quo with regard to the general arrangement of international monetary order. Rather, I envision China as some combination of a "rule-maker" (promoting global reforms), and a "rule-breaker," (in that it will create its own arrangements), though "breaker" is perhaps too strong a word for the expectations here, as that implies a "demand for wholesale transformation," and is suggestive of a petulant withdrawal from existing institutions. More likely China will work for reform within existing institutions, while simultaneously pursuing its own international arrangements on a parallel and not incompatible track.[2] Although a variety of factors will influence the disposition and trajectory of Chinese policy, this chapter emphasizes what the introduction describes as "external" sources of motivation. In particular, the global financial crisis (which was a critical juncture that altered thinking about international monetary relations) and the country's geostrategic context (its continuing emergence as a great power) are the main engines of policy choice emphasized here.

The Political Economy of Monetary Ambition

States that pursue leadership of regional (or global) monetary orders are almost always motivated by *political* concerns—in particular, the desire

---

2. China is a major stakeholder in the stability of the current system and the viability of the US dollar. In this sense especially, it has no incentive to "break" the system, even as it seeks greater voice, influence, authority, and autonomy, and even as it anticipates the RMB encroaching on the dollar's influence.

to gain enhanced influence over other states, and for greater autonomy more generally; that is, for the greater freedom of action provided by a buffer from external pressures and constraints. Indeed, such currency fiefdoms are typically money-losers, as leaders knowingly and willingly offer perks and otherwise spend cash in an unacknowledged effort to purchase power and influence. Thus although leadership of a currency area does provide new levers of coercive power, the appeal and pursuit of "structural" power, as I have argued previously, is so coveted that it inhibits the overt or coercive exercise of currency power within zones of monetary influence.[3] Following logic first articulated by Hirschman with regard to international trade, small states can become conditioned upon and vulnerable to the whims of their larger partners in asymmetric economic relations. Hirschman, for the most part, emphasized vulnerability: the implicit threat by the larger state to terminate the relationship, the consequences of which would be disproportionately felt by the smaller. But in practice, it is the conditioning rather than the vulnerability that is both more cultivated and more politically consequential. Within small states, actors that benefit from participation tend to thrive and are empowered. And at the aggregate level, although it is true that states may fear offending their larger patrons, much more profoundly, over time, they quite voluntarily come to recalculate the definition of their own national interests. Given their external economic associations and shifts in the balance of domestic political power, small states can increasingly see their own interests as progressively more in accord with those of their most intimate economic associates.[4]

With notable consistency, most states that have been in a position to extend their monetary influence have attempted to do so.[5] As early as the

---

3. Inhibits, in that the overriding desire for structural power creates strong disincentives, but this does not rule out the possibly that overt coercive power will be exercised. See Kirshner 1995.

4. Kirshner 1995; Hirschman 1980 [1945]; Abdelal and Kirshner 1999, 119–56.

5. Benjamin Cohen, in this volume, emphasizes that this need not be the case. He notes German reluctance, and Japanese ambivalence, regarding the internationalization of their currencies in the 1980s. Eric Helleiner is also skeptical about overstating claims regarding the inevitability of internationalization, adding US postwar discouragement of Latin American dollarization as another example. These points are well taken, but I would argue that for states with growing international political ambitions, the default setting remains that they will seek to extend the influence of their currencies abroad, and that exceptions are, indeed, exceptional. For example, had global economic trends from the 1980s continued, it is likely that the yen would have taken on a much larger global role. The foreign policy of postwar Germany was greatly influenced by the fact that it

1860s, France's efforts to establish the Latin Monetary Union reflected an "express desire to see all continental Europe united in a franc area which would exclude and isolate Germany." French leaders made every effort to manage the union and keep it alive; the modest 1930s notion of a "gold bloc" was a coda to those efforts. France also cultivated the use of the franc or franc-based currencies first in its colonies, and later, at considerable expense, in the franc zone of former colonies. (Even critics of participation in the franc zone acknowledged that from an economic perspective, the affiliation was beneficial to its members.) Nazi Germany and imperial Japan extended their monetary influence in support of their interwar grand strategies, and, after spending the first few decades after World War II in the penalty box, by the 1980s each was harboring renewed (if considerably more benign) monetary ambitions. The German mark was the anchor of the European Monetary System; the yen, whose experience provides important insights into contemporary Chinese motives, choices, and behavior, seemed for a time on the cusp of mounting a challenge to the dollar. British sterling, of course, served as the world's currency for over a century, before diminishing to the sterling area and then the sterling zone, which, even when reduced to a smaller, defensive organization, provided a crucial source of financing during World War II. Finally, the United States, even with an immature and skeletal domestic financial system, during the first third of the twentieth century extended, if on an ad hoc basis, its monetary reach within the Western Hemisphere and sought to promote New York City as an international financial center. In the second half of the century, the Americans bankrolled the dollar-based gold exchange standard of the Bretton Woods system, and spent a decade tolerating exceptions and waiting for its Cold War allies to recover to an extent that would permit them to play by its rules.[6]

The experiences of Britain and the United States also call attention to the potentially extractive, exploitative, and ultimately burdensome attributes of sitting at the center of a monetary order. Britain called upon the financial resources of the sterling system during World War II without so much

---

was, in Peter Katzenstein's phrase, a "semi-sovereign state," and as the United States was discouraging Latin dollarization, it was also mounting heroic efforts to organize the entire global monetary order around the dollar as the world's currency.

6. Kirshner 1995, 244, 246, 261, 268; De Cecco 1984, 44; Willis 1901; Rosenberg 1985.

as asking, and was saddled with the difficulties of managing the postwar "sterling balances," a significant overhang of liabilities that hampered its economic policymaking for decades. And the United States forced the burden of adjustment upon others—and not for the last time—when it suddenly ended the Bretton Woods system by closing the gold window.[7] But these elements and observations, important for a comprehensive accounting of the political economy of international currency use, are of limited or ironic relevance for China's emerging monetary ambitions. When states embark on the project of extending their monetary influence, then and now, they are usually, as is contemporary China, on the rise, and invariably looking to enhance their structural power. Efforts at economic exploitation would undercut, not enhance, such ambitions, and the opportunities and/or headaches of mature or even senescent monetary arrangements are unlikely to factor as significant considerations given the time horizons of the confident leadership present at the creation. But immediate reactions to perceived exploitation by the issuer of a currency that is perhaps past the peak of its appeal—this, ironically, can serve to spur states into taking on more of an ambitious monetary role. In addition, and as a separate matter, the instabilities associated with the age of globalized finance have created an additional incentive for states to increase the supply of regional monetary arrangements; as well as increased the demand of smaller states for opportunities to shelter from global financial storms.[8] These concerns have contributed to successive phases of European monetary integration, and have spurred both Japan and now China into thinking more about monetary leadership in East Asia.

The Japanese experience from the late 1980s holds a number of lessons that provide insight into the case of contemporary China. There are some remarkable parallels between the two episodes. As Japan emerged as the second largest economy in the world—and by many heady accounts of the day was seemingly poised to become "number one"—the sky seemed the limit, and many Japanese officials imagined an internationalized yen as a major currency as a means of further enhancing Japan's growing influence. But with the stagnation of the Japanese economy in the 1990s (and

---

7. Strange 1971, Walter 1991.

8. On structural power in monetary affairs, see Helleiner 2006a, 84; on the increased demand for insulation see Cooper 2006; Kirshner 2006, 171, 174, 156.

the resurgence of growth in the United States), such attitudes fell into re-mission, only to resurface, in a very different guise, in the wake of the Asian financial crisis. After that crisis, a revived interest in a larger role for the yen was rooted in defensive motivations—the search for greater insu-lation, autonomy, and more distance from the American vision of global financial order. As William Grimes explained, the revived debate was now "fundamentally about *insulation*," rooted in disenchantments—with the instability associated with (American-championed) uninhibited financial globalization and deregulation, with the US ability to shift macroecono-mic burdens of adjustment abroad (and chronic American pressure over ex-rate issues), and with the more general implications of the ideological divergence between the United States and Japan over their respective reac-tions to the Asian financial crisis. Throughout Asia in general there was "profound resentment" over the American response to the crisis, which created new incentives for and receptivity to greater regional cooperation that would provide some distance from the American model. This all also was in part a reaction to US behavior that followed a pattern described by Andrew Walter: when building an international monetary order, sys-tem leaders start out with considerable self-restraint; at the height of their power, they are increasingly tempted to exploit the advantages presented by their privileged status; and in relative decline, the accumulation of such transgressions encourages "the emergence of rival lead currencies and as-sociated financial centers."[9]

The aborted Japanese efforts at a more capacious, internationalized yen offer crucial lessons for understanding the likely behavior of China in the coming years. Once again, such efforts illustrate the tendency for ambi-tious plans for a more assertive presence in the international money game to flow naturally from the momentum and confidence of more general economic rise. They serve as a reminder that such ambitions have impor-tant defensive components—ones that Japan then shares with China now: the desire for insulation from the instabilities associated with financial glo-balization; irritation with the American tendency to use its key currency status to force burdens of adjustment abroad; and ideological alienation

9. Grimes 2003, 177, 180, 181 (quote), 183–84, 193–94; Henning 2006, 133 (resentment), 138; Walter 2006, 69. See also Kirshner 2006, 151; Katada 2002, 86; Helleiner 1992, 434–37.

from the US vision of a completely unmediated global financial order. Finally, even as China's continued economic and political rise seems like the most likely trajectory, the Japanese experience serves as a reminder of the mistakes analysts can make in casually projecting underlying trends indefinitely into the future. Nor should this admonition be taken lightly. It is easy—all too easy—to imagine circumstances that would lead to an interruption of China's decades-long string of remarkable economic growth.

China's Monetary Ambitions and Their Acceleration

Prior to the global financial crisis, RMB internationalization was already a gleam in the eye of elites in China, but it was understood that the yuan was a long way off from serving as an important international currency. The dominant position of the dollar, the emergence of the euro, and the fragility of China's sheltered, murky domestic financial sector (in contrast with the venerable institutions and market powerhouses to be found in the West) tempered expectations about how quickly the RMB might take its place as a currency widely used in international transactions, let alone held as a reserve asset. Nevertheless, such ambitions, however distant, were clearly harbored, and as China continued its rise to great power status it was natural to assume that a greater international role for a maturing RMB would be part of that process.

On the one hand, before the global financial crisis, it was understood that the Anglo-American financial model was the only game in town, and that convergence toward that model was the path that China was taking. On the other hand, China had always been wary of exposing itself to international capital markets, and had understood that its controls had spared it from the Asian financial crisis and other tumult that had characterized global finance in a succession of crises since the mid-1990s. From the early 2000s, China embarked on a cautious path that accommodated controlled RMB appreciation and modest movements toward financial liberalization—if nevertheless always alert to concerns about the tendency of the United States to shift the burden of adjustment abroad. The example of Japan, pressured by the United States into appreciations that were seen as contributing to that country's economic malaise, was routinely invoked. Pushing further into the decade, China's continued economic growth and its massive and increasing holdings of dollar assets assured that, at the very least, discussions of the country's role as a potential powerhouse would take place. On the eve of the crisis, it would be hard to take issue with the assessment of Chin and Helleiner, who argued that China's position as a creditor had increased its autonomy and influence, that it would seek greater financial independence from the United States, and look, cautiously, to enhance its regional role, but that nevertheless it also faced considerable challenges on this path. In sum, they concluded, "China's power in the international financial system, certainly growing, should not be overestimated."[10]

But the global financial crisis changed this. It accelerated the process of RMB internationalization, *and* it ended the project of convergence toward the American model. Thus the crisis both provided a new impetus to and urgency regarding the promotion of the yuan, and it also altered the trajectory of its path. (Gregory Chin, in this volume, also sees a "significant shift" in Beijing's disposition with regard to international monetary reform more generally in the wake of the crisis.) By exposing profound flaws in the American model, the crisis elicited what can be called "buyer's remorse" in China, with regard to its development model that had bound it so tightly to the (weaker than previously assumed) US economy and made it such a stakeholder in the (even more vulnerable than once thought) US dollar. The crisis also redoubled the (already robust) wariness of Chinese elites about the risk of exposure to the global financial economy and reinforced demands for insulation. And the relative rates of recovery in the half-decade that followed the crisis—swift in China, sluggish in the United States (and Europe)—magnified the preexisting trends that were already suggestive of a rising China. Its rate of economic growth might yet slow down—might even likely slow down—but to a large extent, China is not simply emerging, it has arrived as major player on world markets.[11]

---

10. Chin and Helleiner 2008, 87 (quote), 92, 97–98, 99. See also Walter and Howie 2011, ix–x, 3; Foot and Walter 2011, 117, 120, 123, 265–70.

11. In the ten years leading up to the global financial crisis (1998–2007), China's economic growth averaged 9.95 percent per year while the US averaged 3.02 percent. China was becoming an important engine of global economic growth and the gap between the absolute size of the two economies was narrowing. The crisis only accelerated those trends. From 2008 to 2012, the Chinese economy averaged an annual rate of growth of 9.26 percent; the American economy 0.58 percent. Put another way, at the end of 2012, China's economy was 55 percent larger than it had been in 2007; the US economy was not quite 3 percent larger. Other factors tell a similar story of China's astonishing rise. Its imports, for example, soared from $132 billion in 1995 to $561 billion in 2004 to $1.7 trillion in 2011; in 2009, China became the world's second importer, behind only the United States.

Finally, and crucially, the crisis delegitimized the American model that China had been cautiously tacking toward right up until the crisis, if invariably at a rate deemed inadequate by its American tutors. Just months before the crisis, US Treasury Secretary Paulson was (again) lecturing that "the risks for China are greater in moving too slowly than in moving too quickly" with financial liberalization. This was revealed to be transparently wrong, and the American black eye from the financial crisis was not just material, but ideational. Since the end of the Cold War, the United States had benefited from what Ikenberry and Kupchan dubbed "hegemonic socialization"—its power enhanced by the fact that foreign elites had bought into the merits of its model. With the American model at the epicenter of the catastrophic global financial crisis, the reverse was taking place, as elites, especially in Asia, now searched for alternatives to and distance from that delegitimized approach.[12]

RMB internationalization is seen as a necessary corrective for buyer's remorse. "When we were elated about the rapid growth in foreign reserves, China had unconsciously fallen into a 'dollar trap,'" explained Yu Yongding, former Director of the Institute of World Economics and Politics at the Chinese Academy of Social Sciences. It was now necessary to hold fewer dollar assets, and, to promote this, "the internationalization of the RMB truly is an important option for China." This conclusion has been reached by a number of elites, academics, and public officials throughout the People's Republic. "As the U.S.'s largest official creditor, the Chinese government has discovered that it relies too much on the dollar in international trade, international capital flows, and foreign exchange reserve management," another well-placed observer concluded, "and that this overreliance contained a huge risk."[13]

Buyer's remorse also reflects a greater disenchantment with the US management of the dollar and its role in the international financial system more generally, two things about which Chinese observers are increasingly critical. These reassessments have contributed to a desire for insulation from anticipated future instability caused by American mismanagement

---

12. Geoff Dyer, "Paulson Urges Beijing to Speed Up Reform," *Financial Times,* March 8, 2007; Ikenberry and Kupchan 1990.

13. Yu 2011 (first quote); Zhang 2009b (second quote); see also Lieberthal and Wang (2012, 15) on concerns for the future of the dollar and "some urgency to internationalize the Renminbi."

and to demands for reform of the global macroeconomic order for similar reasons. The United States, from this perspective, is also inadequately attentive to the global implications of its management of the dollar. American policies force others to adjust "in accordance with the needs of the U.S. dollar," argues Li Ruogu, chairman and president of the China Export-Import Bank; "the U.S used this method to topple Japan's economy, and it wants to use this method to curb China's development." RMB internationalization is necessary to reform, and to pluralize, the international monetary system. "Only by eliminating the U.S. dollar's monopolistic position" can the system be reformed. Li Yang, vice president of the Academy of Social Sciences, offers a similar analysis. Attributing the unsatisfactory response of the International Monetary Fund to the Asian financial crisis to the underrepresentation of Asian voices and interests, he holds that "actively promoting the internationalization of the RMB is not only the necessary choice for China's economic and financial development, but it is also an important step to systematically raise Asia's position within the international financial system." The global financial crisis reveals an obvious need for basic reform of the international system, with a greater emphasis on regional needs and arrangements. Many Chinese academics have stressed these themes—that the management of the dollar as the world's currency "lacks necessary constraints," and is an important source of volatility in the world economy. RMB internationalization is seen as a necessary step toward a multiple currency system that would reduce the influence of the dollar, contribute to systemic stability, increase China's voice, and provide some insurance against a dollar crisis.[14]

The crisis has also encouraged a new ambitiousness about the rate at which the RMB might ascend to the world stage, because it reinforced an underlying geopolitical trend that had been much talked about for some time—the astonishing rise of China and the relative decline of the United States. (As noted above, this is not to be dismissive of China's own economic and political challenges.)[15] This subtext, often creeping into the text, has

---

14. Li Ruogu 2010; Li Yang 2010; Qu 2009 ("restraints"); Li and Yin 2010.

15. A wild card in all of this remains a more radical, disruptive, indefinitely sustained downshift in China's growth, a possibility that can't be ruled out. Instability in its domestic financial sector, internal labor/migration bottlenecks, and disruptive environmental distress are some of the myriad problems that might cause a major disruption in China's economic growth. See for example Shirk 2007. Short of a major disruption of the Chinese economy, however, current trends will

informed discussions about the role of the dollar in supporting US power, and whether and how global economic governance ought to better reflect the changing international balance of power. A relatively benign interpretation suggests that China's record of "tiding over two financial crises" and "three decades of growth," as contrasted with "weakened confidence in the dollar" and in "the soundness of Washington's macroeconomic policies," offers compelling logic in favor of reform. (Some more nationalistic voices see the dominance of the dollar as a crucial lever of American hegemony.) Others observe that emerging from the crisis, the United States is seen as weaker, and the IMF ineffective, which again, suggests a revisiting of the rules of the game. Chinese academics see a troubled American financial order and a vulnerable greenback, and share the assessment of the World Bank that a multiple currency system is likely to emerge in the not too distant future. In all cases, the rise of China's economic and political power in the context of the global financial crisis is suggestive of a greater role for the RMB and a distinct regional flavor to global financial organization, anticipating a central Chinese role in Asian monetary and financial cooperation.[16] But to focus solely on power (which, certainly, is an essential variable) risks missing the crucial role of ideology in the recalculation of China's strategy with regard to its management of domestic and global monetary and financial affairs, and to how it envisions the future of the RMB. The global financial crisis exposed the emperor's new clothes, revealing to the eyes of Chinese elites the true (and dangerous) nature of uninhibited financial deregulation. Chen Siqing, executive vice president of the Bank of China, attributed the financial crisis to "six surface-level reasons"—familiar items including excessive leverage and conflict

---

continue. Most projections of economic growth—even those that are cautious about China and optimistic about the United States—suggest that even if US growth tracks toward the high end of its potential, and even if China's growth rate checks in closer to the lower end of its commonly anticipated trajectory, each year (and over the years) China will grow faster than the United States For examples of projected rates of growth, see Congressional Budget Office 2013, 64; National Intelligence Council 2012.

16. Wu 2010, 157 (quote), 159 (quote), 161; Lieberthal and Wang 2012, 15 (hegemony); Song 2008; World Bank 2011, 7, 126; Lu 2009 ("Establishing a diverse international monetary system is the realistic choice. . . . Mutual restraint and competition among currencies will be good"); Li and Yin 2010 ("The foundations of U.S. credit have already entered a long path of decline"); Qu 2009 ("financial and monetary cooperation in Asia will grow stronger, and the RMB's status as a regional currency will rise"); Zhang 2009a.

of interest–ridden credit rating agencies. But he also went on to describe "deeper problems" that made the crisis "inevitable"—ones that implicate the basic assumptions of the US economic model, which, among other defects, encourage a disregard for systemic risk. His analysis speaks forcefully in favor of both creating some space between the Chinese and American economies, and altering the trajectory of China's financial model—away from the path of convergence with the Anglo-American approach, and toward something different. This perspective was echoed quite explicitly by Li Ruogu of the Exim Bank—"Blindly believing and even following the models and theories extolled by the west can only result in failure, I'm afraid"—he concluded, a widespread assessment among Chinese elites and academics. "The Anglo-Saxon model is not the only one; and it should not be the final model for emulation," one observer insisted; "China cannot simply use Harvard University's teaching materials to guide the development of Chinese finance," opined another.[17] This perception is not limited to China; many in Korea, for example, have been reaching similar conclusions; and the delegitimization of the American model in Asia has been noted by numerous Western experts.[18]

The Heart of the Matter: Delegitimization of the American Model

> "Well, I don't think it's quite fair to condemn a whole program because of a single slip-up."
>
> GENERAL TURGIDSON TO PRESIDENT MUFFLEY, *DR. STRANGELOVE*

Were the global financial crisis a singular, unpredictable, essentially random catastrophe—the legendary "black swan"—it might not have been

---

17. Chen 2008; Li Ruogu 2010; Yu 2008; (Anglo-Saxon); Xia 2011 (Harvard). See also Zhang 2009b ("One of the root causes of the subprime crisis was that global financial regulatory authorities held a laissez-faire attitude about financial innovations").

18. Kim and Lee 2009, 153, 162–63; Bottelier 2009, 71, 100 ("From China's perspective, the United States has lost credibility in the economic and financial arena. The crisis has confirmed Chinese leaders in their belief that they were correct in resisting U.S. pressure."); Williamson 2012, 3 ("discredit Western views"); Birdsall and Fukuyama, 2011, 45 ("the American version of capitalism is, if not in full disrepute, then at least no longer dominant"); Foot and Walter 2011, 271 ("major blow to the credibility and legitimacy"); see also Walter and Howie 2011, 74, 213; Chin and Helleiner 2008, 96.

enough, in and of itself, to fundamentally change many attitudes about the legitimacy of the American model.[19] But it was not singular, not all that surprising, and random only in its timing and specifics. Three observations are crucial for understanding the context and the interpretation of the crisis. First, a major financial crisis is an *unsurprising* outcome of the American financial deregulation project, which has its roots in the 1970s and 1980s, but which came to full flower in the 1990s and 2000s. The dismantling of financial regulations in the United States, the abdication of oversight, and the financialization of the American economy created an open invitation to financial crisis. Second, this domestic agenda had an international counterpart. With the end of the Cold War, the United States embarked on a sharp-elbowed enterprise to force other countries to open up and deregulate their own financial sectors. Third, for most of the world, and especially Asia, the global financial crisis was not a "single slip-up"— the age of globalized finance was characterized by ubiquitous financial crises, most notably (but not exclusively) the Asian crisis of 1997–98. This crisis of unregulated capital, coming just ten years before the global financial crisis, had already sowed the seeds of disenchantment with the American model, which was further cultivated by resentment at the US response to that disaster. Wariness of the American model, irritation with aggressive US financial diplomacy, and concerns about the merits of unregulated capital, then, did not begin with the global financial crisis. Rather, they were confirmed by it—several times over.

The financialization of the American economy is beyond the scope of this chapter, but it is important to note that it shared ideological underpinnings with the foreign policy agenda that the United States pursued in parallel.[20] In the 1990s the United States pressed countries to dismantle

---

19. Although it might have; the magnitude of the crisis is not to be underestimated.

20. The financialization of the American economy, marking the period in which finance became the largest and fastest-growing sector in the US economy, was the result of a bipartisan project that stretched across the Clinton and George W. Bush administrations. Crucial players include Robert Rubin, Lawrence Summers, Phil Gramm, and Alan Greenspan; landmark moments include the repeal of the Glass-Steagall Act and the passage of the Commodity Futures Modernization Act (which assured that derivatives would not be subject to regulation). But the period was shaped and characterized, most crucially, by an ideological convergence among financiers, government officials, and attendant academics, which contributed to a broader national culture of celebrated, and unregulated, finance.

their capital controls and to create opportunities and access for the giants of the American financial services sector. Not coincidentally, at the same time, the International Monetary Fund, in a radical and bold power play, moved to force its member states to completely eliminate their capital controls.

The confluence of forces—ideas, interests, and power—that led the United States and the IMF to push, hard, for universal, uninhibited, capital deregulation, like so many questions about monetary affairs, is not easily disentangled.[21] But after the Cold War, the triumphant United States, shaking off the malaise of the 1970s and the declinist discourse of the 1980s, set out, as it had after World War II, to reshape the international economy. This new order, however, was quite ideationally distinct from the previous American model. As with domestic deregulation, it was rooted in the rejection of Keynesian perspectives—regarding expectations, the behavior of the financial sector, and, more broadly, embedded liberalism—in favor of rational expectations, the efficient markets hypothesis, and the idea that markets, even financial markets, are always right and always know best. The convergence toward this intellectual position, in the academy, in Washington, and among the professional staff at the IMF, was a crucial building block of what would become the second US postwar order.[22] But interests and power are not to be underestimated. The ascendant American financial services sector was pushing its friends and patrons in Washington to fight to make the world more hospitable to its business—and those friends, commonly former and future colleagues, needed little pushing. And the stewards of the American economy could not fail to see the comparative advantages on the table—the giant and growing US financial sector was world-class and a world-beater. Thinking even more broadly, in a post–Cold War world of American unipolarity, the promotion of globalization, financial and otherwise, was recognized as even further enhancing the US geopolitical position.

In this context, the Clinton administration was very assertive in its diplomatic efforts, throughout the world but especially in Asia, to expand opportunities for American banks, insurance companies, and brokerage houses. "Our financial services industry wanted into these markets," the

---

21. On these themes see Kirshner 2003.
22. On the central role of ideas and of the elite convergence toward the ideology of capital liberalization, see Abdelal 2007, Chwieroth 2010.

head of Clinton's Council of Economic Advisers explained. But it was not, at least initially, an easy sell. At a conference in Hawaii in 1994, hosted by American Treasury Secretary Lloyd Bentsen, finance ministers from Japan, Thailand, Malaysia, and Indonesia all expressed reluctance about swift liberalization, and raised concerns about the possibility of destabilizing financial flows and the dangers of "hot" money and speculation. But prying open growing Asian markets remained at the center of US efforts. In 1996, as Korea sought to become a member of the Organization for Economic Cooperation and Development, the United States insisted as a condition of entry that the country speed the pace of financial deregulation and provide increased access for American firms. "These areas are all of interest to the U.S. financial services community," the Treasury's internal negotiating memo explained. Such efforts were the rule, not the exception. "Working through the IMF or directly with other countries," one account described, Treasury Secretary Robert Rubin and his deputy Lawrence Summers, with the encouragement and support of Alan Greenspan, "pushed tirelessly for . . . free capital flows."[23]

In on this was an institution dominated by the United States, the International Monetary Fund. In May 1997, the IMF announced its intention to amend its Articles of Agreement. Instead of expecting and accommodating the judicious use of capital controls by its members—the intent of Keynes and the other founding architects of the institution—the Fund would resolve "to make the promotion of capital account liberalization a specific purpose of the IMF and give it jurisdiction over capital movements."[24]

What is remarkable about all of this is that there was, and is, precious little economic theory to support the contention that completely unregulated capital is optimal economic policy. In fact, there are good reasons to expect that the opposite is true—that completely unregulated capital is suboptimal, from the perspective of economic efficiency—given the

23. Nicholas Kristof and David Sanger, "How U.S. Wooed Asia To Let Cash Flow In," *New York Times,* February 16, 1999 (quotes); Tim Cribb, "Thorny Issues Await APEC finance ministers," Agence France Presse, March 20, 1994; Kenneth Klee and Rich Thomas with Stefan Theil, "Defending the One True Faith," *Newsweek,* September 14, 1998, 22 (last quote).

24. International Monetary Fund 1997, 131–32. Note that both Abdelal (2007) and Chwieroth (2010) each emphasize that the IMF came to support capital deregulation independent of American pressure. (Though they do acknowledge that the Fund certainly could not make such a move without explicit US permission and support.)

pressures for conformity that it would generate across states' macroeconomic policies, the potentially ephemeral nature of the value of financial assets, and the fact that financial markets are vulnerable to collectively catastrophic, if individually rational herding behavior. Moreover, empirical studies consistently fail to find associations between unregulated capital and improved economic performance. What such studies do reveal, on the other hand, are reasons to tread cautiously.[25] Worse, individual countries liberalizing their capital accounts are more likely to experience a financial crisis, even when the government is pursuing "sound" policies. And for the global economy as a whole, periods of high capital mobility are associated with an increased number of financial crises. As Charles Kindleberger convincingly demonstrated long ago, and recent, comprehensive scholarship has only reconfirmed, financial crises are the rule of history, not the exception—they are a "hardy perennial." In sum, the US model—and the IMF push—was built on a leap of faith.[26]

The IMF project was ill-timed, as pressures to further accelerate capital liberalization coincided with the emergence of the Asian financial crisis. Sparked by events in Thailand in July 1997 and then quickly and unexpectedly spreading throughout the region, this was a crisis that the IMF did not see coming. It had only recently pronounced that "international capital markets appear to have become more resilient and are less likely to be a source of disturbances." (The Fund also assessed, with an unintended ironic nod to the global financial crisis that would emerge a decade later, that "Although the scale of financial activity continues to grow, market participants—including high-risk high-return investment funds—are more disciplined, cautious, and sensitive to market fundamentals.")[27]

The Asian financial crisis also exposed an important ideological fissure. Many in Asia saw the crisis for what it was—a classic international financial crisis—common throughout history and, as noted, especially common during periods of particularly high capital mobility. The IMF/American perspective saw it differently. Representative of this view, Alan Greenspan explained that the "root" causes of the crisis could be found

---

25. Rodrik 1998, 61; Cooper 1999; Rodrik and Subramanian 2009, 113, 116, 125, 136. On good reasons to be cautious, see for example Williamson and Mahar 1998, Willett 2000.

26. Blyth 2003; Kindleberger 1978; Reinhart and Rogoff 2009, 155.

27. International Monetary Fund 1996, 1, 2.

in the "poor public policy" within the Asian states themselves. Indeed, for market fundamentalists, following an efficient markets hypothesis perspective, the very idea that there could even be international sources of financial crisis was an alien concept. (Similarly, the standard macroeconomic models widely in vogue before the global financial crisis ten years later simply could not account for the events that unfolded.) IMF accounts were similarly myopic, not to mention amnesic, placing the blame for the crisis exclusively on the domestic economic policies of states whose economies and macroeconomic management the Fund had only recently been lauding. "I emphatically reject the view," First Deputy Managing Director Stanley Fischer argued, "that recent market turbulence in the region" suggests caution with regard to capital account liberalization. The fault lay with the Asian model of development, not with globalized finance. As Greenspan testified before Congress, "One consequence of this Asian crisis is an increasing awareness in the region that market capitalism, as practiced in the West, especially in the United States, is the superior model."[28]

But this was not the case, neither with regard to the Asian model nor with local attitudes toward it. Elites in Asia could recognize an international financial crisis when they saw one, had their doubts about completely unregulated capital and the efficient markets hypothesis, and could also recognize the exercise of power as well. Japanese Minister of Finance Kiichi Miyazawa attributed the crisis to "general problems inherent in today's global system," and called for "reforming the international financial architecture." His vice minister, Eisuke Sakakibara, stated plainly that "free capital movements do not always bring about optimum allocation of resources." He also spoke of the "inherent instability of liberalized capital markets," and argued that the Asian crisis could not be "explained only by . . . structural problems" within the affected economies. Japanese officials (and, it should be recalled, Japan did not need or seek the assistance of the Fund during the crisis) were among the many in Asia who were also very alert to (if powerless to do anything about), the nakedly opportunistic US responses to the crisis, and to the gratuitously deflationary measures imposed by the IMF that made a bad situation worse. Nor were these

---

28. Greenspan 1998, 1999, Fischer 1997.

observations lost on countries such as China, which (like most Asian states that had retained their capital controls) was spared the worst of the crisis.[29]

The heavy hand of American power was seen, and felt, most clearly and acutely in Korea. Once again, no one, least of all the IMF, thought the crisis would spread to Korea. (An IMF mission visited Korea just a month before the country was swept up in the spreading crisis, and concluded that "Korea would avoid being seriously affected by the crisis then spreading through Southeast Asia.") But the crisis did spread, and the Korean economy, "an economy to envy" as Martin Feldstein would describe it in his critique of the IMF policies that followed, was overtaken by a crisis of "temporary illiquidity," which he distinguished from "fundamental insolvency." Feldstein urged that the Fund "should eschew the temptation to use currency crises as an opportunity to force fundamental and structural reforms on countries." But that is exactly what the Fund did, along with a heap of deflationary medicine that added to the country's distress, when Korea arrived, hat in hand, in need of exactly the kind of emergency help—bridge loans and coordination with creditors—that the Fund was, in theory, designed to provide.[30]

The Fund insisted on structural reforms—especially, it turned out, ones that would open up a reluctant Korea to US financial firms. It was an IMF operation, but in this case, the United States was calling the shots. It was the Americans at the IMF who insisted on the conditions imposed on the Koreans in exchange for the Fund's support, and US officials arrived in Seoul to press the same demands. With little choice, Korea agreed to a raft of IMF demands quite unrelated to the crisis at hand, such as eliminating barriers to foreign direct investment, opening up its markets in insurance and securities dealings, and accelerating the liberalization of foreign exchange transactions. As Robert Gilpin observed, the IMF letter of intent signed by Korea "included specific items that the United States had long demanded of Asian governments, and that the latter had rejected." It is not surprising to learn, then, that "many Koreans consider" the day the letter was signed to be "Korea's 'Second National Humiliation Day' the first being that of its colonization by the Japanese."[31]

---

29. Miyazawa 1998; Sakakibara 1999a, b. See also Kuroda 2000; Beeson 2000, 339, 348.

30. International Monetary Fund 2003a, 18 (quote); Feldstein 1998, 24, 25, 27, 31, 32.

31. Blustein 2001, 143–44, 155–56; Gilpin 2000, 157, 159; Kirk 1999, 35, 36–38, 43, 46; Sheng 2009, 40 (humiliation), 162.

More evidence that the Asian crisis exposed nascent fissures in the foundations of the American order of globalized finance can be found in the divergent reactions to and interpretations of Malaysia's deployment of capital controls during the crisis. On September 1, 1998, Malaysia introduced capital controls in order to pursue pro-growth policies, which would have been otherwise unsustainable in the wake of the punishing capital flight that would have been touched off in response to such a departure from orthodoxy. The reaction of officials in the United States, the IMF, and Western credit rating agencies was withering and vehemently negative (to such an extent that it is difficult to dismiss the idea that the measures touched a rather sensitive nerve). In contrast, many voices in Asia were strongly supportive of the new policy. One Chinese official observed with approval that "Malaysia is returning to the route which China has been taking." Japan also explicitly endorsed the controls, with Finance Minister Miyazawa speaking out in favor of "market friendly controls" more generally. Despite the fact that Western credit agencies downgraded Malaysia's sovereign debt to junk bond status, Japan provided the country with $1.5 billion in new financial support. And despite the "unanimous condemnation" and warnings of imminent ruin from Western markets, authorities, and institutions, the Malaysian economy performed well after the imposition of controls. As with Korea, very different lessons were learned from the experience in Washington and in Asia.[32]

The drive to amend the IMF's Articles of Agreement stalled in the wake of the Korean crisis, which rendered increasingly implausible the idea that capital liberalization was always and everywhere wise and undangerous, suspicions reconfirmed by crises that immediately followed in Russia, Brazil, and Argentina. But even without a new mandate the fundamentalist ideology at the IMF and in the United States was unshaken. A strong case could be made that temporary exchange controls might have spared Russia from the worst of its crisis—but "the IMF and the U.S. Treasury could not accept that option at the time, having drawn a firm line against" such policies.[33] Into the twenty-first century, the IMF, serially

32. See Abdelal and Alfaro 2002, 2, 11; Tourres 2003, 3, 104, 229–30, 234–35, 288; Sheng 2009, 189, 194, 212–13, 215 (unanimous); Wade and Veneroso 1998; Miyazawa 1998; Johnstone 1999, 132; Hughes 2000, 241, 242.

33. Desai 2000, 52; International Monetary Fund 2003b, 3; Blustein 2001, 9, 337, 348, 374.

embarrassed, expressed these views sotto voce, while the United States, if anything more confident in the American model and the ability of unregulated financial markets to look after themselves, pressed its perceived advantages still more. In 2003, completing free trade agreements with Chile and Singapore (and setting a precedent for negotiations with other states), the United States pushed hard, and over the vociferous objections of its counterparties, for clauses that demanded each country renounce the right to introduce any form of capital controls.[34]

But the United States overplayed its hand, unaware of or indifferent to the depth of concerns about deregulated finance and the degree of resentment that its muscular financial diplomacy was engendering abroad. The crisis thus did not bring about an ideological consensus on the singular wisdom of the American model, but instead greased the wheels of future opposition to it. This was not immediately obvious, because the United States emerged from the numerous crises associated with uninhibited financial globalization stronger than ever—unipolar, hegemonic—and there was something irresistible about American influence. But the subtext of a sharp ideological divide, and a craving for some insulation from the hyperpower, endured.[35]

China, an increasingly important player in the world economy in the twenty-first century, was relatively shielded from crises by its own controls, and, looking forward, hedged its bets. On the one hand, the American financial model did look like the only one left standing, but the Chinese Communist Party was not about to shed its cautious spots, especially when it came to finance capital. After the Asian crisis, China would initially bend toward the American model, but slowly to be sure, incrementally and with caution. When the global financial crisis, in America, of America, and from America, confirmed the worst fears of the skeptics of the American model, actors and critics drew upon preexisting reservoirs of ideological and political opposition. Among other problems, the West is "still living with the consequences of its decision to call the East Asian crisis a comeuppance for

34. Weintraub 2004, 87; Elizabeth Becker and Larry Rohter, "U.S. and Chile Reach Free Trade Accord," *New York Times,* December 12, 2002; Wayne Arnold, "Rift on Capital Controls Snags Singapore Trade Pact," ibid., January 9, 2003.

35. David Sanger, "U.S. and Japanese Confer but Differ on Economic Cures," *New York Times,* September 6, 1998; Higgott 1998, 333–4, 339, 347, 351; Grimes 2003, 187, 188, 194; Katada 2002, 86; Bowles 2002, 230–1, 248–9.

crony capitalism," as John Williamson reflected. Recognizing it as a panic then would have been much better.[36]

Toward RMB Internationalization

Rejection of the American model, desire for greater distance from the US economy, and the acceleration of the rise of China's relative power and influence have all stimulated visions of a more important, international RMB. It remains to be seen how quickly this will come about, and the economic template it would follow. But as Benjamin Cohen argues in this volume, "in both words and deeds, the Chinese have appeared to underscore a dissatisfaction with the status quo that goes well beyond anything expressed by earlier newcomers." And in the wake of the crisis, there was a clear increase in official rhetoric about the RMB, although questions remained about how that talk might be translated into action, especially given potential barriers such as the yuan's limited convertibility and uncertainty about the stability of China's domestic financial sector. But some tangible moves designed to increase the international role of the RMB, especially a series of bilateral swap agreements, are visible signs that, to some extent, official talking up of the RMB is not just talk. After the global financial crisis, there is both an increase on the supply side—China's willingness to have the RMB deployed in a greater role internationally—and at the same time a clearly increased demand—a greater desire by states to find ways to transact business in ways that do not bind them tightly to, or at least provide some diversification away from, the dollar, the American financial model, and the US economy. (An illustration of the rhetorical support for diversification is provided by Gregory Chin in this volume, with his observation that communiqués from BRIC meetings invariably call for international monetary reform and a more multipolar global order.)

On March 23, 2009, Zhou Xiaochuan, governor of the People's Bank of China, released an essay titled "Reform of the International Monetary System." The essay, which was essentially seconded by statements from

---

36. Williamson 2012, 15; see also Birdsall and Fukuyama 2011, 47. On China's bending toward the American model, and subsequent pause, see Walter and Howie 2011, 10, 13, 14.

other leading officials, attracted, appropriately, considerable media attention. Nominally a call for a greater role for the SDR, the Governor's statement was properly understood as a challenge to the dollar. If not a call for a greater international role for the RMB (which would have been rather heavy-handed), it was nevertheless an explicit call to move away from the dollar, which, as a practical matter, amounted to the same thing. "The frequency and increasing intensity of financial crises following the collapse of the Bretton Woods system suggests the costs of such a system to the world may have exceeded its benefits," Zhou argued; more to the point, he attributed the crisis to "the inherent vulnerabilities and systemic risks in the existing international monetary system." And if that was not clear enough, he added that the crisis was "an inevitable outcome of the institutional flaws" of relying on a single national currency to serve as the world's money.[37]

Zhou's essay was also notable for two additional reasons. First, the governor repeatedly invoked Keynes ("the Keynesian approach may have been more farsighted"). This, admittedly, was specifically in defense of a supranational currency—but the recurring appeal to Keynes stands notably in contrast with the fundamental anti-Keynesian ideological underpinnings of the second US order. Second, as Chin and Wang have argued, the essay reflects "the consensus Chinese view . . . that a multi–reserve currency era is coming, even if only gradually, and that it would be in China's strategic interests to promote such a scenario." Publications by Chinese elites and academics increasingly illustrate this perspective, calling attention to the observable facts on the ground ("To mainland Chinese economists, the issue of the international monetary system and the so-called post-dollar era is not only possible but is already showing its first signs"); assessing government policy ("The aim of this strategy is to promote the RMB on an international scale, and to decrease . . . reliance on the dollar"); and, often, including prescriptive support for such measures rooted not only in economics but also in politics ("As a major power, China urgently needs to carry out internationalization of the RMB as a national strategic priority").[38]

---

37. Zhou 2009, 1; David Barboza, "China Urges New Money Reserve to Replace Dollar," *New York Times,* March 24, 2009; Chin and Wang 2010, 4, 5, 11, 12.

38. Chin and Wang 2010; Zhang 2010 (Chinese economists; Zhang also adds that "a significant majority of Chinese economists support the internationalization" of the RMB); Zhang 2009a

Despite all this, there remain potential bumps on the road to the emergence of the RMB. To some extent, this remains a question of pace and scope—that is, the trajectory is clearly there for the yuan to become a much more important currency on the world stage, but questions remain about how quickly this will occur, and just how influential it will become. (And, to repeat, this discussion is about the emergence of the RMB as an important international and potentially dominant regional currency, not about its supplanting the dollar and becoming *the* global key currency.) Helleiner and Malkin, while acknowledging that the Chinese government has taken steps to promote the international use of the RMB, argue that the relative dearth of domestic economic interest groups lobbying in favor of internationalization suggests an underappreciated lack of political wind behind the sails of the enterprise. A more treacherous potential disruption of the yuan's trajectory is the extent of the weakness in and discomforting opacity of Chinese banks and of its domestic financial sector more generally. China's controls (once again) allowed its institutions to weather the storms of the global financial crisis. But the state holds a major stake in many of China's banks, which rely on government protection, carry considerable loans to state-owned enterprises of uncertain promise, and would likely come under pressure if fully exposed to market pressures and foreign competition.[39]

This matters, in and of itself as a barometer of future of the Chinese economy, but also because most experts consider rich, deep, and stable financial institutions to be crucial foundations for an international currency. In particular, most Western analysts consider full currency convertibility and completely open capital markets as virtual prerequisites to establish the international financial centers that would be the platforms for and

---

(aim of the strategy); Zhang and Zhang 2008 (major power). See also Lu 2009; Xia 2011; and Wu 2010, all of whom advocate for a greater international role for the yuan. Wu (writing in an American outlet), argues that the global financial crisis marked the end of the post–Cold War order, invalidated the American economic model at home and the one-size-fits-all Washington consensus aggressively promoted abroad, and anticipates that "China's deepening economic connections with its regional partners promise to expand its political clout in East Asia" (155, 156, 160 [quote]).

39. Helleiner and Malkin 2012, 49, 50, 52. (This argument assumes, of course, that domestic sectoral politics is an important factor in explaining currency internationalization.) Walter and Howie 2011, 25, 27, 38, 77–8, 80, 138–39; Martin 2012.

hubs of international money. Many see this as the rate limiting factor of the yuan's rise, and even as suggestive of a ceiling for its ultimate status. For the RMB "to become a genuine international currency," one such study concluded, "China must . . . lift capital controls completely."[40]

As a matter of practice, this may or may not be the case. China seems poised to act as if, in fact, it is not the case, and seems set to embark on a course of considerable internationalization of the RMB without first, or perhaps without even ever intending, to fully liberalize its capital account.[41] In a very telling essay, Governor Zhou sought to redefine the meaning of capital account convertibility in a way that would accommodate these ambitions. "The definition of capital account convertibility is something that can be discussed, and how standards should be set should have a certain degree of flexibility," he wrote, noting that the IMF charter itself is vague on the definition, inviting national interpretation. Moreover, "capital account convertibility does not equal the abandonment of oversight or controls on transnational financial transactions." In particular, "when international markets experience abnormal volatility or when problems occur with a country's balance of international payments, it is reasonable to apply appropriate controls to short-term, speculative capital flows." And finally, and crucially, "China has to have its own voice in the establishment of international standards." This may be part of what rejecting the American model of financial governance looks like: putting the infrastructure in place for the yuan to become more internationalized, promoting its use as a vehicle currency, and encouraging other central banks to hold RMBs as reserves—while retaining some capital controls and other market-inhibiting devices. One way to encourage this would be through bilateral swap agreements, which China has quite actively pursued.[42]

40. Mallaby and Wethington 2012, 136, 137; Frankel 2011, 13; World Bank 2011, 139; Bottelier 2009, 100; Ito 2011, 11 (quote).

41. On the relationship between internationalization and liberalization, see also He 2012; McNally 2012, 760–62.

42. Zhou 2012. On internationalization ahead of liberalization, see McCauley 2011, 1, 3 ("In internationalizing the Renminbi within a system of capital controls, the Chinese authorities set out on a path with no signposts"), 13, 21; Eichengreen 2012, 129, 130 (infrastructure, vehicle, reserves, swaps); World Bank 2011, 140.

After the global financial crisis, Chinese leaders decided to step up the pace of RMB internationalization, promote regional monetary cooperation, and encourage reform of global monetary management, all in an effort to begin to reduce dependence on the US dollar and to establish an alternative to the American model. Crucially, China's willingness to increase the supply of international monetary options coincided, for similar reasons, with greater demand, especially but not exclusively in Asia, for alternatives to the dollar and to the ideology of unbridled financial globalization as well. The desire for diversified options, as well as assessments of "credibility" that derive from different sources than the lack of capital controls, might further facilitate a distinct path to RMB internationalization. "I would rather bet on China's authorities—who ignored the prediction . . . [of] the US Treasury Secretary, that they risked trillions of dollars in lost economic potential unless they freed their capital markets," explained the former prime minister of Thailand. "That seems wiser than praying to god that the U.S. soon finds a credible model of economic growth and regulation of financial institutions."[43]

The signature move in China's new "deliberate" and "aggressive" promotion of the use of the yuan has been the bilateral currency swap. These and other arrangements encourage greater use of the RMB and allow China and its trading partners to settle their accounts without moving in and out of dollars, without requiring multilateral negotiations, and without necessitating ambitious or comprehensive commitments to financial liberalization. Such pacts are welcomed by China's trading partners, of which there are many—the People's Republic is the world's second largest importer and the most important trading partner for an increasing number of major economies, who share most if not all of China's motives for diversifying

43. Zhang 2009a, 23, 24, 27, 29, 31; Pieter Bottelier, "Future of the Renminbi as an International Currency," China US Focus, April 29, 2011, http://www.chinausfocus.com/finance-economy/future-of-the-renminbi-as-an-international-currency/; Keith Bradsher, "In Step to Enhance Currency, China Allows Its Use in Some Foreign Payments," New York Times, July 7, 2009; George Koo and Henry Tang, "How Shall America Respond to Chinese Yuan as a Global Currency," China US Focus, February 29, 2012, http://www.chinausfocus.com/finance-economy/how-shall-america-respond-to-chinese-yuan-as-a-global-currency/; Thaksin Shinawatra, "An Asia Bond Could Save Us from the Dollar," Financial Times, October 6, 2008 (quote).

away from the dollar. Notable among these many agreements—throughout Asia, and also in Latin America, the Middle East, and the Former Soviet Union—was the one reached with Japan. China recently overtook the United States as that country's largest trading partner, and Japan also requested, and received, the right to purchase yuan-denominated bonds, which will result in Japan including RMB in its foreign exchange reserves.[44]

In 2011, more than 9 percent of China's total trade was settled in yuan, up from less than 1 percent the year before, a figure that seems poised to continue to grow. And in addition to its expanding roster of swap agreements, and the increasing (if still very modest) international use of the RMB in some countries' foreign exchange reserves, China is also taking advantage of the distinct status of Hong Kong, permitting some local banks there (and Chinese banks based in the city), to issue RMB-denominated bonds. Singapore (boasting new free trade and currency swap agreements with Beijing) is also jockeying for position to serve as a regional hub for RMB business in Southeast Asia.[45] Yang Jiang, in this volume, offers a skeptical assessment of these measures, labeling them "shallow" and "largely symbolic," and argues that Beijing's appetite for bilateral deals, controls on its currency, and capital account restrictions fundamentally circumscribe the international role that the yuan can hope to play. In contrast, and in accord with the emphasis that Hongying Wang (also in this volume) places on the role of economic ideology in shaping China's development model, I argue that China need not fully liberalize in order for the RMB to emerge as an important international

44. Ito 2011, 2 (quotes), 4–5, 16; Koo and Tang, "Yuan as a Global Currency"; Edward Wong and Natasha Singer, "Currency Agreement for Japan and China," *New York Times,* December 27, 2011; Simon Rabinovitch, "China and Japan Agree on Currency Push," *Financial Times,* December 27, 2011; Wang Xiaotian and Gao Changxin, "China-Japan Currency Deal Ushers in a New Era," *China Daily,* May 30, 2012, http://europe.chinadaily.com.cn/business/2012-05/30/content_15418505.htm; "China and Australia in $31bn Currency Swap," *Financial Times,* May 22, 2012; "China and Brazil in $30bn Currency Swap Agreement," BBC News, June 22, 2012, http://www.bbc.co.uk/news/business-18545978.

45. Takahashi 2012; Chin and Wang 2010, 13; Ito 2011, 8; Bottelier, "Future of the Renminbi as an International Currency"; Zhang 2010, 6; Gregory Chin, "Off to the RMB Races—the Singapore Stock Exchange," CIGI, July 23, 2012, http://www.cigionline.org.

currency.[46] In that light, actions taken by both China and its economic partners suggest the prepositioning of an apparatus that would support the emergence of the yuan as the key currency in Asia—if cautiously, slowly, and in a form somewhat different from the American model of completely uninhibited finance.

The Politics of a Greater RMB

Barring a major internal economic setback, the RMB will emerge as an important international currency, and has the potential to become the money of preference in East Asia. From China's perspective, the logic of international politics, the desire for some insulation from globalized financial markets, and a preference to foster an ideological alternative to the American model all motivate public policy in this direction. The rate at which the RMB will emerge will be most likely determined by politics, regionally, and economics, globally. That is, if China's foreign policy in Asia becomes clumsy and heavy-handed (which it occasionally threatens to do), then regardless of the eagerness with which China is willing to supply international money, the demand side will atrophy, as regional players seek to avoid becoming more intimately enmeshed with an intimidating regional giant. On the economic side of the equation, if cracks at the foundations of China's economic order visibly widen, that will tend to temper the pace of the RMB's increasing reception abroad; conversely, renewed economic distress elsewhere, such as a new financial crisis that implicates Europe and/or the United States, will further accelerate all of the trends that have encouraged the yuan's emergence. At whatever rate, however, regional monetary arrangements in Asia, anchored in Beijing, with features, practices, and norms recognizably distinct from the second postwar American model, are very likely to emerge in the coming years.

---

46. There are many historical examples of important regional and global monetary arrangements that have been designed and operated in the absence of full capital account convertibility—indeed in some cases these arrangements have had substantial illiberal qualities. This is not to suggest that China's approach to an internationalized RMB will not (or should not) be market-friendly; but history suggests that there are many different ways to orchestrate such arrangements. See Kirshner 1995, chap. 4. McNally (2012, 763–64) also suggests divergence from the US model.

REFERENCES

Abdelal, Rawi. 2007. *Capital Rules: The Construction of Global Finance.* Cambridge, MA: Harvard University Press.

Abdelal, Rawi, and Laura Alfaro. 2002. *Malaysia: Capital and Control.* Case no. N9 702–040. Cambridge, MA: Harvard Business School.

Abdelal, Rawi, and Jonathan Kirshner. 1999. "Strategy, Economic Relations, and the Definition of National Interests." *Security Studies* 9 (1–2): 119–56.

Aguado, Iago Gol. 2001. "The Creditanstalt Crisis of 1931 and the Failure of the Austro-German Customs Union Project." *Historical Journal* 44 (1): 199–221.

Ahuja, Ashvin, Nigel Andrew Chalk, Nathan Porter, Papa N'Diaye, and Malhar Nabar. 2012. *An End To China's Imbalances.* IMF Working Paper No. 12-100. Washington, DC: IMF.

Aizenman, Joshua, and Jaewoo Lee. 2007. "International Reserves: Precautionary versus Mercantilist Views, Theory and Evidence." *Open Economies Review* 18:191–214.

Aizenman, Joshua, and Nancy Marion. 2003a. "Foreign Exchange Reserves in East Asia: Why the High Demand?" Federal Reserve Bank of San Francisco, http://www.frbsf.org/economic-research/publications/economic-letter/2003/april/foreign-exchange-reserves-in-east-asia-why-the-high-demand/.

———. 2003b. "The High Demand for International Reserves in the Far East: What Is Going On?" *Journal of the Japanese and International Economies* 17 (3): 370–400.

Amyx, Jennifer. 2008. "Regional Financial Cooperation in East Asia since the Asian Financial Crisis." In *Crisis as Catalyst: Asia's Dynamic Political Economy,* ed. Andrew Macintyre, T. J. Pempel, and John Ravenhill. Ithaca, NY: Cornell University Press.

Andrews, David, ed. 2006. *International Monetary Power.* Ithaca, NY: Cornell University Press.

Angell, Norman. 1910. *The Great Illusion.* New York: Putnam.

Bagby, Wesley. 1992. *The Eagle-Dragon Alliance: America's Relations with China in World War II.* Newark: University of Delaware Press.

Baldwin, David A. 2013. "Power and International Relations." In *Handbook of International Relations,* 2d ed., ed. Walter Carlsneas, Thomas Risse, and Beth A. Simmons. Los Angeles: Sage Publications.

Bank for International Settlements. 2011. *Annual Report 2010/11.* Basel: Bank for International Settlements.

Bank for International Settlements. 2013. *Triennial Central Bank Survey—Foreign Exchange Turnover in April 2013: Preliminary Global Results.* Basel: Bank for International Settlements.

Beckley, Michael. 2011/12. "China's Century?" *International Security* 36 (3): 41–78.

Beeson, Mark. 2000. "Mahathir and the Markets: Globalization and the Pursuit of Economic Autonomy in Malaysia." *Pacific Affairs* 73 (3): 335–51.

Bell, Stephen, and Hui Feng. 2013. *The Rise of the People's Bank of China.* Cambridge, MA: Harvard University Press.

Bergsten, C. Fred. 1975. "The United States and Germany: The Imperative of Economic Bigemony." In *Toward a New International Economic Order: Selected Papers of C. Fred Bergsten, 1972–1974,* ed. C. Fred Bergsten. Lexington, MA: D. C. Heath.

———. 2008. "A Partnership of Equals: How Washington Should Respond to China's Economic Challenge." *Foreign Affairs,* July–August: 57–69.

Bernanke, Ben. 2005. "The Global Saving Glut and the U.S. Current Account Deficit." Sandridge Lecture, Virginia Association of Economics, Richmond, VA. http://www.federalreserve.gov/boarddocs/speeches/2005/200503102/.

———. 2007. "Global Imbalances: Recent Developments and Prospects." Speech at Bundesbank Berlin. http://www.federalreserve.gov/newsevents/speech/bernanke20070911a.htm.

Bernhard, W. J., J. Lawrence Broz, and William Clark. 2002. "The Political Economy of Monetary Institutions." *International Organization* 56 (4): 693–723.

Bernstein, Thomas, and Xiaobo Lü. 2003. *Taxation without Representation in Contemporary Rural China.* Cambridge: Cambridge University Press.

Bhagwati, Jagdish N., and Hugh T. Patrick. 1991. *Aggressive Unilateralism: America's 301 Trade Policy and the World Trading System.* Ann Arbor: University of Michigan Press.

Birdsall, Nancy, and Francis Fukuyama. 2011. "The Post-Washington Consensus: Development After the Crisis." *Foreign Affairs,* 90 (2): 45–53.

Blustein, Paul. 2001. *The Chastening: Inside the Crisis that Rocked the Global Financial System and Humbled the IMF.* New York: Public Affairs.

———. 2012. *A Flop and a Debacle: Inside the IMF's Global Rebalancing Efforts.* CIGI Papers no. 4. Waterloo, Ont.: Centre for International Governance Innovation.

Blyth, Mark. 2003. "The Political Power of Financial Ideas: Transparency, Risk and Distribution in Global Finance." In *Monetary Orders: Ambiguous Economics, Ubiquitous Politics,* ed. Jonathan Kirshner. Ithaca, NY: Cornell University Press.

Bo, Zhiyue. 2002. *Chinese Provincial Leaders: Economic Performance and Political Mobility since 1949.* Armonk, NY: M. E. Sharpe.

Borgwardt, Elizabeth. 2005. *A New Deal for the World; America's Vision for Human Rights.* Cambridge: Belknap Press of Harvard University Press.

Bottelier, Pieter. 2009. "China and the International Financial Crisis." In *Strategic Asia 2009–10: Economic Meltdown and Geopolitical Stability,* ed. Ashley Tellis, Andrew Marble, and Travis Tanner. Seattle: National Bureau of Asian Research.

Boughton, James. 2001. *Silent Revolution: The International Monetary Revolution, 1979– 1989.* Washington, DC: IMF.

Bowles, Paul. 2002. "Asia's Post-Crisis Regionalism: Bringing the State Back In, Keeping the (United) States Out." *Review of International Political Economy* 9 (2): 230–256.

———. 2012. "Rebalancing China's Growth: Some Unsettled Questions." *Canadian Journal of Development Studies/Revue canadienne d'études du développement* 33 (1): 1–13.

Bowles, Paul, and Baotai Wang. 2006. " 'Flowers and Criticism': The Political Economy of the Renminbi Debate." *Review of International Political Economy* 13 (2): 233–257.

———. 2008. "The Rocky Road Ahead: China, the US and the Future of the Dollar." *Review of International Political Economy* 15 (3): 335–353.

Brahm, Laurence J. 2002. *Zhu Rongji and the Transformation of Modern China.* Hoboken: Wiley.

Brender, Anton, and Florence Pisani. 2010. *Global Imbalances and the Collapse of Globalised Finance.* Brussels: Centre for European Policy Studies.

Breslin, Shaun. 2012. "Government-Industry Relations in China: A Review of the Art of the State." In *East Asian Capitalism: Continuity, Diversity and Change,* ed. Andrew Walter and Xiaoke Zhang. Cambridge: Cambridge University Press.

BRIC Leaders. 2009. "Joint Statement of the BRIC Countries' Leaders." Yekaterinburg, Russia, 16 June 2009. Moscow: President of Russia. http://archive.kremlin.ru/eng/text/docs/2009/06/217963.shtml.

———. 2010. "Second BRIC Summit of Heads of State and Government—Joint Statement." Press Release No. 212. Brasilia: Ministry of External Relations, Government of the Federative Republic of Brazil, April 15.

BRICS Development Banks. 2012. "Agreements Between BRICS Development Banks." Issued by Ministry of External Affairs, Government of the Republic of India, New Delhi, March 29.

BRICS Leaders. 2011. "Sanya Declaration of the BRICS Leaders Meeting." China Daily, April 14, 2011. http://www.chinadaily.com.cn/china/brics2011/2011–04/14/content_12329531.htm.

Broz, J. Lawrence, and Jeffry A. Frieden. 2001. "The Political Economy of International Monetary Relations." *Annual Review of Political Science* 4(1): 317–343.

Bueno de Mesquita, Bruce, Alastair Smith, Randolph M. Siverson, and James D. Morrow. 2003. *The Logic of Political Survival.* Cambridge, MA: MIT Press.

Cai, Hongbin, and Daniel Treisman. 2006. "Did Government Decentralization Cause China's Economic Miracle?" *World Politics* 58: 505–535.

Cai, Yongshun. 2004. "Managed Participation in China." *Political Science Quarterly* 119 (3): 425–451.

Calvo, Guillermo A. 1991. "The Perils of Sterilization." *IMF Staff Papers* 38: 921–26.

Chan, Anita. 2001. *China's Workers Under Assault: The Exploitation of Labor in a Globalizing Economy.* Armonk, NY: M. E. Sharpe.

Chen, Feng. 2003. "Between the State and Labour: The Conflict of Chinese Trade Unions' Double Identity in Market Reform." *China Quarterly* (176): 1006–28.

Chen, Siqing. 2008. "Meiguo jinrong weiji de shencengci yuanyin fenxi ji dui zhong-guo yinhangye de qishi" [Deeper-level analysis of the reasons for the U.S. financial crisis and its lessons for China's banking industry]. *Guoji jinrong yanjiu* [Studies of International Finance] 12.

Cheung, Yin-Wong, and Xingwang Qian. 2009. "Hoarding of International Reserves: Mrs. Machlup's Wardrobe and the Joneses." *Review of International Economics* 17 (4): 824–43.

Chin, Gregory. 2008. "China's Evolving G8 Engagement." In *Emerging Powers in Global Governance,* ed. Andrew Cooper and Agata Antkiewicz. Waterloo, Ont.: Wilfred Laurier University Press.

———. 2010. "Remaking the Architecture: Emerging Powers, Self-Insuring and Regional Insulation." *International Affairs* 86 (3): 693–716.

———. Forthcoming. "Asian Regionalism after the Global Financial Crisis." In *The Political Economy of Asian Regionalism,* ed. Giovanni Capannelli and Masahiro Kawai. New York: Springer/Series of the Asian Development Bank.

Chin, Gregory, and Eric Helleiner. 2008. "China as a Creditor: A Rising Financial Power?" *Journal of International Affairs* 62 (1): 87–102.

Chin, Gregory, and Wang Yong. 2010. "Debating the International Currency System: What's in a Speech?" *China Security* 6 (1): 2–20.

Chinn, Menzie, and Jeffrey A. Frankel. 2008. "Why the Euro Will Rival the Dollar." *International Finance* 11 (1): 49–73.

Chinn, Menzie D., and Jeffry A. Frieden. 2011. *Lost Decades: The Making of America's Debt Crisis and the Long Recovery.* New York: Norton.

Christensen, Thomas J. 2001. "Posing Problems without Catching Up: China's Rise and Challenges for U.S. Security Policy." *International Security* 25 (4): 5–40.

———. 2006. "Fostering Stability or Creating a Monster? The Rise of China and U.S. Policy toward East Asia." *International Security* 31 (1): 81–126.

Chung, Connie Wee-Wee, and Jose L. Tongzon. 2004. "A Paradigm Shift for China's Central Banking System." *Journal of Post Keynesian Economics* 27 (1): 87–103.

Chwieroth, Jeffrey M. 2010. *Capital Ideas: The IMF and the Rise of Financial Liberalization.* Princeton, NJ: Princeton University Press.

Cline, William. 2012. *Projecting China's Current Account Surplus.* Policy Brief 12-7. Washington, DC: Peterson Institute for International Economics.

Cohen, Benjamin J. 1986. *In Whose Interest? International Banking and American Foreign Policy.* New Haven, CT: Yale University Press.

———. 2008. "The International Monetary System: Diffusion and Ambiguity." *International Affairs* 84 (3): 453–70.

———. 2011. *The Future of Global Currency: The Euro Versus the Dollar.* London: Routledge.

———. 2012. "The Yuan Tomorrow?: Evaluating China's Currency Internationalization Strategy." *New Political Economy* 17 (3): 361–71.

———. 2014. "The Yuan's Long March." In *Power in a Changing World Economy: Lessons from East Asia,* ed. Benjamin J. Cohen and Eric M. P. Chiu. London: Routledge.

Commission on Growth and Development. 2008. *The Growth Report: Strategies for Sustained Growth and Inclusive Development.* Washington, DC: The World Bank.

Congressional Budget Office. 2013. *The Budget and Economic Outlook: Fiscal Years 2013–2023.* Washington, DC: United States Congress.

Cooper, Richard N. 1999. "Should Capital Controls Be Banished?" *Brookings Papers on Economic Activity* (1): 89–141.

Cooper, Scott. 2006. "The Limits of Monetary Power: Statecraft within Currency Areas." In *International Monetary Power,* ed. David Andrews. Ithaca, NY: Cornell University Press.

Craig, R. Bruce. 2004. *Treasonable Doubt: The Harry Dexter White Spy Case.* Lawrence: University Press of Kansas.

Cristadoro, Riccardo, and Daniela Marconi. 2012. "Household Savings in China." *Journal of Chinese Economic and Business Studies* 10 (3): 275–99.

Cumings, Bruce. 1999. *Parallax Visions.* Durham, NC: Duke University Press.

Dahl, Robert A. 1957. "The Concept of Power." *Behavioral Science* 2, 201–215.

Dai Xianglong. 2002a. "Statement by Mr. Dai Xianglong, Governor of the People's Bank of China." International Monetary and Financial Committee (5th Meeting), April 20, 2002. Washington, DC: IMF. http://www.imf.org/external/spring/2002/imfc/stm/eng/chn.htm.

———. 2002b. "Statement by Mr. Dai Xianglong, Governor of the People's Bank of China, September 28, 2002." International Monetary and Financial Committee. Washington, DC: IMF. http://www.imf.org/external/am/2002/imfc/state/eng/chn.htm.

De Cecco, Marcello. 1984. *The International Gold Standard.* New York: St. Martin's Press.

———. 2012. "Global Imbalances: Past, Present and Future." *Contributions to Political Economy* 31: 29–50.

Desai, Padma. 2000. "Why Did the Ruble Collapse in August 1998?" *American Economic Review* 90 (2): 48–52.

Development Research Center of the State Council. 2011. *The Regionalization of RMB.* Beijing: China Development Press.

Dickson, Bruce. 2003. *Red Capitalists in China.* Cambridge: Cambridge University Press.

Ding, Xueliang. 1994. *The Decline of Communism in China: Legitimacy Crisis 1977–1989.* Cambridge: Cambridge University Press.

Dooley, Michael P., David Folkerts-Landau, and Peter Garber. 2003. *An Essay on the Revived Bretton Woods System.* NBER Working Paper Series, No. 9971. Washington, DC: NBER.

———. 2004. *The Revived Bretton Woods System*. NBER Working Paper Series, No. 10332. Washington: NBER.

Downs, Anthony. 1957. "An Economic Theory of Political Action in a Democracy." *Journal of Political Economy* 65 (2): 135–50.

Drezner, Daniel W. 2009. "Bad Debts: Assessing China's Financial Influence in Great Power Politics." *International Security* 34 (2): 7–45.

———. 2010. "Will Currency Follow the Flag?" *International Relations of the Asia-Pacific* 10: 389–414.

Duckett, Jane. 1998. *The Entrepreneurial State in China*. London: Routledge.

Eichengreen, Barry. 2005. "Is a Change in the Renminbi Exchange Rate in China's Interest?" *Asian Economic Papers* 4 (1): 40–75.

———. 2011. *Exorbitant Privilege: The Rise and Fall of the Dollar and the Future of the International Monetary System*. New York: Oxford University Press.

———. 2012. "When Currencies Collapse: Will We Replay the 1930s or the 1970s?" *Foreign Affairs* 91 (1): 117–34.

Einzig, Paul. 1931. *The World Economic Crisis*. London: Macmillan.

Ekbladh, David. 2010. *The Great American Mission: Modernization and the Construction of an American World Order*. Princeton, NJ: Princeton University Press.

European Council on Foreign Relations. 2012. "European Foreign Policy Scorecard 2012." www.ecfr.eu/page/-/ECFR_SCORECARD_2012_WEB.pdf.

Fairbank, John King. 1968. *The Chinese World Order: Traditional China's Foreign Relations*. Cambridge, MA: Harvard University Press.

Feldstein, Martin. 1998. "Refocusing the IMF." *Foreign Affairs* 77 (2): 20–33.

Fewsmith, Joseph. 2008. *China since Tiananmen*. 2d ed. Cambridge: Cambridge University Press.

Fischer, Stanley. 1997. "Capital Account Liberalization and the Role of the IMF." IMF Seminar. September 19. Washington, DC: IMF. http://www.iie.com/Fischer/pdf/Fischer141.pdf.

Foot, Rosemary, and Andrew Walter. 2011. *China, the United States, and Global Order*. Cambridge: Cambridge University Press.

Frankel, Jeffrey. 2011. *Historical Precedents for Internationalization of the RMB*. CGS/IIGG Working paper. New York: Council on Foreign Relations.

Frankel, Jeffrey, and George Saravelos. 2012. "Can Leading Indicators Assess Country Vulnerability? Evidence from the 2008–09 Global Financial Crisis." *Journal of International Economics* 87 (2): 216–31.

Frazier, Mark. 2010. *Socialist Insecurity: Pensions and Politics of Uneven Development in China*. Ithaca, NY: Cornell University Press.

Freeman, Charles W. III, and Wen Jin Yuan. 2011. *China's Exchange Rate Politics: Decoding the Cleavage Between the Chinese Ministry of Commerce and the People's Bank of China*. Washington, DC: Center for Strategic and International Studies.

Friedberg, Aaron. 2011. *A Contest for Supremacy: China, America, and the Struggle for Mastery in Asia*. New York: Norton.

Frieden, Jeffry. 1991. "Invested Interests." *International Organization* 45 (4): 425–51.

Gallagher, Mary. 1999. *Contagious Capitalism*. Princeton, NJ: Princeton University Press.

Gardner, Richard. 1980. *Sterling-Dollar Diplomacy in Current Perspective.* New York: Columbia University Press.

Geddes, Barbara. 1999. "What Do We Know About Democratization After Twenty Years?" *Annual Review of Political Science* 2 (1): 115–44.

Gilley, Bruce, and David Murphy. 2001. "Why China Needs a Real Central Bank." *Far Eastern Economic Review,* May 24, 48–52.

Gilpin, Robert. 2000. *The Challenge of Global Capitalism: The World Economy in the 21st Century.* Princeton, NJ: Princeton University Press.

———. 2001. *The Global Political Economy: Understanding the International Economic Order.* Princeton, NJ: Princeton University Press.

Goldsmith, Raymond. 1983. *The Financial Development of Japan, 1868–1977.* New Haven, CT: Yale University Press.

Goldstein, Avery. 2005. *Rising to the Challenge: China's Grand Strategy and International Security.* Stanford, CA: Stanford University Press.

Gourinchas, Pierre-Olivier, and Maurice Obstfeld. 2012. "Stories of the Twentieth Century for the Twenty-First." *American Economic Journal: Macroeconomics* 4 (1): 226–65.

Gowa, Joanne. 1983. *Closing the Gold Window.* Ithaca, NY: Cornell University Press.

Green, Michael. 2003. *Japan's Reluctant Realism: Foreign Policy Challenges in an Era of Uncertain Power.* New York: Palgrave.

Green, Stephen. 2007a. "A Happy (and Prosperous) New Year at the PBoC." In *On the Ground: China,* ed. Standard Chartered Bank. Shanghai.

———. 2007b. "Calling all PBoC FX Sterilisation Geeks." In *On the Ground: China,* ed. Standard Chartered Bank. Shanghai.

———. 2007c. "More Inflation, More Hikes, More Sleepless Nights." In *On the Ground: China,* ed. Standard Chartered Bank. Shanghai.

———. 2008. "CNY NEER Gains to Slow Sharply into 2009." In *FX Alert—Chinese Yuan,* ed. Standard Chartered Bank. Shanghai.

Green, Stephen, and David Mann. 2004. "Pressure Increasing to Revalue the CNY." In *Standard Chartered CNY Barometer Update,* ed. Standard Chartered Bank. Shanghai.

Greenspan, Alan. 1998. "The Current Asia Crisis and the Dynamics of International Finance." Testimony before the Committee on Banking and Financial Services, U.S House of Representatives, January 30. www.federalreserve.gov/boarddocs/testi mony/1998/19980130.htm.

———. 1999. "Do Efficient Financial Markets Mitigate Financial Crises?" Remarks before the 1999 Financial Markets Conference of the Federal Reserve Board of Atlanta, Georgia. October 19. www.federalreserve.gov/boarddocs/speeches/1999/19991019. htm

Grey, Austin. 1944. "The Monetary Conference and China." *Far Eastern Survey* 13 (18): 165–67.

Gries, Peter. 2005. *China's New Nationalism: Pride, Politics, and Diplomacy.* Berkeley: University of California Press.

Grimes, William. 2001. *Unmaking the Japanese Miracle: Macroeconomic Politics 1985–2000.* Ithaca, NY: Cornell University Press.

———. 2003. "Internationalization of the Yen and the New Politics of Monetary Insulation." In *Monetary Orders: Ambiguous Economics, Ubiquitous Politics,* ed. Jonathan Kirshner. Ithaca, NY: Cornell University Press.

———. 2006. "East Asian Financial Regionalism in Support of the Global Financial Architecture? The Political Economy of Regional Nesting." *Journal of East Asian Studies* 6: 353–80.

———. 2008. *Currency and Contest in East Asia: The Great Power Politics of Financial Regionalism.* Ithaca, NY: Cornell University Press.

———. 2009. "Japan Confronts the Global Economic Crisis." *Asia-Pacific Review* 16 (2): 42–54.

Group of Five. 2009. "G5 Declaration," July 8, 2009.http://www.g8.utoronto.ca/summit/2009laquila/2009-g5declaration.pdf.

Group of Twenty. 2011. "Communiqué." Finance Ministers and Central Bank Governors Meeting. Washington, DC, 14–ß15 April. http://www.g20.utoronto.ca/2011/2011-finance-110415-en.html.

Guo, Kai, and Papa N'Diaye. 2009. *Is China's Export-Oriented Growth Sustainable?* IMF Working Paper WP/09/172. Washington, DC: IMF.

Haggard, Stephan, and Robert R. Kaufman. 1995. *The Political Economy of Democratic Transitions.* Princeton, NJ: Princeton University Press.

Hamada, Koichi, and Hugh Patrick. 1988. "Japan and the International Monetary Regime." In *The Political Economy of Japan,* vol. 2, ed. Takashi Inoguchi and Daniel Okimoto. Stanford, CA: Stanford University Press.

He, Dong. 2012. *Renminbi Internationalization: A Primer.* Hong Kong: Hong Kong Institute for Monetary Research.

He Xingqiang. 2011. "The RMB Exchange Rate: Interest Groups in China's Economic Policymaking." *China Security* 19: 23–36.

Healy, Andrew, and Neil Malhotra. 2009. "Myopic Voters and Natural Disaster Policy." *American Political Science Review* 103 (3): 387–406.

Helleiner, Eric. 1992. "Japan and the Changing Global Financial Order." *International Journal* 47 (2): 420–44.

———. 2003. *The Making of National Money.* Ithaca, NY: Cornell University Press.

———. 2006a. "Below the State: Micro-Level Power." In *International Monetary Power,* ed. David Andrews. Ithaca, NY: Cornell University Press.

———. 2006b. *Towards North American Monetary Union?* Montreal: McGill-Queen's University Press.

———. 2011. "Understanding the 2007–2008 Global Financial Crisis: Lessons for Scholars of International Political Economy." *Annual Review of Political Science* 14: 67–87.

———. 2014a. *Forgotten Foundations of Bretton Woods: International Development and the Making of the Postwar Order.* Ithaca, NY: Cornell University Press.

———. 2014b. *The Status Quo Crisis: Global Financial Governance after the 2008 Meltdown.* Oxford: Oxford University Press.

Helleiner, Eric, and Jonathan Kirshner, eds. 2009. *The Future of the Dollar.* Ithaca, NY: Cornell University Press.

Helleiner, Eric, and Anton Malkin. 2012. "Sectoral Interests and Global Money: Renminbi, Dollars and the Domestic Foundations of International Currency Policy." *Open Economies Review* 23 (1): 33–55.

Henning, C. Randall. 1994. *Currencies and Politics in the United States, Germany and Japan.* Washington, DC: Institute for International Economics.

———. 2006. "The Exchange-Rate Weapon and Macroeconomic Conflict." In *International Monetary Power,* ed. David Andrews. Ithaca, NY: Cornell University Press.

———. 2014. "Choice and Coercion in East Asian Exchange Rate Regimes." In *Power in a Changing World Economy: Lessons from East Asia,* ed. Benjamin J. Cohen and Eric M. P. Chiu. London: Routledge.

Herd, Richard. 2010. *A Pause in the Growth of Inequality in China?* Economic Department Working Papers, No. 748. Paris: OECD.

Herrerias, Maria J., and Vicente Orts. 2011. "The Driving Forces Behind China's Growth." *Economics of Transition* 19 (1): 79–124.

Higgott, Richard. 1998. "The Asian Economic Crisis: A Study in the Politics of Resentment." *New Political Economy.* 3 (3): 333–56.

Hirschman, Albert. 1980 [1945]. *National Power and the Structure of Foreign Trade.* Berkeley: University of California Press.

Holbig, Heike, and Bruce Gilley. 2010. "Reclaiming Legitimacy in China." *Politics & Policy* 38 (3): 395–422.

Horsefield, J. Keith, ed. 1969. *The International Monetary Fund 1945–1965: Twenty Years of International Monetary Cooperation.* Vol. 3. Washington, DC: International Monetary Fund.

Howson, Susan, and Donald Moggridge, eds. 1990. *The Wartime Diaries of Lionel Robbins and James Meade, 1943–45.* London: Macmillan.

Hu Angang and Shaoguang Wang. 1993. *Zhongguo Guojia Nengli Baogao* [Chinese National Capacity Report]. Shenyang: Liaoning Renmin Chubanshe.

Hu Jintao. 2008. "Hu Jintao Addresses the G20 Summit on Financial Markets and the World Economy," November 16. Ministry of Foreign Affairs of the People's Republic of China, http://www.fmprc.gov.cn/eng/wjdt/zyjh/t522600.htm.

———. 2009. "Cooperating Hand in Hand and Pulling Together at Times of Trouble," April 3. Speech summarized in "The Second Financial Summit Takes Place in London," Ministry of Foreign Affairs of the People's Republic of China, http://www.fmprc.gov.cn/eng/wjdt/zyjh/t556209.htm.

Hu, Xiaolian. 2007. "Cujin guoji shouzhi jiben pingheng, shixian guomin jingji youhao youkuai fazhan" [Promote a basic balance in the international balance of payments, achieve good and rapid development of the national economy]. Speech at the national conference on foreign exchange management in Beijing, January 21, 2007, http://news.xinhuanet.com/politics/2007-01/21/content_5633601.htm.

Huang, Yasheng. 2008. *Capitalism with Chinese Characteristics.* Cambridge: Cambridge University Press.

Hufbauer, Gary Clyde, and Claire Brunel. 2008. "The US Congress and the Chinese Renminbi." In *Debating China's Exchange Rate Policy* ed. Morris Goldstein and Nicholas R. Lardy. Washington, DC: Peterson Institute for International Economics.

Hughes, Christopher W. 2000. "Japanese Policy and the East Asian Crisis: Abject Defeat or Quiet Victory?" *Review of International Political Economy* 7 (2): 219–53.

Hung, Ho-fung. 2009. "America's Head Servant: The PRC's Dilemma in the Global Crisis." *New Left Review* 60: 5–25.

Ikenberry, G. John. 1992. "A World Order Restored: Expert Consensus and the Anglo-American Postwar Settlement." *International Organization* 46 (1): 289–321.

———. 2008. "The Rise of China and the Future of the West: Can the Liberal System Survive?" *Foreign Affairs* 87 (1): 23–37.

———. 2013. "The Rise of China, the United States, and the Future of the Liberal International Order." In *Tangled Titans: The United States and China,* ed. David Shambaugh. New York: Rowman & Littlefield.

Ikenberry, G. John, and Charles Kupchan. 1990. "Socialization and Hegemonic Power." *International Organization* 44 (3): 283–315.

Independent Evaluation Office of the IMF. 2007. *IMF Exchange Rate Policy Advice.* Washington, DC: IEO.

———. 2011. *IMF Performance in the Run-Up to the Financial and Economic Crisis.* Washington, DC: IEO.

———. 2013. *The Role of the IMF as Trusted Advisor.* Washington, DC: IEO.

International Monetary Fund. 1977. *Surveillance Over Exchange Rate Policies—Executive Board Decision No. 5392-(77/63).* Washington, DC: IMF.

———. 1996. "International Capital Markets Charting a Steadier Course." *IMF Survey* (September 23): 1–4.

———. 1997. "IMF Wins Mandate to Cover Capital Accounts, Debt Initiative Put in Motion." *IMF Survey* (May 12): 129–32.

———. 2003a. *The IMF and Recent Capital Account Crises: Indonesia, Korea, Brazil.* Washington, DC: IMF.

———. 2003b. *Lessons from the Crisis in Argentina.* Washington, DC: IMF.

———. 2005. *People's Republic of China: 2005 Article IV Consultation—Staff Report; Staff Statement; and Public Information Notice on the Executive Board Discussion.* Country Report No. 05/411, 17. Washington, DC: IMF.

———. 2006. *People's Republic of China: 2006 Article IV Consultation—Staff Report; Staff Statement; and Public Information Notice on the Executive Board Discussion.* Country Report No. 06/394. Washington, DC: IMF.

———. 2008. *Statement by Dr. Yi Gang, Deputy Governor of the People's Bank of China, at the Eighteenth Meeting of the International Monetary and Financial Committee.* Washington, DC: IMF.

———. 2011a. *G20 Mutual Assessment Process: From Pittsburgh to Cannes—IMF Umbrella Report.* Washington, DC: IMF.

———. 2011b. *People's Republic of China: 2011 Article IV Consultation.* Country Report No. 11/192. Washington, DC: IMF.

———. 2011c. *People's Republic of China Sustainability Report.* Washington, DC: IMF.

———. 2012a. *Decision on Bilateral and Multilateral Surveillance.* IMF Public Information Notice No.12/89, 30 July. Washington, DC: IMF.

———. 2012b. *IMF Executive Board Concludes 2012 Article IV Consultation with People's Republic of China.* IMF Public Information Notice No.12/86, 24 July. Washington, DC: IMF.

———. 2012c. *People's Republic of China 2012 Article IV Consultation.* IMF Country Report No.12/195, July. Washington, DC: IMF.

———. 2012d. *Transcript of a Conference Call on the 2012 Article IV Consultations with China.* Washington, DC: IMF.

———. 2012e. *Transcript of the International Financial and Monetary Committee (IMFC) Press Conference.* October 13. Washington, DC: IMF.

———. 2013a. "Currency Composition of Official Foreign Exchange Reserves (COFER)," September 30. http://www.imf.org/external/np/sta/cofer/eng.

———. 2013b. *Fact Sheet: A Guide to Committees, Groups and Clubs.* September 27. Washington, DC: IMF.

Ito, Takatoshi. 2011. *The Internationalization of the RMB: Opportunities and Pitfalls.* CGS/IIGG Working Paper. New York: Council on Foreign Relations.

Jacobson, Harold K., and Michel Oksenberg. 1990. *China's Participation in the IMF, the World Bank, and the GATT: Toward a Global Economic Order.* Ann Arbor: University of Michigan Press.

James, Harold. 2009. *The Creation and Destruction of Value.* Cambridge, MA: Harvard University Press.

Jian, Chen. 2001. *Mao's China and the Cold War.* Chapel Hill: University of North Carolina Press.

Jiang, Yang. 2010. "Response and Responsibility: China in East Asian Financial Cooperation." *Pacific Review* 23 (5): 603–23.

Jiang, Yong. 2011. "Guoyou qiye shi guojia jingji anquan de zhongliu dizhu" [State-owned enterprises are the pillars of national economic security]. *Guoyou zichan guanli* [State Assets Management] (12): 46–49.

Jiang Zemin. 2002. "Build a Well-Off Society in an All-Rounded Way and Create a New Situation in Building Socialism with Chinese Characteristics." In *Documents of the Sixteenth National Congress of the Communist Party of China: Jiang Zemin.* Beijing: Foreign Languages Press.

Johnston, Alastair Iain. 2003. "Is China a Status Quo Power?" *International Security* 27 (4): 5–56.

———. 2008. *Social States: China in International Institutions, 1980–2000.* Princeton, NJ: Princeton University Press.

Johnstone, Christopher. 1999. "Strained Alliance: U.S.-Japan Diplomacy in the Asian Financial Crisis." *Survival* 41 (2): 121–37.

Kaplan, Stephen B. 2006. "The Political Obstacles to Greater Exchange Rate Flexibility in China." *World Development* 34 (7): 1182–1200.

Katada, Saori. 2002. "Japan and Asian Monetary Regionalization: Cultivating a New Regional Leadership after the Asian Financial Crisis." *Geopolitics* 7 (1): 85–112.

Katzenstein, Peter. 1987. *Policy and Politics in West Germany; The Growth of a Semi-Sovereign State.* Philadelphia: Temple University Press.

Keefer, Philip. 2007. "Elections, Special Interests, and Financial Crisis." *International Organization* 61 (3): 607–41.

Kennedy, Scott. 2008. *The Business of Lobbying*. Cambridge, MA: Harvard University Press.

Kent, Ann. 2007. *Beyond Compliance: China, International Organizations, and Global Security*. Stanford, CA: Stanford University Press.

Keohane, Robert O., and Joseph S. Nye. 1977. *Power and Interdependence: World Politics in Transition*. Boston: Little, Brown.

Kessler, Timothy P. 1998. "Political Capital: Mexican Financial Policy Under Salinas." *World Politics* 51 (1): 36–66.

Kim, Icksoo. 2002. "Accession into the WTO: External Pressure for Internal Reforms in China." *Journal of Contemporary China* 11 (32): 433–58.

Kim, Joon-Kyung, and Chung H. Lee. 2009. "Between Two Whales: Korea's Choice in the Post-Crisis Era." In *Strategic Asia 2009–10: Economic Meltdown and Geopolitical Stability,* ed. Ashley Tellis, Andrew Marble, and Travis Tanner. Seattle: National Bureau of Asian Research.

Kindleberger, Charles P. 1972. "The International Monetary Politics of a Near–Great Power: Two French Episodes, 1926–1936 and 1960–1970." *Economic Notes* 1 (2–3): 30–44.

———. 1973. *The World in Depression, 1929–1939*. Berkeley: University of California Press.

———. 1978. *Manias, Panics and Crashes: A History of Financial Crises*. New York: Basic Books.

———. 1981. *International Money: A Collection of Essays*. Boston: George Allen & Unwin.

Kirk, Donald. 1999. *Korean Crisis: Unraveling of the Miracle in the IMF Era*. New York: Palgrave.

Kirshner, Jonathan. 1995. *Currency and Coercion: The Political Economy of International Monetary Power*. Princeton, NJ: Princeton University Press.

———, ed. 2003. *Monetary Orders: Ambiguous Economics, Ubiquitous Politics*. Ithaca, NY: Cornell University Press.

———. 2006. "Currency and Coercion in the Twenty-First Century." In *International Monetary Power,* ed. David Andrews. Ithaca, NY: Cornell University Press.

———. 2007. *Appeasing Bankers: Financial Caution on the Road to War*. Princeton, NJ: Princeton University Press.

———. 2008. "Dollar Primacy and American Power." *Review of International Political Economy* 15 (3): 418–38.

———. 2009. "After the (Relative) Fall: Dollar Diminution and the Consequences for American Power." In *The Future of the Dollar,* ed. Eric Helleiner and Jonathan Kirshner. Ithaca, NY: Cornell University Press.

———. 2012. "The Tragedy of Offensive Realism: Classical Realism and the Rise of China." *European Journal of International Relations* 18 (1): 53–75.

———. *American Power after the Financial Crisis*. Ithaca, NY: Cornell University Press.

Krasner, Stephen. 1977. "US Commercial and Monetary Policy: Unravelling the Paradox of External Strength and Internal Weakness." *International Organization* 31 (4): 635–71.

Krugman, Paul. 1979. "A Model of Balance-of-Payments Crises." *Journal of Money, Credit and Banking* 11 (3): 311–25.

Kuroda, Haruhiko. 2000. "Information Technology, Globalization, and International Financial Architecture." Speech delivered at Foreign Correspondents Club of Japan, June 5. http://www.mof.go.jp/english/international_policy/convention/summit/if018.htm.

Lake, David. A. 2009. "Open Economy Politics: A Critical Review." *Review of International Organizations* 4 (3): 219–44.

Lardy, Nicholas. 1998. *China's Unfinished Revolution.* Washington, DC: Brookings Institution Press.

———. 1999. "China and the International Financial System." In *China Joins the World: Progress and Prospects,* ed. Elizabeth Economy and Michel Oksenberg. New York: Council on Foreign Relations Press.

———. 2008. *Financial Repression in China.* Peterson Institute Policy Brief 08-8. Washington, DC: Peterson Institute for International Economics.

———. 2012. *Sustaining China's Economic Growth after the Global Financial Crisis.* Washington, DC: Peterson Institute for International Economics.

Lardy, Nicholas, and Nicholas Borst. 2013. *A Blueprint for Rebalancing the Chinese Economy.* Institute for International Economics, Policy Brief 13-02, February. Washington, DC: Institute for International Economics.

Lawton, Thomas C., James N. Rosenau, and Amy C. Verdun, eds. 2000. *Strange Power: Shaping the Parameters of International Relations and International Political Economy.* Burlington, VT: Ashgate.

League of Nations. 1932. *Report of the Gold Delegation of the Financial Committee.* Geneva: League of Nations.

Lee, Ching Kwan. 2012. "Durable Subordination: Chinese Labour Regime through a South Korean Lens." In *East Asian Capitalism: Continuity, Diversity and Change,* ed. Andrew Walter and Xiaoke Zhang. Cambridge: Cambridge University Press.

Lee, Il Houng, Murtaza Syed, and Liu Xueyan. 2012. *Is China Over-investing and Does it Matter?* Working Paper 12/277. Washington, DC: IMF.

Leng Zhaosong. 2013. "Guojin Mintui Zhuyan Fenqi Zongshu [A summary analysis of the controversies over 'Guojin Mintui']," *Hongqi Wengao* (Red Flag Presentation) (1).

Li, Cheng. 2005. "The New Bipartisanship within the Chinese Communist Party." *Orbis* 49 (3): 387–400.

———, ed. 2008. *China's Changing Political Landscape: Prospects for Democracy.* Washington, DC: Brookings Institution.

———. 2012. *The Battle for China's Top Nine Leadership Posts.* Washington, DC: Center for Strategic and International Studies.

Li, Choh-Ming. 1943. "China in World Economy." *Foreign Policy Reports* 19 (16): 218–23.

Li, Daokui, and Yin Xingzhong. 2010. "Guoji huobi tixi xin jiagou: Hou jinrong weiji" [New structure of the international monetary system: Research on the post–financial crisis era], *Jinrong yanjiu* [Journal of Financial Research] 2.

Li Ruogu. 2003. "Statement of Mr. Li Ruogu, Assistant Governor of the People's Bank of China." April 12. Washington, DC: IMF.

———. 2005. "Statement by Mr. Li Ruogu, Deputy Governor of the People's Bank of China." Eleventh Meeting of the International Monetary and Financial Committee, April 16. http://www.imf.org/external/spring/2005/imfc/stmt/eng/chn.pdf.

——. 2010. "Jinrong weiji yu guoji huobi tixi gaige" [The financial crisis and international monetary system reform]. *Zhongguo jinrong* [China Finance] 5.

Li Shaojun. 2003. "International Regimes of Nuclear Nonproliferation and China." In *Construction within Contradiction: Multiple Perspectives on the Relationship between China and International Organizations,* ed. Wang Yizhou. Beijing: China Development Publishing House.

Li Xing. 2010. "The Rise of China and the Capitalist World Order: The 'Four-China' Nexus." In *The Rise of China and the Capitalist World Order,* ed. Li Xing. Burlington, VT: Ashgate.

Li Yang. 2010. "Quanjiu jinrong tixi gaige ji yazhou de xuanze" [Reform of the global financial system and Asia's choices: we need deeper thinking], *Guoji jinrong yanjiu* [Studies of International Finance] 10.

Lieberthal, Kenneth, and Jisi Wang. 2012. *Addressing US-China Strategic Distrust.* China Center Monographs, No. 4. Washington, DC: The Brookings Institution.

Liew, Leong H. 2004. "Policy Elites in the Political Economy of China's Exchange Rate Policymaking." *Journal of Contemporary China* 13 (38): 21–51.

Lin, Li-Wen, and Milhaupt, Curtis J. 2011. *We Are the (National) Champions: Understanding the Mechanisms of State Capitalism in China.* Columbia Law and Economics Working Paper No. 409. New York: Columbia Law School.

Ljungwall, Christer, Yi Xiong, and Zou Yutong. 2013. "Central Bank Financial Strength and the Cost of Sterilization in China." *China Economic Review* 25 (1): 105–16.

Lu Dong and Wang Hao. 2012. "Shuangbian benbi jiesuan moshi yu fazhan" [The patterns and development of bilateral currency settlement]." *Zhongguo jinrong* [China Finance] 4: 63–64.

Lu Qianjin. 2009. "Lun guoji jinrong tixi de gaige he renminbi guojihua zhanlue" [Discussion of international financial system reform and RMB internationalization strategy]. *Shehui kexue* [Social Science] (4).

Ma, Guonan, and Wang Yi. 2010. "China's High Saving Rate: Myth and Reality." *International Economics* 122: 5–39.

Mallaby, Sebastian, and Olin Wethington. 2012. "The Future of the Yuan: China's Struggle to Internationalize Its Currency." *Foreign Affairs* 91:1.

Martin, Michael. 2012. *China's Banking System: Issues for Congress.* Washington, DC: Congressional Research Service.

McCauley, Robert N. 2011. *Internationalizing the Renminbi and China's Financial Development Model.* CGS/IIGG Working Paper. New York: Council on Foreign Relations.

McKinnon, Ronald I. 2005. *Exchange Rates under the East Asian Dollar Standard: Living with Conflicted Virtue.* Cambridge, MA: MIT Press.

McKinnon, Ronald, and Kenichi Ohno. 1997. *Dollar and Yen: Resolving Economic Conflict Between the U.S. and Japan.* Cambridge, MA: MIT Press.

McNally, Christopher A. 2012. "Abstract Sino-Capitalism: China's Reemergence and the International Political Economy." *World Politics* 64 (4): 741–76.

McNamara, Kathleen. 1998. *The Currency of Ideas.* Ithaca, NY: Cornell University Press.

Mertha, A. 2009. "'Fragmented Authoritarianism 2.0': Political Pluralization in the Chinese Policy Process." *China Quarterly* 200: 995–1012.

Metzler, Mark. 2006. *Levers of Empire: The International Gold Standard and the Crisis of Liberalism in Prewar Japan.* Berkeley: University of California Press.

Mikesell, Raymond. 1994. *The Bretton Woods Debates: A Memoir.* Essays in International Finance, No.192. Princeton, NJ: International Finance Section, Department of Economics, Princeton University.

Miyazawa, Kiichi. 1998. "Towards a New Financial Architecture." Speech delivered at the Foreign Correspondents Club of Japan, December 15. http://www.mof.go.jp/english/if/e1e057.htm.

Momani, Bessma. 2013. "China at the International Monetary Fund: Continued Engagement In Its Drive for Membership and Added Voice at the IMF Executive Board." *Journal of Chinese Economics* 1 (1): 125–50.

Montinola, Gabriella, Yingyi Qian, and Barry R. Weingast. "Federalism, Chinese Style: the Political Basis for Economic Success in China." *World Politics* 48 (1) (1995): 50–81.

Morgan, Peter J. 2012. "The Role of Macroeconomic Policy in Rebalancing Growth." *Journal of Asian Economics* 23 (1): 13–25.

Nathan, Andrew J., and Andrew Scobell. 2012. *China's Search for Security.* New York: Columbia University Press.

National Intelligence Council. 2012. *Global Trends 2030: Alternative Worlds.* http://www.dni.gov/index.php/about/organization/global-trends-2030.

National Security Council. 2006. *The National Security Strategy of the United States of America*, Washington, DC, March. http://georgewbush-whitehouse.archives.gov/nsc/nss/2006/index.html.

Naughton, Barry. 2008a. "China's Economic Leadership after the 17th Party Congress." *China Leadership Monitor* (23): 1–12.

———. 2008b. "SASAC and Rising Corporate Power in China." *China Leadership Monitor* (24): 1–9.

———. 2011. "What Price Continuity?" *China Leadership Monitor.* (34): 1–11.

———. 2013. "Signaling Change: New Leaders Begin the Search for Economic Reform." *China Leadership Monitor,* (40): 1–11.

Noland, Marcus. 1996. *US-China Economic Relations.* Peterson Institute Working Paper No. 6. Washington, DC: Peterson Institute for International Economics.

Obstfeld, Maurice. 1996. "Models of Currency Crises with Self-fulfilling Features." *European Economic Review* 40 (3): 1037–47.

Obstfeld, Maurice, and Kenneth Rogoff. 2005. "Global Current Account Imbalances and Exchange Rate Adjustments." *Brookings Papers on Economic Activity* (1): 67–146.

———. 2009. *Global Imbalances and the Financial Crisis: Products of Common Causes.* CEPR Working Paper No. 7606. London: CEPR.

Obstfeld, Maurice, Jay C. Shambaugh, and Alan M. Taylor. 2010. "Financial Stability, the Trilemma, and International Reserves." *American Economic Journal: Macroeconomics* 2 (2): 57–94.

Odell, John. 1982. *U.S. International Monetary Policy: Markets, Power, and Ideas as Sources of Change.* Princeton, NJ: Princeton University Press.

Oi, Jean. 1999. *Rural China Takes Off.* Berkeley: University of California Press.

Olson, Mancur, Jr. 1982. *The Rise and Decline of Nations.* New Haven, CT: Yale University Press.

Parello-Plesner, Jonas. 2012. "China and Europe in the Eurocrisis." Testimony before the US-China Economic and Security Review Commission, Hearing on the China-Europe Relationship and Transatlantic Implications, April 19, 2012. http://origin. www.uscc.gov/sites/default/files/transcripts/4.19.12HearingTranscript.pdf.

Pearson, Margaret M. 1999. "The Major Multilateral Economic Institutions Engage China." In *Engaging China: The Management of an Emerging Power,* ed. Alastair Iain Johnston and Robert Ross. New York: Routledge.

———. 2000. *China's New Business Elite.* Berkeley: University of California Press.

Pei, Minxin. 2011. "Inside the Black Box; A Guide to Policy-making in China." Macquarie Economics Research, http://macq.wir.jp/l.ut?t=dVMxcYq.

———. 2012. "China's Politics of the Economically Possible." http://www.project-syndi cate.org/commentary/china-s-politics-of-the-economically-possible.

People's Bank of China. 2009. *2009 nian zhongguo jinrong wending baogao* [China Financial Stability Report 2009]. http://www.pbc.gov.cn/publish/jinrongwendingju/ 370/2010/20100712145051297162094/20100712145051297162094_.html.

People's Bank of China, Wuhan Branch. 1995. "A View of the Effects of the New Exchange Rate Policy in 1994." *Review of Economic Research* 28: 38–46.

Pepinsky, Thomas. 2009. *Economic Crises and the Breakdown of Authoritarian Regimes.* New York: Cambridge University Press.

Pettis, Michael. 2007. "China's Last Option: Let the Yuan Soar." *Far Eastern Economic Review* 170 (5): 10–15.

———. 2008. "Chinese Inflation: It's Money, Not Pork." *Far Eastern Economic Review* 171 (3): 42–45.

———. 2011. "The Contentious Debate over China's Economic Transition." Carnegie Endowment for International Peace, http://carnegieendowment.org/2011/03/25/ contentious-debate-over-china-s-economic-transition/37hy.

———. 2012. "What Is Financial Reform in China?" China Financial Markets, 4 July. http://blog.mpettis.com.

———. 2013. *Restructuring the Chinese Economy: Economic Distortions and the Next Decade of Chinese Growth.* Washington: Carnegie.

Pineau, G., Ettore Dorrucci, Fabio Cornelli, and Angelika Lagerblom. 2006. *The Accumulation of Foreign Reserves.* European Central Bank Occasional Paper Series, No. 43. Frankfurt: ECB.

Pollard, Robert. 1985. *Economic Security and the Origins of the Cold War, 1945–1950.* New York: Columbia University Press.

Prasad, Eswar. 2011. "Rebalancing Growth in Asia." *International Finance* 14 (1): 27–66.

Qu, Fengjie. 2009. "Guoji huobi jinrong tixi de bianhua qushi yu woguo duice" [Trends of change in the international financial system and China's policy responses]. *Xin jinrong* [New Finance] 5.

Reinhart, Carmen M, and Vincent R. Reinhart. 1998. "Some Lessons for Policy Makers Who Deal with the Mixed Blessing of Capital Inflows." In *Capital Flows and Financial Crises,* ed. Miles Kahler. Manchester: Council of Foreign Relations.

Reinhart, Carmen, and Kenneth Rogoff. 2009. *This Time is Different: Eight Centuries of Financial Folly.* Princeton, NJ: Princeton University Press.

Rodrik, Dani. 1998. "Who Needs Capital Account Mobility?" In *Should the IMF Pursue Capital Account Liberalization?* ed. Peter Kenen. Essays in International Finance, No. 207 Princeton, NJ: Princeton University Press.

———. "Social Cost of Foreign Exchange Reserves." *International Economic Journal* 20: 253–66.

———. 2008. "The Real Exchange Rate and Economic Growth." *Brookings Papers on Economic Activity* (2): 365–412.

———. 2010. "Making Room for China in the World Economy." *American Economic Review* 100 (2): 89–93.

———. 2013. "The New Mercantilist Challenge." http://www.project-syndicate.org/commentary/the-return-of-mercantilism-by-dani-rodrik.

Rodrik, Dani, and Arvind Subramanian. 2009. "Why Did Financial Globalization Disappoint?" *IMF Staff Papers* 56 (1). Washington, DC: IMF.

Rosenberg, Emily. 1985. "Foundations of United States International Financial Power: Gold Standard Diplomacy, 1900–1905." *Business History Review* 59: 169–202.

Ross, Robert S., and Zhu Feng. 2008. "The Rise of China: Theoretical and Policy Perspectives." In *China's Ascent: Power, Security, and the Future of International Politics,* ed. Ross and Feng. Ithaca, NY: Cornell University Press.

Roubini, Nouriel, and Stephen Mihm. 2010. *Crisis Economics.* New York: Penguin Press.

Roubini, Nouriel, and Brad Setser. 2005. "Will the Bretton Woods 2 Regime Unravel Soon? The Risk of a Hard Landing in 2005–2006" *Federal Reserve Bank of Chicago Proceedings* (1).

Royal Institute of International Affairs. 1932. *The International Gold Problem.* London: Oxford University Press.

Ruggie, John G. 1983. "International Regimes, Transactions, and Change: Embedded Liberalism in the Postwar Economic Order." In *International Regimes,* ed. Stephen D. Krasner. Ithaca, NY: Cornell University Press.

Sakakibara, Eisuke. 1999a. "Reform of the International Financial System." Speech delivered at the Manila Framework Meeting, Melbourne, March 26. https://www.mof.go.jp/english/international_policy/financial_cooperation_in_asia/manila_framework/e1e070.htm.

———. 1999b. "Reform of the International Financial Architecture." Speech delivered at the Symposium on Building the Financial System of the 21st Century, Kyoto, June 25. http://www.mof.go.jp/english/international_policy/new_international_financial_architecture/if004.htm.

Schuler, Kurt, and Andrew Rosenberg, eds. 2012. *The Bretton Woods Transcripts.* New York: Center for Financial Stability.

Schwartz, Herman. 2009. *Subprime Nation.* Ithaca, NY: Cornell University Press.

Scissors, Derek. 2012. *Chinese Outward Investment: Acceleration Features the U.S.* Issue Brief 3656. Washington: Heritage Foundation.

Sester, Brad. 2008a. "China: Creditor to the Rich." *China Security* 4 (4): 17–23.

———. 2008b. *Sovereign Wealth and Sovereign Power: The Strategic Consequences of American Indebtedness.* New York: Council on Foreign Relations Press.

Shambaugh, David. 2008. *China's Communist Party: Atrophy and Adaptation.* Berkeley: University of California Press.

———. 2013. *China Goes Global: The Partial Power.* New York: Oxford University Press.

Sheng, Andrew. 2009. *From Asian to Global Financial Crisis: An Asian Regulator's View of Unfettered Finance in the 1990s and 2000s.* Cambridge: Cambridge University Press.

Sheng, Yumin. 2010. *Economic Openness and Territorial Politics in China.* Cambridge: Cambridge University Press.

Shih, Victor C. 2008. *Factions and Finance in China: Elite Conflict and Inflation.* Cambridge: Cambridge University Press.

Shih, Victor. 2009. *Factions and Finance in China: Elite Conflict and Inflation.* Cambridge: Cambridge University Press.

Shih, Victor, and David Steinberg. 2012. "The Domestic Politics of the International Dollar Standard: A Statistical Analysis of Support for the Reserve Currency, 2000–2008." *Canadian Journal of Political Science* 45 (4): 855–80.

Shinjo, Hiroshi. 1962. *History of the Yen: 100 Years of Japanese Money-Economy.* Tokyo: Kinokuniya Bookstore Co.

Shirk, Susan. 1993. *The Political Logic of Economic Reform in China.* Berkeley: University of California Press.

———. 2007. *China, Fragile Superpower: How China's Internal Politics Could Derail Its Peaceful Rise.* Oxford: Oxford University Press.

Shiroyama, Tomoko. 2009. *China in the Great Depression: Market, State, and the World Economy, 1929–1937.* Cambridge, MA: Harvard University Press.

Smethurst, Richard. 2007. *From Foot Soldier to Finance Minister: Takahashi Korekiyo, Japan's Keynes.* Cambridge, MA: Harvard University Press.

Sohn, Injoo. 2008. "Learning to Co-operate: China's Multilateral Approach to Asian Financial Co-operation." *China Quarterly* 194: 309–326.

Song Guoyou. 2008. "Guoji jinrong tixi xianlu chongsu yixiang" [The international financial system shows signs of being remolded]. *Xibu Luncong* [Western Forum] 11.

Spiro, David E. 1999. *The Hidden Hand of American Hegemony: Petrodollar Recycling and International Markets.* Ithaca, NY: Cornell University Press.

State Administration of Foreign Exchange. 2003. "2002 nian zhongguo guoji shouzhi zhuangkuang fenxi" [An analysis of the state of China's international balance of payments in 2002]. http://news.xinhuanet.com/zhengfu/2003-05/23/content_883902.htm/.

Steinberg, David, and Victor Shih. 2012. "Interest Group Influence in Authoritarian States: The Political Determinants of Chinese Exchange Rate Policy." *Comparative Political Studies* 45 (11): 1405–34.

Strange, Susan. 1971. *Sterling and British Policy: A Political Study of an International Currency in Decline.* Oxford: Oxford University Press.

———. 1987. "The Persistent Myth of Lost Hegemony." *International Organization* 41: 551–74.

———. 1988. *States and Markets.* New York: Pinter.

Subramanian, Arvind. 2010. *New PPP-Based Estimates of Renminbi Undervaluation and Policy Implications.* Peterson Institute Policy Brief 10-8. Washington, DC: Peterson Institute for International Economics.

———. 2011. *Eclipse: Living in the Shadow of China's Economic Dominance.* Washington: Peterson Institute for International Economics.

Summers, Lawrence. 2004. "The United States and the Global Adjustment Process." Speech at the 3rd Annual Stavros S. Niarchos Lecture, Institute for International Economics, March 23, 2004. http://www.iie.com/publications/papers/paper. cfm?researchid=200.

Sun Lujun. 1995. "Some Thoughts on Central Bank's Regulation of Foreign Exchange." *Review of Economic Research* 193: 2–8.

Sun Yat-sen. 1922. *The International Development of China.* New York: G. P. Putnam's Sons.

Takahashi, Kosuke. 2012. "Japan and China Bypass U.S. in Direct Currency Trade." *Asia-Pacific Journal* 10, 24 (3).

Taylor, John B. 2007. *Global Financial Warriors: The Untold Story of International Finance in the Post-9/11 World.* New York: Norton.

Thorbecke, Wilem, and Gordon Smith. 2010. "How Would an Appreciation of the Renminbi and Other East Asian Currencies Affect China's Exports?" *Review of International Economics* 18 (1): 95–108.

Thornton, Alistair. 2012. "Anaemic Ascent: Why China's Currency Is Far from Going Global." Lowy Institute Analysis (August). http://lowyinstitute.cachefly.net/files/ thornton_anaemic_ascent_web.pdf.

Tourres, Marie-Aimée. 2003. *The Tragedy That Didn't Happen: Malaysia's Crisis Management and Capital Controls.* Kuala Lumpur: Institute of Strategic and International Studies.

Tsai, Kellee. 2007. *Capitalism Without Democracy.* Ithaca, NY: Cornell University Press.

US State Department. 1948. *Proceedings and Documents of the United Nations Monetary and Financial Conference, Bretton Woods, New Hampshire, July 1–22, 1944.* Washington, DC: US Government Printing Office.

———. 1966. *Foreign Relations of the United States: Diplomatic Papers, 1944: China: Volume VI.* Washington: US Government Printing Office.

US Treasury. 1990. *Report to the Congress on International Economic and Exchange Rate Policy.* Washington, DC: Department of the Treasury.

———. 1991. *Report to the Congress on International Economic and Exchange Rate Policy, May 1991.* Washington, DC: Department of the Treasury.

———. 1994. *Seventh Annual Report to the Congress on International Economic and Exchange Rate Policy, December 1994.* Washington, DC: Department of the Treasury.

Vogel, Ezra. 2011. *Deng Xiaoping and the Transformation of China.* Cambridge, MA: Belknap Press of Harvard University Press.

Von Glahn, Richard. 1996. *Fountain of Fortune: Money and Monetary Policy in China 1000–1700.* Berkeley: University of California Press.

Wade, Robert, and Frank Veneroso. 1998. "The Gathering World Slump and the Battle Over Capital Controls." *New Left Review* (September–October): 124–37.

Walter, Andrew. 1991. *World Power and World Money: The Role of Hegemony and International Monetary Order.* London: Palgrave Macmillan.

———. 2006. "Domestic Sources of International Monetary Leadership." In *International Monetary Power,* ed. David Andrews. Ithaca, NY: Cornell University Press.

Walter, Carl E., and Fraser Howie. 2011. *Red Capitalism: The Fragile Financial Foundation of China's Extraordinary Rise.* Singapore: Wiley.

Walter, Stefanie. 2008. "A New Approach for Determining Exchange-Rate Level Preferences." *International Organization* 62 (3): 405–38.

Wang, Chun-Hsuan, Chun-Hung A. Lin, and Chih-Hai Yang. 2012. "Short-run and Long-run Effects of Exchange Rate Change on Trade Balance: Evidence from China and Its Trading Partners." *Japan and the World Economy* 24 (4): 266–73.

Wang Gungwu. 1995. *The Revival of Chinese Nationalism.* Leiden: International Institute for Asian Studies.

Wang, Hongying. 2003. "China's Exchange Rate Policy in the Aftermath of the Asian Financial Crisis." In *Monetary Orders: Ambiguous Economics, Ubiquitous Politics,* ed. Jonathan Kirshner. Ithaca, NY: Cornell University Press.

Wang Xin. 2007. "China as a Net Creditor: An Indication of Strength or Weakness." *China & World Economy* 15 (6): 22–36.

Wang, Yaping 1995. "An Analysis and Solution to the Change in RMB's Value." *Review of Economic Research* 91: 12–18.

Weintraub, Sidney. 2004. "Lessons from the Chile and Singapore Free Trade Agreements." In *Free Trade Agreements: U.S. Strategies and Priorities,* ed. Jeffrey Schott. Washington, DC: Institute for International Economics.

Wen Jiabao. 2011. "Report on the Work of the Government." Speech delivered at the Fourth Session of the Eleventh National People's Congress, March 5, http://www.china.org.cn/china/NPC_CPPCC_2011/2011-03/15/content_22143099.htm.

Westad, Odd Arne. 1993. *Cold War and Revolution.* New York: Columbia University Press.

Wilbur, C. Martin. 1976. *Sun Yat-sen: Frustrated Patriot.* New York: Columbia University Press.

Willett, Thomas D. 2000. *International Financial Markets as Sources of Crises or Discipline: The Too Much Too Late Hypothesis.* Essays in International Finance, No. 218. Princeton, NJ: International Finance Section, Department of Economics, Princeton University.

Williamson, John. 2012. "Is the 'Beijing Consensus' Now Dominant?" *Asia Policy* 13: 1–16.

Williamson, John, and Molly Mahar. 1998. *A Survey of Financial Liberalization.* Essays in International Finance, No. 211. Princeton, NJ: International Finance Section, Department of Economics, Princeton University.

Willis, Henry Parker. 1901. *A History of the Latin Monetary Union.* Chicago: University of Chicago Press.

Wilsdon, James, and James Keeley. 2007. *China: The Next Science Superpower.* London: Demos.

Wong, Christine. 2007. "Budget Reform in China." *OECD Journal on Budgeting* 7 (1): 1–24.

World Bank. 2011. *Global Development Horizons 2011—Multipolarity: The New Global Economy.* Washington: World Bank.

World Bank. 2012. *World Development Indicators Database.* http://databank.world bank org.

World Bank and Development Research Center of the State Council, the People's Republic of China. 2012. *China 2030: Building a Modern, Harmonious, and Creative High-Income Society.* Washington, DC: World Bank.

Wright, Logan. 2009. "The Elusive Price for Stability." Ph.D. diss., Department of Political Science, George Washington University.

Wu, Ching-Chao. 1943. "Internal Economic Development." *Foreign Policy Reports* 19 (16): 214–18.

Wu Xinbo. 2010. "Understanding the Geopolitical Implications of the Global Financial Crisis." *Washington Quarterly* (October), 33 (4): 155–63.

Xia Bin. 2011. "Zhongguo fazhan yu guoji jinrong zhixu" [China's development and the international monetary order], *Lilun shijiao* [Theoretical Horizon] 1.

Xiang Huaicheng. 2011. "Zhongguo caizheng tizhi gaige liushinian" [Sixty years of reform of the Chinese fiscal system)]. http://www.chinareform.org.cn/economy/tax/practice/201112/t20111202_129043.htm.

Xiao Gang. 2000. "Statement by Mr. Xiao Gang, Deputy Governor of the People's Bank of China and Alternate Governor of the Fund for China." International Monetary and Financial Committee, April 16. Washington, DC: IMF. http://www.imf.org/external/spring/2000/imfc/chn.htm.

Xing, Yuqing. 2012. "Processing Trade, Exchange Rates and China's Bilateral Trade Balances." *Journal of Asian Economics* 23 (5): 540–47.

Xiong, Xianlong. 1995. "The Market Exchange Rate of RMB and the Internal and External Equilibrium of the Chinese Economy." *Review of Economic Research* 66: 2–8.

Yam, Joseph. 2010. *The International Monetary System and the Renminbi.* Paper written for China Development Bank Research Centre Working Paper No. 3, November 3. Beijing: China Development Bank Financial Research Center.

Yang, Dennis Tao, Junsen Zhang, and Shaojie Zhou. 2011. *Why Are Saving Rates So High in China?* NBER Working Paper No. 16771. Washington: National Bureau of Economic Research.

Yeung, Benjamin. 2008. "China in the Era of Globalization: The Emergence of the Discourse on Economic Security." *Pacific Review* 21 (5): 635–60.

Yi Gang. 2011. "Statement by Yi Gang, Deputy Governor, People's Bank of China." Twenty-Third Meeting of the International Monetary and Financial Committee, April 16. http://www.imf.org/External/spring/2011/imfc/statement/eng/chn.pdf.

Yi, Jingtao. 2007. *China's Exchange Rate Policymaking in the Hu-Wen Era.* The University of Nottingham China Policy Institute, Briefing Series Issue 29.

Young, Arthur N. 1963. *China and the Helping Hand: 1937–1945.* Cambridge, MA: Harvard University Press.

Yu Yongding. 2001. "A Review of China's Macroeconomic Development and Policies in the 1990s." *China & World Economy* 6: 3–12.

———. 2003. "Xiaochu shengzhi kongjiu zheng, shixian jingji de ping heng fazhan" [Eradicate the fear of RMB revaluation]. *Guoji jingji pinglun* [International Economic Review] (9–10): 1–10.

———. 2005. "The G20 and China: A Chinese Perspective." *China & World Economy* 13 (1): 3–14.

———. 2006. "Global Imbalances: China's Perspective." Paper prepared for conference on European and Asian Perspectives on Global Imbalances, Beijing, 12–14 July. www.iie.com/publications/pb/pb07-4/yu.pdf.

———. 2008. *Meiguo cihuo weiji: beijing, yuanyin yu fazhan* [US subprime crisis: background, causes and development]. Zhongguo shehuikexueyuan shijie jingji yu zhengzhi yanjiusuo guoji jinrong yanjiu zhongxin [Chinese Academy of Social Sciences, Institute of World Economics and Politics, Research Center for International Finance], Working Paper no. 0817.

———. 2011. "Zai lun renminbi guojihua" [Further discussion on the internationalization of the RMB], *Guoji jingji pinglun* [International Economic Review] (5).

Zanasi, Margherita. 2006. *Saving the Nation: Economic Modernity in Republican China.* Chicago: University of Chicago Press.

Zhang, Bin, and He Fan. 2007. "Is Asian Currency Unit Attractive to East Asian Economies?" *China & World Economy* 15 (1): 62–76.

Zhang, Ming. 2009a. "China's New International Financial Strategy amid the Global Financial Crisis." *China & World Economy,* 17 (5): 22–35.

Zhang, Ming. 2009b. *Quanqiu jinrong weiji beijing xia de guoji huobi tixi gaige* [Reform of the international monetary system under the global financial crisis]. Zhongguo shehuikexueyuan shijie jingji yu zhengzhi yanjiusuo guoji jinrong yanjiu zhongxin [Chinese Academy of Social Sciences, Institute of World Economics and Politics, Research Center for International Finance], Working Paper no. 0919. December 21.

Zhang, Ming. 2012. "Chinese Stylized Sterilization: The Cost-sharing Mechanism and Financial Repression." *China & World Economy* 20 (2): 41–58.

Zhang Yuyan and Zhang Jingchun. 2008. "Guoji huobi de chengben he shouyi" [International currency's costs and benefits], *Shijie zhishi* [World Affairs] (21).

Zhang Yuyan. 2010. "Renminbi guojihua: zantong haishi fandui" [Internationalization of the RMB: Endorse or oppose?]. *Guoji jingji pinglun* [International Economic Review] 1.

Zhao, Suisheng. 2004. *A Nation-State by Construction: Dynamics of Modern Chinese Nationalism.* Stanford, CA: Stanford University Press.

Zheng, Yongnian. 1999. *Discovering Chinese Nationalism in China.* Cambridge: Cambridge University Press.

Zhou Xiaochuan. 2004a. "Statement by Zhou Xiaochuan, Governor of the People's Bank of China at the Ninth Meeting of the International Monetary and Financial Committee." April 24. http://www.imf.org/External/spring/2004/imfc/statem/eng/chne.pdf.

———. 2004b. "Statement by the Hon, Zhou Xiaochuan, Governor of the Fund for the People's Republic of China, at the Joint Annual Discussion." October 3. Annual Meeting, Boards of Governors, International Monetary Fund and World Bank Group. http://www.imf.org/external/am/2004/speeches/pr32e.pdf.

———. 2006a. "Statement by Zhou Xiaochuan, Governor of the People's Bank of China, at the Thirteenth Meeting of the International Monetary and Financial Committee." April 22. http://www.imf.org/external/spring/2006/imfc/statement/eng/chn.pdf.

———. 2006b. "Statement of Mr. Zhou Xiaochuan, Governor of the People's Bank of China at the Annual Joint Discussion." Annual Meetings of the IMF and World Bank Group, Singapore, September 19.

———. 2009. "Reform the International Monetary System." Essay by Dr. Zhou Xiaochuan, Governor of the People's Bank of China, 23 March. http://www.bis.org/review/r090402c.pdf.

———. 2010a. "Statement of the Hon. Zhou Xiaochuan, Governor of the Fund for the People's Republic of China." Press Release No. 47. Annual Meetings of the IMF and World Bank Group, Washington, D.C., October 8. http://www.imf.org/external/am/2010/speeches/pr47e.pdf.

———. 2010b. "Statement of the Honorable Zhou Xiaochuan, Governor of the People's Bank of China and Governor of the IMF for China, at the Twenty-Second Meeting of the International Monetary and Financial Committee." Washington, DC, October 9. http://www.imf.org/External/AM/2010/imfc/statement/eng/chn.pdf.

———. 2011. "On Savings Ratio." *Banque de France Financial Stability Review,* special issue on "Global imbalances and financial stability," (5): 165–70.

———. 2012. "Jinrongye biaozhun zhiding yu zhixing de ruogan wenti" [Several issues in the establishment and implementation of financial industry standards], *Zhongguo jinrong* [China Finance].

INDEX

Page numbers followed by *f* or *t* indicate figures or tables.

266 *Index*

balance of payments *(continued)*
See also foreign reserves; international
macroeconomic policy surveillance
Bank for International Settlements (BIS),
207, 208
Bank of China (BOC), 162–63, 177, 181,
224
Belarus, 169t, 170, 172, 178n59
Bergsten, Fred, 134–35
bilateral surveillance, 13, 134, 136–37, 142
bilateral swap arrangements (BSAs): China's intentions as monetary power and,
42; CMI/CMIM, formation of, 4, 28;
conditionalities of, 157, 171–72, 183;
domestic politics favoring, 159–65;
favored by China generally, 8, 15, 18;
monetary diplomacy of China and, 157;
monetary diplomacy of China favoring, 157–58, 166–72; RMB aid in form
of, 168–72, 169t; RMB, internationalization of, 7, 42, 158, 170, 178–80, 208, 237,
238–39
bilateral trade balance between US and
China, 104, 131, 132–33, 133f
Bo Xilai, 94
Brazil, 47n5, 169t, 170, 178, 195, 196, 203–4,
207, 208, 211, 232. See also BRIC/BRICS
countries
Bretton Woods conference, 13, 47–48,
57, 59. See also International Monetary
Fund; World Bank
BRIC/BRICS countries, 14, 36, 158, 169,
170, 173, 174, 178, 186, 196, 198, 202–7,
210–12, 234. See also Brazil; India; Russia; South Africa
Britain, 30, 31, 33, 47, 50n17, 51, 88, 152,
166n23, 169t, 181, 195–96, 198, 210,
217–18
Brown, Gordon, 196
Bush, George W., 133–34, 135, 136, 192,
226n20

Canada, 33, 47, 50n17, 171, 195–96, 200,
207
Cao Yuanzheng, 163
capital account convertibility, 68, 237,
240n46

Central Bank. *See* People's Bank of China
Chen Deming, 167
Chen Siqing, 224
Chen Yuan, 89, 205, 208, 212
Chi Peng-Fei, 62
Chiang Kai-shek, 48, 60, 62
Chiang Mai Initiative (CMI)/Chiang Mai
Initiative Multilateralization (CMIM)
arrangement, 4, 5, 12, 14, 28, 42, 70,
171–72, 175, 179
China Investment Corporation (CIC), 28,
155
China Securities Regulatory Commission,
121, 159, 163, 177
China's international monetary relations,
vii–viii, 1–22; development priorities in
China and, 18–19; domestic and state-
level influences on, 15–20, 41; external
influences on, 20–21; financial security,
emphasis on, 19, 21, 93; political aspects,
focus on, 2; power gained by China in,
2–8, 27–29; priorities of Chinese government regarding, 8–15; revolution of
1949 and, 12; state control of financial
system, 117, 163; "taker," "maker," and
"breaker" roles open to, 8–10, 22, 41,
128. *See also specific aspects, e.g.* reform of
international monetary system
Chinese Academy of Social Sciences, 88, 94,
177, 200n53, 222, 223
Chinese Communist Party (CCP) and Central Committee: challenges to legitimacy
of, 108, 111; foreign policy of, 190; foreign reserves and, 80, 80–81n26, 83; IMF
and, 46, 58–62, 65, 69; influence on Chinese international monetary policy, 16,
17, 20; international macroeconomic policy surveillance, Chinese stance on, 149;
monetary diplomacy of China and, 160,
162; private businesses and, 122; SASAC
and, 120–21; SOEs and, 121; stability,
premium placed on, 6
Clinton, Bill, 131, 226n20, 227–28
coastal provinces, local governments of, 16,
19, 81, 84, 87, 91, 95, 119–20, 121
Cold War, 46, 60–62, 69, 214, 217, 222, 226,
227